THE MEKONG ARRANGED & REARRANGED

The **Southeast Asian Studies Regional Exchange Program Foundation** (SEASREP), www.seasrepfoundation.org, was initiated in 1994 by four historians from the region with the support of the Toyota Foundation and the Japan Foundation. SEASREP is devoted to the study of Southeast Asia and the development of Southeast Asian scholars in the humanities and social sciences. SEASREP's core program consists of grants for the study of Southeast Asian languages, postgraduate research in the region, and comparative and collaborative research on Southeast Asia. In addition, the organization offers training seminars for undergraduate and postgraduate students. Over the past decade, SEASREP has built an impressive network among scholars, universities and research institutes in the region and has entered into collaborative arrangements with Southeast Asian specialists in other parts of Asia and Europe.

Mekong Press, www.mekongpress.com, was initiated in 2005 by Silkworm Books, Thailand, and the Creativity & Culture Division of Rockefeller Foundation's Southeast Asia Regional Office in Bangkok, to encourage and support the work of local scholars, writers and publishing professionals in Cambodia, Laos, Vietnam and the other countries in the Greater Mekong Subregion. Books published by Mekong Press will be marketed and distributed internationally. In addition, Mekong Press intends to hold seminars and training workshops on aspects of book publishing as well as help find ways to overcome some of the huge challenges for small book publishers in the region. Mekong Press is funded by the Rockefeller Foundation's Learning Across Borders in the Greater Mekong Sub-region progam.

THE MEKONG ARRANGED & REARRANGED

edited by
Maria Serena I. Diokno
Nguyen Van Chinh

MEKONG PRESS
Chiang Mai, Thailand

This publication is funded by The Rockefeller Foundation.

ISBN–10: 974-94804-9-x
ISBN–13: 978-974-94804-9-6

First published in 2006 by
Mekong Press
6 Sukkasem Road, T. Suthep, Chiang Mai 50200, Thailand
E-mail: info@mekongpress.com
Website: http://www.mekongpress.com

Original cover photo of a section of the Mekong River
by Vijit Heng, ©2005 by *Sarakadee Magazine*

Type set in Janson Text 10 pt. by Silk Type
Printed in Thailand by O. S. Printing House, Bangkok

CONTENTS

ACKNOWLEDGEMENTS

We thank the Rockefeller Foundation's Southeast Asia Regional Office, especially Lia Sciortino and Alan Feinstein, for supporting this project and providing the things that do not always come with material support: patience, understanding, and trust. Assembling a group of Southeast Asian scholars with different perspectives on a subject that is open to debate is never easy, but the experience is, no doubt, rewarding. We thank the contributors to this anthology; each piece enriches our knowledge of the Mekong and shows how a complex space like the Mekong can be arranged in different ways. While working on the project, Diana Wong gave us helpful insights and comments; we thank her for her suggestions. Misael Racines and Imelda Adante assisted us in double checking some of the entries. The Mekong Press also deserves our gratitude. Trasvin Jittidecharak and Dayaneetha de Silva took on the (challenging) task of bringing our manuscript to life. We finally wish to acknowledge the SEASREP Foundation, whose 'initiation' into the Mekong has been a most interesting experience and one that we expect to continue over time.

The Editors

INTRODUCTION: MOTHER OF WATERS

MARIA SERENA I. DIOKNO AND NGUYEN VAN CHINH

The Mekong is one of the longest and most magnificent rivers in the world. From its source in China's Qinghai Province in the Tibetan Plateau, the Mekong crosses Yunnan Province (China), Myanmar, Laos, Thailand, Cambodia and Vietnam before emptying into the South China Sea.[1] However, most documents about the Mekong River produced outside China often ignore its upper stretch, focusing instead on its middle and lower reaches. This is partly because not much has been written about the river's source but, more importantly, because the concept of the Mekong was shaped by mid-19th century French explorations of the river and subsequent colonization over much of this area, as Armando Malay and Vatthana Pholsena point out in their contributions here (chapters 1 and 2). To a certain extent that colonial imagery and legacy is still evident today.

The Mekong is often seen as a river of mysteries; its diverse ecology and the cultures yet to be completely explored. It is also a river of many names. People in the upper course (the Tibetan Plateau) call it *Dzachu*, meaning "river of rocks" (Kasetsiri 2003, 6). The Chinese name the section that crosses Yunnan Province *Lan Xang* (or *Lancang Jiang*), which means "turbulent river" (Gargan 2003, 41). The section that crosses Myanmar and Thailand is called *Nam Khong*, perhaps the oldest name of the river in the Tai-Lao language, although the meaning of *khong* is unclear (Kasetsiri 2003, 6). According to Pham Duc Duong, an expert on Southeast Asian languages, Tai-Lao descendants living on both sides of the Mekong River call it *Mae Khong* ("mother of rivers") or *Mae Nam* ("mother of waters") because for them, this is not only the largest but also the most important river. Pham suggests that *Mekong* is actually the way the French articulated *Mae Khong*. He adds that the Vietnamese name for the lower reaches of the river, *Cuu Long* ("Nine Dragons") originated from the transcription of *Mae Khong* from Tai-Lao into Sino-Vietnamese.[2] Naming big rivers "mother river" is common practice in Southeast Asia and elsewhere. The Khmer also call the Mekong *Tonle Thom* or "big river", while the Vietnamese call the Red River *Song Cai* or "mother river".

The Mekong as a region: concept or reality?

The Mekong River is seen not only as a source of livelihood but also a sacred entity with cultural and spiritual significance. It was the site of French explorations, initially, as Malay explains, by individual travelers motivated by curiosity, adventure or missionary zeal, and later in the 19th century, by officials pursuing colonial interest. Indochina, which may be viewed as the immediate predecessor of the Mekong region today, was a creation of the French, whose failed project of a Mekong federation, as Pholsena observes, "served as a cover for what was primarily exploitative rule." The term "Indochina" resurfaced in the "Indochina Wars" of the mid-1950s to the 1970s. "Convenient in its imprecision," Malay writes, the term omitted the role of the two Western countries (and their allies) that engaged the peoples of the area in conflict, and left out as well the fluid nature of the borders that cut across Vietnam, Cambodia and Laos, as evidenced by guerilla forces traversing the jungles of the region. Both Malay and Pholsena interrogate the French notion of "Indochina"; Pholsena takes this investigation further by examining the (failed) communist project of an Indochinese federation.

Although the concept of "the Mekong" as a region—encompassing Myanmar, Laos, Thailand, Cambodia, Vietnam and Yunnan Province (China)—appears everywhere in documents on development cooperation, the term requires critical analysis because many fundamental questions remain about what it connotes. What is the basis for defining the concept, "Mekong region"? Does the "region" refer to the territories bound by or under the influence of the river or the countries that share the benefits from it? Why is the upper course in the Tibetan Plateau not seen as part of the Mekong region? Is the Mekong a "geo-body" (using Thongchai Winichakul's term)—a land in which a common set of natural and social conditions are shared among a number of societies, or a concept artificially created for the purpose of development cooperation (Winichakul 1994; Sangkhamanee 2003)? More fundamentally, do the societies located in the geographical area we refer to as the Mekong region possess any distinct cultural identity?

Moreover, from the point of view of development, can treating the Mekong as an entity make a difference to the socio-economic life of the region and its member countries and bring about much desired change and prosperity? What roles are individual countries, territories, regional and international organizations playing in protecting the natural environment, preserving local cultures, and minimizing conflicts so as to realize cooperation and development? What bearing have the processes of regionalization and globalization had on the conceptualization of the region? These issues have been and continue to be the subject of research on the Mekong, and the contributors to this volume address some of these questions from a variety of disciplinary backgrounds.

A historic-culture area?

While rivers have undoubtedly played a central role in the rise and development of many famous cultures, does proximity to a river bestow common cultural or social patterns? In the case of the Mekong, what constitutes regional identity? This is a difficult question to answer, which explains why it hardly appears in the growing literature on the region. In an effort to address this question, we turn to linguists whose studies suggest theories about the origin and movement of the peoples of the region and how they relate to one another.

As early as 1852, Logan and later Forbes (1881) discovered the close linguistic relationships between the Mon, Khmer, and Viet (Kinh) languages. Their findings created the first premises for Schmidt (1907) to develop the scientific grounds for a language family that he called Austro-Asiatic. For the first time the close connection between the languages spoken by the Paluang, Wa, Riang, Munda, Khasi and the Mon-Khmer peoples was proven. Schmidt held that Austro-Asiatic languages were spoken in a large area from Chota-Nagpour in northern India to southern China and northern Vietnam.

. Based on these findings, the French researcher Georges Coedès (1925) suggested there was a possibility that Austro-Asiatic descendants had had a shared culture, and that the oldest owners of the region were perhaps not Thai and Tibeto-Burmese language speakers, but those who spoke Austro-Asiatic languages. The latter, Coedès believed, had a distinct cultural identity that he named the Austro-Asiatic civilization, characterized by wet rice cultivation, the relatively important position of women in the family and society, animism, the cult of ancestor worship, and common linguistic features (see also Vuong 1963 and Phan 1998). Coedès' theory ignited a lively debate that ensued for many decades. The idea of a conflation between a group of languages and a culture needs to be further discussed at both theoretical and empirical levels because linguistic similarities do not necessarily indicate a common culture (Wolters 1982).

On the one hand, the argument that linguistic similarities can be seen as evidence for common cultural origins has been further developed by recent research. For example, using comparative historical linguistics data, Ha Van Tan and Pham Duc Duong (1978, 64–69) reconstructed the connection between the ethnically diverse speakers of Viet Muong (an Austro-Asiatic language) and came to the conclusion that they had belonged to a common culture that later split up. Similarly, Chatthip Nartsupha (1996), while investigating the historical relationships of Tai-speaking inhabitants in the region, developed the hypothesis that linguistic affinity implies cultural affinity among various Tai-speaking groups.

On the other hand, there is also the opposing view that the various Tai-speaking groups in the region do not necessarily belong to a common culture because each had been assimilated by, or adapted to, distinctive local conditions as the result of historical circumstances (Evans 2000, 11). Yet in the Mekong region, apart from linguistic differences, it is hard to define the cultural boundaries among the myriad local societies. Throughout the thousands of years of its history, massive migration into and across the region, and major conflicts and confrontations as well as peaceful contact and interaction have shaped cultural features distinct from other regions in Asia. For this reason, perhaps Foley's views of mainland Southeast Asia as a "linguistic area" are a useful summing up:

> In this region, languages of four different major language families are spoken: Sino-Tibetan, Thai, Mon-Khmer, and Austronesian. The ancestral languages and earlier stages of these languages from the four families were very different from each other, but centuries of mutual interference have reduced this diversity so that they now share many structural features. (Foley 1997, 391)

Shared artifacts

Apart from linguistic evidence pointing to shared origins, the peoples of the Mekong have other historical and cultural commonalities. Archaeological findings indicate that similar large ceremonial bronze drums are distributed widely in the Mekong region, from Myanmar, Thailand, Laos and southern China to northern Vietnam. Although opinions regarding the origin of these drums are heavily influenced by nationalism, and was once the topic of a heated and prolonged debate between Vietnamese and Chinese scholars (Han 1998), for example, it is hard to deny that the bronze drums are part of the Mekong region's cultural heritage. It is, however, surprising that for more than a century now since the findings about the drums were first announced, research has mainly focused on two issues: the type and age of the drums, and the meaning of their decorations. In Vietnam, there has also been some speculation about the music produced by the drums and how they were played (Ha 1994, 370).

Archaeologists of mainland Southeast Asia seem to have an implicit though strong belief that the culture which created these bronze masterpieces no longer exists. This seems to ignore the fact that bronze drums are still in use, not as quaint reminders of the past in some tourist show, but as a popular musical instrument of many ethnic groups in the Mekong region. In fact, the Karen in Myanmar still produce bronze drums, which are exchanged and traded actively among various Mekong peoples. Large numbers of bronze drums are kept by local communities who use them in festivals and ritual performances during sacrificial ceremonies, harvest festivals, receptions for distinguished guests, the consecration of new houses, and funerals. Legends about the drum, the art of playing the drum, and the rules of behavior with respect to the drum are still present in the life of many ethnic groups (Simina and Preisig 2004). That is why the drums, and the music and rituals associated with them, are deemed a unique and shared part of the cultural heritage of the Mekong region.

Another general feature of the region's culture can be gleaned from the thousands of Buddhist pagodas and monasteries that stretch from the snow-covered heights of the Tibetan Plateau to the vast tropical rice fields in villages downstream. In this sense the Mekong could also be called the "river of Buddhism". Despite the differences between Tibetan and Theravada or Mahayana Buddhism, the omnipresence of Buddhist architecture in the region indicates similar or shared cultural practices. Religious practices by hosts of Buddhist monks and their followers are an indispensable part of the lives of millions of people living along the Mekong River. Buddhism has arguably exerted the strongest overarching influence over many centuries on the cultures of the peoples of the Mekong, regardless of whether they are Thai, Khmer, Lao, Vietnamese, Burmese or Chinese.

The present day shape of societies and nations in the region cannot be understood without knowledge of their age-old relationships and similar histories. While colonial and post-colonial nation-state borders heightened differences and disparities in the region, they did not break down centuries of interaction and a common past. To sum up, the Mekong region, therefore, is not simply a vast stretch of territory on which different ethnic groups live next to one another. The Mekong can indeed be said to be a geo-body in which societies have evolved and now share a certain set of traits, what historians and anthropologists would define as a 'culture area' or an 'ethno-historic region'.[3]

Vanishing borders

Commercial routes took shape in the Mekong region long before the explorations by the French. Cross-border trading featured such well-known local commodities as drugs, silk, and green tea. They were brought upstream and created famous trading routes, such as the ancient route for trading tea, which is still mentioned in documents in Yunnan. Nevertheless, the idea of exploiting the Mekong region's commercial possibilities was best evidenced by the explorations of the French in the mid-19th century. Though the "grand commercial future" of tapping the Chinese market failed to materialize, the Mekong is once again considered a river full of potential for commerce and tourism.

Almost all the countries that share borders with China, including Myanmar, Laos, and Vietnam, consider it an advantage to develop trading ties with China. The centuries-old petty trading has grown rapidly since the opening of the borders between China and mainland Southeast Asia in the 1990s. Cities along the Mekong with official crossings, such as Chiang Khong in Thailand, are regarded as important gateways in this commerce. As observed by Kuah Khun Eng (2000, 73):

In the border regions, trading has increased significantly and become a part of life among the border residents. It is not uncommon to see 50 to 80 percent of the border residents engaged in some kind of petty trading in the region. Likewise, border trading has become an important source of revenue for local and provincial governments. In Yunnan and Guangxi, border trading and related activities contributed over 50 percent of their provincial and country revenue.

Similarly, Andrew Walker (2000) documents and points out the continued popularity of long-distance river-based trading in the border regions between Laos and Thailand, in which women play an important role as traders and entrepreneurs. Mya Than's research also shows how many of the laborers hired to smuggle goods in today's border trade are women aged 20 to 45 (chapter 6). Recently, these informal trading activities have been incorporated into regional development cooperation projects. However, the river is not only for informal or individual trading activities. The Thais look upon the river as a major transport route for trade with China because it is shorter, faster and cheaper than the alternatives. Of the five channels of product distribution from Thailand to southern China—by river, road, sea, air and rail—the Mekong River route ranks first, accounting for 95 percent of the total value of goods distributed. Commerce between the upper part of northern Thailand and southern China has increased continuously from 2000. In his discussion of intra-regional commerce, Mya Than suggests that this trade is even more significant to some of the Mekong countries than their trade with countries outside the region. Indeed, as he explains, the most interesting and, to some, the most meaningful, feature of the economic renaissance of the Mekong riparian countries is this cross-border trade.

Region vis-à-vis nation

Parallel to the swift development of the cross-border trade is the rising potential of tourism. First and foremost, the cultures of the Mekong riparian countries rank among the most diverse in the world. The Mekong countries (except Thailand, with its well developed tourism industry), and Yunnan are now promoting tourism with encouraging results. Yunnan is a good example. From only 1,299 tourists in 1979, the number of tourists that flocked to the province skyrocketed to

213,000 in 1994, rising to 520,000 in 1997, and 1,266,000 in 2001. The annual growth rate of tourists coming to Yunnan is 29 percent (Nguyen and Kieu 2001, 51). Most notable is the increase in Asian tourists, especially from Japan, China and Thailand. The idea of the Mekong region as a single, easily accessible travel destination—rather than being made up of individual, nationally demarcated tourist spots, each with its own visa requirements and procedures—is gaining ground.

Coupled with the ever-increasing flow of commodities and tourism is more cross-border migration, which has both positive and negative features. The Asian Migration Research Center in Bangkok estimates that, excluding refugees, 1.6 to 2 million people are involved in intra-Mekong regional migration, most of them illegal (Harima et al. 2003, 226). Another report places the figure of migrants in the region at approximately 10 million (Archavanikul and Guest 1999). These large population movements are contributing to such existing problems as poverty and human trafficking. However, the attractions of existing or emerging economic centers like Bangkok and the cities of Yunnan are difficult to resist, especially for a Mekong region labor force badly in need of work. It is also important to note that improving inter-country transport infrastructure and the opening of the borders has made this population mobility easier.

With their rapidly expanding populations and economies, many frontier towns of the Mekong region are no longer deserted and property prices are rising. Bustling border posts have also changed deep-rooted images of frontier regions traditionally thought to be remote. Apart from border guards who defended national security, those who came to these areas were chiefly the poor in search of land, prisoners sent into exile, and groups of 'less civilized' communities living in isolation from the outside world. Researchers have noted that in the process of regional exchanges, such frontiers are disappearing and cultural borders, which did not exist in the past, have become fragile today. As the anthropologist Evans observes:

> ...political borders do not coincide with cultures—Vietnamese overlap into Chinese and vice versa, Hmong, Akha, Yao, Lue, and so on all overlap the borders of the region, just as languages flow back and forth across them. At a cultural and social level, the frontiers have been borderless for a long time. (Evans et al. 2000, 2)

Mya Than affirms this in his chapter, when he talks about an emerging "center-periphery" relationship in which the center is no longer the national capital distant from (and alien to) the border town but rather, the capital closest (and most familiar) to the border, that is, the capital of the neighboring country. From intra-regional mobility and trade, new notions of nationhood and of one's neighbor are also evolving alongside older, perhaps more traditional ideas. Only recently, a Chinese farmer who married a Burmese woman who had been smuggled into Xincai county was surprised to learn that his wife was a foreigner; Burma, he had thought, was part of Yunnan province (*Bangkok Post*, 17 June 2006). The ambivalence of neighborly relations, such as the "closeness" and "strangeness" of Lao-Thai relations observed by Pholsena, may well apply to other peoples in the Mekong region. Pholsena argues that "identity boundaries are becoming blurred, so much so that national belonging appears to be superseded to some degree by a more pervasive sense of community." In the final analysis, it is this sense of community that makes regional cooperation possible.

Different faces of regional cooperation

The initiative of establishing a formal institution for cooperation in the Mekong region emerged in 1957 by four countries in the lower stretch of the river: Laos, Cambodia, Thailand and the former Southern Authorities of Vietnam (Nguyen and Kieu 2001, 75). The Mekong Committee, as it was then called, initially focused its efforts on flood control and in the early 1960s, commissioning a study of the social and economic aspects of the Mekong River basin. Apart from flood monitoring and preparedness, specific recommendations from that study included human resource and agricultural development. Perhaps its lasting legacy was the systematic collection of data on the Mekong and its tributaries (Jacobs 2002, 357).

The activities of the Committee were interrupted after the end of the Indochina war in 1975, and three years later, Laos, Thailand and Vietnam put up an Interim Mekong Committee. Preoccupied with internal strife, Cambodia was left out of this interim body. Despite its limited efforts, the Interim Committee produced an Indicative Basin Plan in 1987, which called for a shift to smaller dams with less harmful effects on the environment and reduced human dislocation (Jacobs 2002, 358). In October 1992, on the initiative of the Asian

Development Bank (ADB), a ministerial-level meeting of the Mekong countries was convened in Manila to discuss cooperation for regional development. The Greater Mekong Subregion (GMS) was thus conceived; it included Vietnam, Laos, Cambodia, Thailand, Myanmar and China (Yunnan Province). Three years later, the Mekong River Commission (MRC) succeeded the old Mekong Committees and in 1996, the ASEAN Mekong Basin Development Cooperation was officially formed, proof of ASEAN's commitment to the development of the Mekong basin. The MRC has a broader scope for it covers all matters relating to the Mekong, while the ASEAN Mekong Basin Development Cooperation is confined to the river basin, a subset of the region. The GMS, on the other hand, is a subregional grouping smaller than ASEAN but larger than the MRC. Although the GMS is perhaps the least formally organized, because of the ADB's support, it seems to possess easier access to foreign funding than the MRC.

Geopolitics, however, lies at the underbelly of regional cooperation. From the time of the earliest Mekong Committee, which was sponsored by the United States as part of its drive against communism, to SEATO (ASEAN's predecessor) and the present day GMS, geopolitical considerations have propelled the moves of various actors, international and regional. Nguyen Phuong Binh (chapter 3) examines these, pointing out the significance of individual national interests vis-à-vis those of the region as a whole. In his discussion of the national context and framework of China's engagement in the GMS, for example, He Shengda (chapter 4) cites regional stability and development as China's twin goals in the region, best captured in the words of Chinese Premier Wen Jiabao: "friendly neighbors, stable nation and wealthy neighbors". But He makes it clear that it is to China's (Yunnan's) advantage to develop the Mekong basin, Yunnan being one of the least developed provinces of the country.

Against the backdrop of political transition in the former Indochina states, Doung Chanto Sisowath (chapter 5) examines the role of these regional institutions and evaluates their contribution in two key areas: the reduction or prevention of conflict in the subregion, and the reconstruction of the region itself. Conflict resolution, Chanto asserts, is a pressing concern especially with regard to the effects on downstream countries of upstream hydropower projects. Yet none of the regional organizations have the mandate or capacity to resolve conflict—their major concern being conflict prevention—leaving the settlement of disputes to the concerned parties themselves. The MRC, adds Binh, does not even represent the entire subregion (just countries in the lower basin); and the MRC has no authority to engage in political matters even if these impinge heavily on the development of the Mekong region. The ASEAN Vision 2020 of a "community of caring societies", concludes Chanto, is a far cry from reality for too many in the region.

Disparities are inevitable when huge and vital resources (such as those of the Mekong River) are shared among neighboring, unevenly developed states. Binh and He call attention to these facts: Laos contributes 35 percent of the water flow, the largest, and also occupies the largest basin area (26 percent). Myanmar, in contrast, contributes the smallest flow (two percent) and controls the smallest land area (also two percent). Control of the river and the basin area by the other riparian countries ranges from 8 to 18 percent (Goh 2001, 471–476). China, on the other hand, is a gigantic player in the region and enjoys the advantage of its geographical position upstream. While Binh and Chanto view the upstream-downstream issue as a thorn in the side of regional cooperation, He Shengda plays down the effects of Yunnan's hydropower projects on the lower basin, preferring to tackle cooperation in terms of conditions that favor and discourage it. While admitting that Yunnan's dams have raised concerns among the lower basin countries, He nonetheless argues that coal is a worse alternative than hydropower and questions the view that dams cause serious environmental damage.

Obviously this debate is unresolved. Describing the Mekong area as one of the "most dammed" in the world, journalist John Vidal (2006) writes about the impact of more than a hundred water-related projects on downstream communities. The three dams built by China (with six more on the horizon) have brought down the water level and threaten the livelihoods of nearly 100 million people in the region. Even among MRC members, adherence to agreed upon principles and mechanisms is questionable. Barry Wain reported in 2004 that Vietnam, for example, failed to inform Cambodia of its dam construction on the Sesan, a tributary of the Mekong which flooded communities in northeastern Cambodia in August of that year. Even Thailand, Wain points out, attempted to circumvent the need for MRC approval by building its water diversion projects on two tributaries of the Mekong (Wain 2004). He Shengda's optimistic outlook about regional cooperation in the GMS and between China and the GMS is balanced by concerns raised by Binh and Chanto, who cite, among other issues, the persistent lack of coordination between regional bodies amid competing national interests.

The GMS, poverty and water

What then is the "Greater Mekong Subregion"? Like any other concept, it is a construct that serves a distinct purpose, depending on who or which institution applies the term. The construction of the GMS was instigated by the ADB with the Mekong member countries in mind, in order to facilitate the design and delivery of comprehensive rather than piecemeal programs aimed at the entire region instead of individual states. The Mekong River indisputably lies at the core of the GMS, not just as a natural resource to be developed, preserved and shared, but also as a source of livelihood, a means of trade and movement of people, and as potential for further economic development.

The term GMS itself is an interesting one. The word "Greater" presumably refers to the participation of China in the GMS, which does not belong to the other two Mekong regional bodies, the MRC and the ASEAN Mekong Basin Development Cooperation. The term "subregion", again presumably, indicates that the Mekong is only part of a larger whole, that whole being Southeast Asia. Underneath this visible layer of labels, the GMS image of the Mekong is not that of a rich social and cultural space but rather a huge land area, a resource with vast potential, a huge development site. For this reason, Chaiyan Rajchagool's provocative analysis (chapter 7) of the ADB discourse on poverty alleviation and water management—two central concerns of the GMS—is useful. There is inconsistency between the use of universal yardsticks of growth and the maintenance of diversity of riparian peoples and states in the region. The tension between producing wealth and sharing it is also visible. While some may not find Chaiyan's juxtaposition of the ADB 'text' with religious metaphors a comfortable idea, he implicitly raises an important question that poses a challenge to the Bank: how to blend its prescriptions ("sacred teaching") for poverty eradication with the adverse effects of these prescriptions (such as water pricing guidelines) on the poor.

Solving the complex problems of the region requires, fundamentally, a perspective not just of what the Mekong River obviously *presents*—a large reservoir of water—but also what it *represents* to communities, foremost those who live alongside the river. More than nature or the potential for prosperity, the river represents the spirit of life. Water worship and water processions are not a thing of the past; they continue to this day because they hold meaning for residents of the

Mekong. Yet, when governments plan large-scale projects to control the benefits brought about by the section of the Mekong River that flows past their respective countries, the communities living along the riverbanks usually receive unsatisfactory answers to their concerns about the impact of these projects. Planners tend to forget that these communities know the river best and are its staunchest protectors. Chaiyan challenges the notion that farmers waste water and hence must pay for its use, arguing instead that if water use is to be charged, a rational basis must be devised.

A more complete understanding of the Mekong thus has to take into account not just its geographical elements, but also its cultural and social dimensions and, above all, the people who live in the area, with their distinct identities, a common past, a shared culture, and a history that has alternated between peace and conflict:

> The Mekong region is more than the Mekong River, and more than the Mekong basin. It is a social and political construct with wider scope and implications. The regional context is being shaped by a wider range of historical and contemporary forces. Partly as a consequence of relative peace, but owing also to various other global and regional drivers, there is increasing transnational regionalism. The surge in regional connections is led either by the state, business or civil society. (Kaosa-ard and Dore 2003, 2)

Up ahead

The Mekong is, above all, a region in the making. It is neither an ADB development construct nor that of the states that comprise it. Every day the concept is molded and remolded on the ground as individuals and communities arrange and rearrange their images of themselves. Several years ago, anti-Thai riots saw Cambodians ransacking the Thai embassy and business establishments in Phnom Penh, because of a remark attributed to a popular Thai actress that Angkor Wat, the national heritage and symbol of Cambodia, belonged to Thailand. The affront was not just cultural or historical. (After all, Siem Reap, home to Angkor, means "flatten Siam".) The riots reopened deep-seated resentment over Thailand's dominance in the region: its currency, goods, television and films abound. Concomitant to the perception of Thai affluence is the Cambodian self-image of a lesser, weaker, poorer neighbor. The "burden of proximity", observed a Singapore journalist, "is, in fact, also a burden of history made worse by inventive Thai history books....Cambodian journalists are no less guilty in fabricating untrue stories" (Lee 2003). More recently, a Thai magazine published a guide for local readers about how to relate to their neighbors northeast. Among other matters, Thai men were advised to address Lao women as *e dok thong* ("golden flower" or, in Thai slang, "you little whore"), a form of flattery supposedly welcomed by Laotian women. The Lao government demanded a public apology from the publisher through the Thai Embassy (Hongthong 2005).

Animosities of this sort no doubt have historical roots. In his essay on French explorations of the Mekong in the 19th century, Malay cites Francis Garnier's "distress over the Siamese kingdom's 'suffocating oppression' of the Laotians," whom he viewed as an "intelligent and gentle race" in contrast to the Cambodians, all of whose "qualities have disappeared, and all vitality seems to be extinguished." Accurate or not, perceptions of the self and the other have hounded the region throughout its history. The "spectre of an Indochinese entity (either in the form of an empire or a federation)," Vatthana Pholsena maintains, "belongs to the history of French colonialism, anti-colonial struggle and Cold War conflict in Southeast Asia." Today's requirements of regional cooperation in the Mekong—the "hardware" (massive transportation and other infrastructure) and "software" (less red tape in customs and visa requirements)—are in a sense not original; they bring to mind Garnier's recommendations to construct a railway from Saigon to Stung Treng in Cambodia and streamline customs procedures along the Mekong. Indeed, the unrealized explorers' dream of transforming the Mekong into the direct water route to the attractive Chinese market upstream may yet be fulfilled.

It can be said that wars and poverty have constituted the two largest obsessions for the peoples of the region. The Indochina wars lasted many decades, destroying Vietnam, Laos and Cambodia, and involving other countries in a whirlpool of conflict and division. Thirty years have elapsed since the end of this war but its wounds have not completely healed. They include not only the wounds of the flesh of millions of victims, of the forests and water sources, but also, and most painfully, of the human spirit. Turning this area from a battlefield into not merely a marketplace[4] but a space of thriving humanity in both an individual and collective sense would be one of the greatest achievements of this century.

The struggle against poverty in the Mekong region is no less fierce than past wars for national liberation. Even Thailand, whose annual average income per capita is the highest in the region, has parts located in the Mekong basin capture area (chiefly in the north and northeast) that are much poorer than the national average. As Mya Than correctly points out, these areas of Thailand would more easily fit the characteristics of the other GMS members. The danger of poverty is that it brings along other social evils, such as trafficking in women and children, drug smuggling, and the incidence of HIV/ AIDS, all of which are growing at an alarming rate in the Mekong region. The transit trade in goods that Mya Than discusses applies as well to people. A recent workshop in Vietnam focused on the use of Vietnam as a transit point for the trafficking of children and women to China (*Viêt Nam News*, 22 June 2006).

In their analyses of institutions, policies and strategies of development cooperation in the region, Nguyen Phuong Binh, Doung Chanto Sisowath and He Shengda accept that national interests are at play and sometimes get in the way of regional cooperation. Economic disparities in the Mekong are equally imposing obstacles, with Thailand at one end as the most developed Southeast Asian country in the Mekong and huge China at the other commanding a chunk of the market and water up north. But the authors here also all agree that cooperation is essential to the success of development efforts in the region. Expanding the role of the Mekong River, writes Binh, from a source of water to "a source of friendship, cooperation and prosperity as the name of the river itself implies", is one message of this book. This may sound trite but the need for it is unquestionable. The other message is to interrogate the very idea of the Mekong region because, as the various chapters in this volume demonstrate, conceptual arrangements and rearrangements of the Mekong help explain not just what the region is (and is not), but also why things happen the way they do. The same issue or event will appear again and again in this collection, but handled differently by each contrubutor; for underneath the same concept lie real differences that neither public professions of goodwill nor bureaucratic solutions alone can address.

Notes

1   The Mekong river can be divided into three parts: the upper stretch from the
    Tibetan headwaters to the Golden Triangle; the middle stretch running through
    the flat terrain from Ubon, Thailand to Champasak in Laos; and the lower reaches
    at the Khone Falls, plunging into Cambodia and Vietnam and then flowing into the
    sea (Kasetsiri 2003).
2   Discussions with Dr. Pham Duc Duong, Professor of Linguistics at the Institute of
    Southeast Asian Studies, Hanoi, 2005.
3   According to Thomas Barfield (1997, 103), a culture area is "a geographic region
    in which a common set of traits, often called a 'culture complex,' is found shared
    among a number of societies". More concretely, Adam Kuper (1992, 13) explains:
    "Culture areas are defined in part by historical relationships, and they may exhibit
    profound continuities despite superficial changes. Structural continuities within
    a region may signal shared roots, though local variants may be shaped by direct
    interactions, exchanges, even confrontations between communities."
4   The phrase "from battlefield to marketplace" is attributed to Thai Prime Minister
    Chatichai Choonhavan.

References

Archavanikul, Kritaya and Philip Guest. 1999. *Managing the Flow of Migration: Regional
    Approaches.* Bangkok: Mahidol University Institute of Population and Social
    Research.
Barfield, Thomas, ed. 1997. *The Dictionary of Anthropology.* Oxford: Blackwell.
Coedès, Georges. 1925. "Documents sur l'histoire politique et réligieuse du Laos
    occidental." *Bulletin de L'École Française D'Extrême-Orient* 1–2, 25: 1–201.
Cunningham, Philip. 2003. "Rising Tide of Intolerance." *South China Morning Post,*
    10 February.
Evans, Grant, ed. 2000. *Laos: Culture and Society.* Singapore: Institute of Southeast
    Asian Studies.
Evans, Grant, Christopher Hutton and Kuah Khun Eng, eds. 2000. *Where China Meets
    Southeast Asia: Social and Cultural Change in the Border Regions.* Bangkok: White
    Lotus; Singapore: Institute of Southeast Asian Studies.
Foley, William. A. 1997. *Anthropological Linguistics: An Introduction (Language in Society).*
    Oxford: Blackwell.
Forbes, Charles James Forbes Smith. 1881. *Comparative Grammar of the Languages of
    Further India: A Fragment, and Other Essays.* London: W.H. Allen.
Gargan, Edward A. 2003. *The River's Tale: A Year on the Mekong.* New York: Vintage
    Books.
Goh, Evelyn. 2001. "The Hydro-Politics of the Mekong River Basin: Regional
    Cooperation and Environmental Security." In *Non-Traditional Security Issues
    in Southeast Asia,* edited by Andrew T.H. Tan and J.D. Kenneth Boutin, pp.
    468–506. Singapore: Select Publishing for Institute of Defence and Strategic
    Studies.
Ha Van Tan, ed. 1994. *Van hoa Dong Son o Viet Nam* (Dong Son Culture in Vietnam).
    Hanoi: Khoa hoc Xa hoi.

Han Xiaorong. 1998. "The Present Echoes of the Ancient Bronze Drum: Nationalism and Archaeology in Modern Vietnam and China." *Explorations in Southeast Asian Studies* 2, 2 (Fall). http://www.hawaii.edu/sceas/pubs/explore/han/html.

Harima, Reiko, Rex Varona and Christina DeFalco. 2003. "Migration." In *Social Challenges for the Mekong Region*, edited by Mingsarn Kaosa-ard and John Dore, pp. 225–261. Chiang Mai: Chiang Mai University Social Research Institute.

Hongthong, Pennapa. 2005. "Laos Jokes Spotlight Thai Insensitivities." *The Nation*, 7 July.

Jacobs, Jeffrey W. 2002. "The Mekong River Commission: Transboundary Water Resources Planning and Regional Security." *Geographical Journal* 168, 4 (December): 354–364.

Kasetsiri, Charnvit. 2003. "Will the Mekong Survive Globalization?" http://kyotoreview.cseas.kyoto-u.ac.jp/issue3/article_297.html.

Kaosa-ard, Mingsarn and John Dore, eds. 2003. "Editors' Introduction." In *Social Challenges for the Mekong Region*, pp. 1–12. Chiang Mai: Chiang Mai University Social Research Institute.

Kuah Khun Eng. 2000. "Negotiating Central, Provincial, and Country Policies: Border Trading in South China." In *Where China Meets Southeast Asia: Social and Cultural Change in the Border Regions*, edited by Grant Evans et al., pp. 72–97. Bangkok: White Lotus; Singapore: Institute of Southeast Asian Studies.

Kuper, Adam, ed. 1992. *Conceptualizing Society*. London: Routledge.

Lee Kim Chew. 2003. "Burden of Proximity." *Straits Times*, 9 February.

Logan, James Richardson. 1852. "Ethnology of the Indo-Pacific Islands." *Journal of the Indian Archipelago 2*.

Nartsupha, Chatthip. 1996. "On the Study of Tai Cultural History." *Thai-Yunnan Project Newsletter* 32 (June): 15.

Nguyen Tran Que and Kieu Van Trung. 2001. *Song va tieu vung Mekong. Tiem nang va hop tac phat trien quoc te* (The Mekong River and the Greater Mekong Subregion: Potentials for International Development Cooperation). Hanoi: Khoa hoc Xa hoi.

Pham Duc Duong and Ha Van Tan. 1978. "Ve ngon ngu tien Viet-Muong" (On the Proto Viet-Muong Language). *Journal of Ethnology* 1: 64–69.

Phan Huu Dat. 1998. "Van de Nam A" (Austro-Asiatic Issues). In Mot so van de ve dan toc hoc Viet Nam (Some Problems of Vietnamese Anthropology), edited by Phan Huu Dat, pp. 645–688. Hanoi: Dai hoc Quoc gia.

Sangkhamanee, Jakkrit. 2003. "Charting the Mekong: A Configuration of the GMS 'Geo-body' for Development." Paper presented at the Regional Center for Social Science and Sustainable Development International Conference, "Politics of the Commons: Articulating Development and Strengthening Local Practice." Chiang Mai University, Chiang Mai, 11–14 July.

Schmidt, Wilhem. 1907. "Les peuples Mon-Khmer, trait d'union entre les peuples de l'Asie centrale et de l'Austronesie." *Bulletin de L'École Française D'Extrême-Orient* 7: 213–263 and 8: 1–35.

Simina, Suksavang and Elisabeth Preisig. 2004. The Old Heritage of the Khmu Called 'Yaan'. Unpublished working paper, Vientiane.

Taesiriphet, Chusri et al. 2005. "Potential Expansion of Distribution Channels between the Upper North of Thailand and the South of China by Applying Geographical Information System." Paper presented at the conference,

"(Re)inventing Tradition, Articulating Modernity in the Mekong Region."
Chiang Mai University Regional Center for Social Science and Sustainable
Development and Angiang University, Long Xuyen City, 21–23 April.

Vidal, John. 2004. ""Dammed and Dying: The Mekong and its Communities Face a
Bleak Future." *The Guardian*, 25 March.

Vuong Hoang Tuyen. 1963. *Cac dan toc nguon goc Nam A o mien Bac Vietnam* (Ethnic
Groups with Austro-Asiatic Origin in the North of Vietnam). Hanoi: Giao
duc.

Wain, Barry. 2004. "River at Risk." *Far Eastern Economic Review*, 26 August.

Walker, Andrew. 2000. "Women, Space, and History: Long-distance Trading in
Northwestern Laos." In *Laos: Culture and Society*, edited by Grant Evans, pp.
79–99. Singapore: Institute of Southeast Asian Studies.

Winichakul, Thongchai. 1994. *Siam Mapped: A History of the Geo-body of a Nation*.
Chiang Mai: Silkworm Books.

Wolters, Oliver W. 1982. *History, Culture, and Region in Southeast Asian Perspectives*.
Singapore: Institute of Southeast Asian Studies.

1

CONFIGURING "INDOCHINA": 19TH CENTURY EXPLORATIONS OF THE MEKONG

ARMANDO MALAY, JR

From the mid-1950s through the 1970s, the concept of a region named *Indochina* regained currency in the term "Indochina War" (often distinguished between its "First" and "Second" phases against the French and against the Americans, respectively). Popularized mainly by the mass media, the term was convenient in its imprecision, signifying as it did an armed conflict which successively engaged the two Western countries and their allies in the geophysical space of three national entities (more or less accepted by the international community as such, in any case): Vietnam, Cambodia and Laos, which had all been colonized by France to one degree or another in the 19th century; and which shifted fluidly across natural and man-made "borders" in a tropical terrain which, especially in its jungles and rural areas, privileged guerilla rather than conventional warfare.

Yet it was not lost on any of the protagonists of the war(s) that "Indochina" was largely shorthand for only one of its constitutive components: the epicenter, the irreducible crux of the conflict was Vietnam (cf Régis Wargnier's 1992 film *Indochine*, which deals with and takes place only in Vietnam). Considering the centrality in the regional drama of this, from 1954 to 1975, artificially divided nation-state—the land and the people, the "geo-body" (Winichakul 1994) and the "social space" (Condominas 1980) that it represents—Vietnam's crucial role was fully deserved. But it was a role that owed much to the effects of the French expansionist project on the discursively constructed notion of "region". In a sense, the projected "Greater Mekong Subregion" is still conceived on a colonial regime designed-grid, only supplanting but not obliterating the grand vision of the "French Indochina" construct. This short essay focuses on the explorations of the Mekong territories between 1866 and 1895 underwritten by the French state, and their intended or unintended consequences for the concept of an ideologically homogenous region.

Explorers' motivations, official and unofficial

Intertwined themes of political bankruptcy and ideological (essentially Confucian) stagnation of the ruling class pervade the conventional historical accounts of Vietnam in the mid-19th century. Likewise, the juxtaposition of Vietnamese decline with Western aggressiveness, the one facilitating if not inviting the other, is a staple of the national history whether written by a communist or a non-communist, a Westerner or a non-Westerner (Le 1981, 1955; Nguyen 1987; Bain 1967, Chesneaux 1955). Certainly the "dialectical" aspect of this crucial turning point suits both Marxist-Leninist interpretations and commonplace understandings of the yin-yang relationship. Yet it is not far-fetched to surmise that French colonialist interests would have attempted to take over the Mekong region territories even in the absence of Vietnamese, or for that matter Cambodian and Laotian, weakness during that particular period. Fierce rivalry with Great Britain, the search for overseas and especially Chinese markets, rapid advances in communications and transportation technology, the universalizing myth of "*mission civilisatrice*": all these factors over-determined the colonization of Indochina[1] and, later, the construction of "French Indochina." Indeed the colonialist impulse was an objective reality, which could only be suppressed at the price of national crisis and retrogression to second- or third-class status, as apologists of expansionism like Jules Ferry warned (Ganiage 1975; Girardet 1972). In any event the Second Empire *did* invest heavily in colonialist ventures, and France thus remained in contention as a Western power possessing territory overseas.

But as in other Western countries' attempts at colonization, the French conquest was preceded by its explorations. Earlier explorers of the Mekong and its adjacent territories were individual travelers seeking adventure or simply indulging their curiosity, or else were missionaries pursuing their evangelical duties. Being unofficial enterprises, these engaged in no "applied research," generated no State policy, and hardly ever figure in the chronicles of colonial history. Among these pioneers are the missionaries Barros, who furnished in 1544 the first geographic descriptions of the Indochinese peninsula; Gaspar da Cruz, OP, in 1555–56; Gerard van Wusthoof

in 1641; Father Chevreul in 1672; Sylvestre d'Azevedo, Tomé
Pires, the naturalist Henri Mouhot in 1858 and not least, a certain
Duyshart whom François Garnier actually met in 1867 in Laos (Lach
1968; Osborne 1975; Garnier 1996). Assuming that their oral or
written accounts, if any, met with popular acclaim in their respective
metropoles, these earlier explorers—with the possible exception of
Mouhot—could not be said to have changed the course of history in
the Mekong riparian countries the way that the de Lagrée-Garnier
and Pavie missions did. For better or for worse, the Frenchmen's
collective project contributed to a multiple (geopolitical and cultural)
reconfiguration of the spatial disposition of the Mekong region, in
the process framing and organizing our present-day cognition of
most of mainland Southeast Asia and its inter-regional problems. In
a sense, of course, all major explorations of so-called terra incognita
(those of Jacques Cartier, Lewis and Clark, Savorgnan de Brazza,
Livingstone, Peary, etc.) have always tended to remap the "unknown"
terrain to suit one purpose or the other. But unknown to whom in the
first place, and why does it matter which colonizer was the first to cast
his peremptory gaze over a particular stretch of land?

Just like the "Dutch East Indies" or "French West Africa",
"French Indochina" was a period-specific artificial construct with
no objective reality outside of the official colonial discourse. But its
usefulness for the ideological schemes of the Second Empire cannot
be understated. For the ruling elites in Paris, to be able to claim
French proprietary rights in the so-called Far East was to appropriate
images of State power and "modernity" on the same footing as the
other European powers; to be able to export French administrative
institutions, capital, merchandise, expertise, soldiers and teachers
was to demonstrate the correctness of its policy of assimilation, itself
based on Enlightenment ideals of supposedly universal value. The
de Lagrée-Garnier and especially the Pavie missions constituted the
spearhead of this ideological thrust: they were groundbreakers, not
outright conquerors (though most of the men had à military—naval—
background). One would be tempted to say this was "colonialism with
a human face," were it not for the awareness that it was organically
part of a larger impersonal system that was little disposed to sensitivity
to local concerns or human rights. In this regard, the recurrent trope
of "penetration" in the written accounts of the 19th century colonizers
may also be considered a telling ideological construct of their times.
It is a moot point to determine if they were aware of their own
assumptions: the prerogatives of the occupier were taken for granted.

Suffice to point out that, in their capacity as young French military
officers sent by their government to tame and bring order to the
territories of a still-to-be-constructed "Indochina" (unequivocally a
feminine noun in their own language), the explorers were acting out
preordained roles in an objectively gendered narrative of the "East-
West encounter." Thus did Francis Garnier and his comrades state
their objective in terms evocative of the *jus primae noctis*: "We come…
to claim the honor of being the first to penetrate central Indochina"
(in Taboulet 1955, 555). The male/female set in this narrative is only
one of many binaries, the most basic of which remains the concept
of the Subject/the Other that is immanent in ethnographic method.
In the words of Edward Said, "The West is the actor, the Orient a
passive reactor. The West is the spectator, the judge and jury, of every
facet of Oriental behavior" (1979, 108–109). Where the Indochina
discourse was concerned, the passivity of the female element was
constitutive of the "decline and decadence" period which had aroused
the Western/French aggression in the first place and which, still
from a Western/French viewpoint, mitigated, if it did not justify, that
aggression.

Doudart de Lagrée-Garnier: geography and power

A propitious intellectual and material climate prevailing in the
European colonialist countries in the mid-19th century encouraged
such Promethean projects as the Mekong expeditions. At the
threshold of the century successive agricultural, commercial and
industrial revolutions in the West had pushed even further the
frontiers of scientific knowledge and technological innovation, all
indicating unprecedented opportunities for territorial expansion
overseas. The twin conquests of time and space in turn spurred
acute interest in geography, both as "neutral" science and as vehicle
of colonialist discourse; this interest led to the founding by Conrad
Malte-Brun (alleged to be the first to coin the term *Indo-Chine*) of
the first association in the world devoted to geography, the Société
de Géographie, in Paris in 1821. The latter's close imbrication with
the "ruling class" was self-evident: all throughout the 19th century
its high officials were dukes, barons, admirals and the like. The
spiritual godfather of the first official Mekong missions was Louis
Napoléon Bonaparte, president of the Second Republic (1848–52),
known subsequently as Napoléon III, emperor of the Second Empire

(1852–70), a patron of prestigious enterprises such as the Suez Canal and the first Alpine tunnel; and who in 1856, foreshadowing the Mekong project, promoted the creation of the Danube Commission for the development of the regions around the famed European river (Guérard 1943).

Significantly, the Société's secretary-general from 1867 to 1896, that is during the de Lagrée-Garnier and Pavie missions, was a functionary of the War Ministry, Charles Maunoir (Girardet 1972, 40). Its president in the 1860s who officially endorsed the de Lagrée-Garnier expedition, the Marquis de Chausseloup-Laubat, was concurrently minister of the Navy; its vice-president in the late 1890s was Henri de Bizemont, a member of the same mission (Taboulet 1955, 553, 557). Between 1871 and 1881, eleven other geographical societies were founded in France, mostly in the provincial cities. Complementing these associations' popular impact was the appearance of the first illustrated mass-media magazines in France with titles like *Le Monde Illustré* and *Le Tour du Monde*, and the publication of the first Jules Verne novels: the entire historical period was characterized by great public enthusiasm for Orientalism, exoticism and imperial conquest (Said 1979, 217–220; Girardet 1972, 39–42).

Although the officially appointed mission chief was Commander Ernest Doudart de Lagrée, the younger officer Garnier was the real initiator of the Mekong project (a controversy over leadership "honors" would envenom the memory of the expedition even after their demise) (Osborne 1975; Garnier 1996). A habitué of the Friday dinners of the Société de Géographie (Girardet 1972, 40), Garnier had attracted attention in Paris with his pamphlet *La Cochinchine française en 1864*, an appeal for French commitment to a higher colonial calling in Asia, namely, the emancipation of what he termed "slaves of ignorance and despotism." Posing his rhetorical question: "Will France extinguish in her own hands the torch of civilization in the face of the deep darkness of Annam? Will she close her eyes to this immense misery?" (in Girardet 1972, 48), Garnier articulated the consensual call for a national (if not racial) *mission civilisatrice*. In the company of a small group of colleagues who spent their evenings carousing, dining and conversing at his Cholon residence, the prefect constructed his vision of regional conquest. Garnier's nationalist sentiment, according to a crony, led him to desire "to give to France, in the Far East, a colonial empire as vast and as flourishing as the English possessions in the Indies," and of which the Mekong was to be the "grand artery" (Taboulet 1955, 553).

Starting in June 1863 Garnier took the group's discussions a step further by writing to his superior, Admiral-Governor Jean de la Grandière, a formal request for permission to organize an expedition with the objective of fulfilling three self-assigned "obligations": "To enlarge the domain of science, enlighten the regions which have remained hitherto unknown and barbaric, [and] penetrate them with the blessings of civilization, well-being and the wealth that results from trade…" (in Taboulet 1955 II, 554). Garnier rather needlessly proposed a methodological principle: "The search for truth must only be undertaken outside of the framework of any preconceived system or idea" (ibid., 555). Apparently not considered a preconception, however, was the self-imposed task of the French to introduce rationality and modernity to the dark terra incognita of Indochina.

Endorsing the mission, de la Grandière set three goals: to determine the river's course "through rapid reconnaissance to the farthest limit possible"; to study the resources of the countries traversed; and to study the routes by which the upper Mekong might be linked to the protectorate of Cambodia and the colony of Cochinchina (i.e., southern Vietnam). Furthermore the admiral admonished the men to maintain strict discipline, avoid violence and "giving a bad example" (for they were representing a "powerful, fair, tolerant nation"); to respect native laws and religious beliefs; and in dealings with native chiefs, to use "persuasion and generosity together with proper firmness" (ibid., 556–557).

The mission which took off from Saigon on 5 June 1866 was composed of six men: Garnier, Doudart de Lagrée, Clovis Thorel, Louis Delaporte, Lucien Joubert, and Louis de Carné. The rest of the expedition was composed of a French escort of two marines, one of whom doubled as interpreter, and two sailors; two other interpreters, a Christian Cambodian and a Laotian named Alevy; and lastly two "Tagal" and seven "Annamite" soldiers or servants (Garnier 1996 I, 4–5). The first major stop was Angkor Wat, reached on 24 June. Like Mouhot before him, Garnier was astounded by its sheer beauty and size, later writing several pages about its smallest details. At the same time the sight of the ruins triggered an outburst of romantic (pre-industrial) musings:

> Mixed with the admiration that one feels for this artistic richness spread out there with so much profusion there is a profound feeling of sadness. Is it regret at being unable to penetrate this grandiose enigma which rises up suddenly before us, evoking an entire civilization, a

whole people, a disappeared past?... Is it the fear that this magnificent
masterpiece of human genius cannot deliver the secret that it hides
before its destruction is complete? (ibid., 22)

The artistically inclined Delaporte similarly rhapsodized about
the Khmer sculptures at Wat Phou (ibid., 187). The explorers did not
have occasion afterwards to admire, to this degree, any contemporary
man-made monuments or artifacts in the Mekong territories that they
visited. This disappointment meshed with their regret over the state
of darkness and decadence that Indochina since the heyday of Angkor
had fallen into—and which thus made French intervention necessary.
Indeed, it is in the same vein that Garnier suggested that the French
government launch a conservation program to save Angkor Wat from
further deterioration (ibid., 24).

At least in his official account, Garnier manifested a high-minded
attitude towards cultural matters. Coming across a vandalized
inscription at Angkor Wat, he recalled that "Our astonishment and
the indignation of Commander de Lagrée was great....Was this
unintelligible act of vandalism the work of a superstitious indigenous
person or of an anglophile [sic] tourist...? We lost ourselves in
speculations about this act" (ibid., 39).

But the strongest expression of indignation that he permitted
himself was on the subject of slavery, which apparently still flourished
on what was nominally French soil. Along the Se Cong affluent in
Cambodia, Garnier noted the commerce in slaves of tribal origin
whom Chinese traders openly sold in the Phnom Penh marketplace,
which was French territory. While admitting that these slaves
were relatively well treated, especially in comparison to African
ones elsewhere, Garnier and Delaporte were anxious for more
than personal reasons. The "dignity of France" was at stake; the
colonialists in Indochina owed it to their national image to put a stop
to it. "The immediate results of abolishing this odious trade would
be the raising of moral standards, the development of the resources
and security of the area and an increase in the prestige of Europeans"
(ibid., 67, 125, 216).

Primacy of trade and control

It is quite clear that Garnier's humanist discourse did not inhibit
his preoccupation with the exploitation of the Mekong region's

commercial possibilities. (Many of his sharper observations touch on the ideal season for navigation, the volume of fluvial traffic and estimated cargo capacity of the vessels encountered.) But development of the Mekong was predicated on the federation of its different populations under a French regime. Garnier's first recorded comment on Cambodia's capital is revealing: "By its position at the confluence of the big stream and the arm from the Great Lake [Tonle Sap], Phnom Penh is without doubt destined for a grand commercial future if French domination can take root in a durable and intelligent way in these locations." (ibid., 48)

Upon arrival at Khong, a provincial capital, the mission observed that on the right bank of the Mekong the province of Tonly Repou was henceforth under Siamese control; but it was now partly deserted, and in the nearby mountains were refugees from bandits. The solution, for Garnier, was obvious: "If we want the trade of the Mekong valley to expand as much as possible, then the French flag must be hoisted on the right bank of the river, below the waterfalls [of Khon]." French rule would then guarantee the protection of goods going up or down the river; facilitate works along the passage, and increase "the extent of the zone of *civilizing influence, which alone* can bring about the development of which these rich areas are capable" (ibid., 74–75, emphasis in the original). In like manner, Cambodian trade downstream to Saigon and across the banks of the rich and immense Tonle Sap appeared to Garnier extremely difficult because the lake was "unfortunately" divided between Siam and Cambodia. In effect, the artificial border across the water was the source of a thousand bureaucratic harassments suffered by Cambodians living on either side (ibid., 142). He thus urged that France exert efforts to make Siam "restore the waters" to Cambodia and to "reunify" the populations of the northwest area of the Tonle Sap basin under the French tricolor. To expand inter-regional trade, Garnier further recommended the streamlining of transport and customs procedures along the Mekong; the improvement of existing roads or construction of new ones; the building of a railway from Saigon to Stung Treng in Cambodia; and perhaps the most ambitious of all, to make the Siamese government stop the forced barter practices engaged in by Bangkok's envoys in Laos; to agree, with the government of the colony of Cochinchina, to abolish the slave trade; and to grant commercial freedom to all the affected regions "in exchange for the regular tax which their conquest has given them the right to impose."

Despite his allusions to Chinese greed, deceit and duplicity (ibid., 54; Garnier, 1996 II, 196), Garnier suggested that Chinese and Annamites be encouraged to immigrate to the Cambodia-Laos border provinces in the expectation that they would stimulate agricultural and industrial activity there (ibid., 124–126). The hardworking Chinese, he acknowledged, were good at inter-regional trade, but high customs duties imposed by the Cambodians had hampered their business. In geopolitical terms Cambodia was precisely crucial to the inter-regional trade circuit, for in its northeast region that protectorate formed the border with the French possessions in Cochinchina, and it was the obligatory transit point of all the merchandise from the Mekong valley to the Saigon market. Hence the importance, for Saigon, of the removal of the impediments put up by the Cambodian customs. If Cambodian trade with countries other than those of French Indochina were to flourish, Garnier argued, a similar measure was necessary (ibid., 66–67).

In any event, by mid-October 1867 the Frenchmen's dream of the Mekong as a waterway leading straight to the Chinese market had to be abandoned: they discovered that the river was non-navigable beyond Xien-Hong in Yunnan, and an armed rebellion of Muslim tribesmen in the same province made further exploration of the Mekong too risky. Commonsense, plus the men's exhaustion, prevailed over Admiral de la Grandière's instructions to follow the Mekong to its very source. The mission came close to trying out another fluvial route instead: the Song-Koi, or Red River to the north, originating in Yunnan, traversing the Tonkin region and emptying into the Bay of Tonkin. But the men never navigated the Red River, and the question of first "discovering" its route generated much controversy. Contrary to the allegation of mission member Dr. Joubert that *they* informed the trader-adventurer Jean Dupuis about its possibility, Dupuis never wavered from his claim that he knew about it as early as 1861, while still living in Hankow in China; and even navigated it twice, halfway in 1868 and completely in 1870, a fact acknowledged by Garnier himself (Tsuboi 1987, 60–63; Garnier 1996 I, 319–320). Also, unknown to the de Lagrée-Garnier mission, in 1863 a French sergeant named Charles Duval had gone on a secret reconnaissance of the lower reaches of the Red River and wrote a report to the Ministry of War suggesting its commercial possibilities. However, his report remained unread for many years (Osborne 1975, 138–139).

Once in China, and particularly in the picturesque Yunnan region which the expedition reached in mid-October 1867, the French found considerably more material incentives for their interests than in the Mekong valley itself. As several other earlier and contemporary explorers' accounts testified, the Chinese were a people whose agricultural and commercial talents had no equal in Asia. "Few races are blessed with energy as great as the Chinese," wrote Garnier, who never marveled in such detail over new sights and discoveries during his voyage as much as he did in Yunnan (Garnier 1996 I, 117). Indeed he thought that the Europeans could learn from the Chinese in building more gracious cities (because of the latter's elegant roofs) and embanking rivers for agricultural purposes (ibid., 113, 146). Gaining access to China's huge internal market, "which will be sufficient to guarantee the wealth and the grandeur of the nation skillful enough to penetrate it first" (and here Garnier referred to Russia and England as rivals) was enough reason for France to persist in its empire-building project in Indochina (ibid., 297). The French had an advantage in that through treaties previously signed with the court of Hué, they exercised influence over the neighboring Tonkin region. These geopolitical considerations were not lost on Garnier, whose argument is worth quoting at length:

> The pacification of Yunnan would provide the vast Song-Koi [Red River] basin with the commercial life and the richness assured it by its varied and precious products. They are offered an easy and economical outlet by the proximity of the mouth of the river and the French port of Saigon. A jealous policy has thus far managed to divert Annamite merchandise from their natural outlet; they have to seek a distant and expensive market in Canton or Shanghai. It is up to us to use our influence on the courts of Peking and Hué to put a stop to this state of affairs. *Our Cochinchinese colony is legitimately destined, by the very force of circumstance, to harvest the heritage of Canton*, and Saigon will offer to the products of Yunnan and southern Indochina a better-located entrepôt for trade against European merchandise.[2] (emphasis in the original; in Taboulet 1955, 564)

The Muslim rebellion resulted in Yunnan's rich copper, silver, tin and iron mines being abandoned. Garnier imagined how, via the Red River, the French could transport these mineral products to Saigon and thence to Europe, thus eventually making Yunnan "the most important metallurgical supplier in the world." But these were to remain idle daydreams: as Garnier ruefully noted, the lack of interpreters prevented Doudart de Lagrée from pursuing his investigation into the matter (Garnier, 1996 II, 166). Furthermore, it was out of the question for the French colonial regime itself, already challenged by a growing resistance movement in Cochinchina, to undertake the "pacification" of the huge Yunnan territory. Rather anticlimactically, towards the end of the expedition—that is, the first half of 1868—Garnier's views of China began to change: it was, he now wrote, an "exhausted, sick civilization," stricken by "lethargy and immobility." A remedy lay in its greater opening up to the world, specifically to European industry and foreign trade (ibid., 266–268). In retrospect, this view does not sound very different from the official French prescription for contemporary Indochina itself.

After reaching Yunnan the expedition had nowhere else to go; minus Doudart de Lagrée who had died en route, and disabused about the possibilities of the Mekong, Garnier's men returned to their Saigon home base in June 1868. By the turn of the century, the grandiose schemes for the Red River as the major artery into China had given way to the realization of the Yunnan railway, a more "modern" but also more profitable means of transportation. Promoted by Governor-General Paul Doumer (1897–1902), a region-wide railway-building program was drawn up to complement a 77-km long route in Cochinchina, the first and till then only track built in the peninsula in 1881–1886. Reflecting his priorities, the Yunnan railway was first on Doumer's list, ahead of the projected Laotian, Cambodian and trans-Indochinese (Saigon-Hanoi) networks. After a mere four-month feasibility study, work on the Yunnan railway commenced in 1905 and was completed in 1910. It did not escape the attention of observers that the French project was at least in part motivated by the possibility that the British might be the first to "penetrate" Yunnan from the south; but eventually, to the relief of the French, their rivals abandoned their Burma-Yunnan railway project (Thompson 1937, 207).

Pavie the amateur geographer and "pacifier"

Auguste Pavie was another Cochinchina veteran, who had served some seven years in that colony before being reassigned in 1879 to Cambodia as chief telegraphist in the port town of Kampot. Encouraged by the intention of Charles le Myre de Vilers, the newly

appointed governor of Cochinchina, to continue the geographic
studies initiated by the de Lagrée-Garnier mission, Pavie submitted a
proposal for the exploration of what he termed the "unknown regions
of Indochina" (Pavie 1901, 1). (Not coincidentally, the governor-
general who approved Pavie's project was secretary-general of the
Société de Géographie, 1906–1908.) The additional task of installing
a telegraph line between Phnom Penh and Bangkok was given to
Pavie; this was a good opportunity for him to explore the "terra
incognita" between the Tonle Sap basin and the Gulf of Siam.

Although an amateur compared to his better educated and better
equipped predecessors, and less given to philosophical speculation
as Garnier, Pavie was a hard worker, single-mindedly dedicated to
recording facts and figures, and above all, making maps. His travel
accounts make for tedious reading as they are almost exclusively
descriptive, with little attempt at analysis. His obsession to master
the subject of the geography of Cambodia ("almost unknown then,
aside from the major arteries of the [Mekong] river and the Great
Lake [Tonle Sap]") was well known in Kampot. Every new arrival in
the port who could inform him on the subject—civil servant, sailor,
trader—was thus brought to him. The indications derived therefrom
he dutifully

> ...noted down on a map which, compared with the existing geographic
> documents, contributed in no small way to my nascent resolution to
> do everything possible to search for the truth in the field, and I hoped
> that nobody would think, before I did, of undertaking the study that
> I was dreaming about. (Pavie 1901, 44)

In his desire to be first to know, Pavie was perhaps unwittingly
experiencing the de Lagrée-Garnier mission's anxiety not to be
beaten by their rivals, the British, in the race to be the first to reach
the source of the Mekong (Garnier 1996 I, 274–275).

Riding an elephant as his mission headed for the banks of the
Mekong, Pavie would ask his mahout the name of every hamlet, of
every mountain near or distant, of streams, their source and their
direction, and "endless details on Cambodia's geography, history,
legends" (Pavie 1901, 47). Such assiduousness led him to think of
himself "better informed about many things about the country than
even the chiefs of several regions which I hoped to travel in could
be" (ibid., 56). Earlier in fact, he considered a neighbor in Kampot to
"know even less" about ancient Cambodian history than he already

did (ibid., 16). All throughout his voyage Pavie recorded empirical data in great detail: widths, lengths and depths of sections of the Mekong and its tributaries; velocity of the water's flow, upstream and downstream, in dry and wet seasons; meteorological patterns, soil conditions, changes in vegetation, and of course, like Garnier before him, prospects for navigability of the different sections of the river. But in a sense he did not fit the profile of the colonialist: a major history of the French protectorate over Cambodia mentions his name only once (Forest 1980). In 1891 he entertained the idea of initiating negotiations with the Chinese over the rearrangement of the Sipsong Pahnas region (now part of the People's Republic of China) mostly populated by Thai/Tay ethnic groups. With his companions Pavie hoped to

> hasten, by means of as complete a geographic study as possible, the future settlement [of the border question] and to make the French loved and desired by the populations who, constantly bothered by internecine wars and piracy, were living in a perpetual state of anxiety. (Pavie 1901, 117)

But as will later be seen, his own government's divide-and-rule designs favored the Vietnamese and only added to the Khmers' resentment of their stronger neighbor.

Well meaning but naïve, Pavie really thought there existed a geo-ethnic "limit" between the Sipsong Pahnas and Yunnan to which, by the 20th century, the region was universally conceded to be attached. In any case his project was "judged premature" (but by whom, Pavie did not say) and the idea was shelved (Pavie 1906, 117, 123). On the other hand, his maps of the region omitted boundary lines between Siam and French Indochina, perhaps his way of leaving the question open for additional claims (Winichakul 1994, 126).

After setting up a Cambodian school, later simply named the Colonial School, in Paris for native colonial administrators, Pavie was promoted to vice-consul in 1865 and posted to the principality of Luang Prabang. Once again he was entrusted with a mission, this time to explore and lay down a route linking the area between the Mekong and the Tonkin provinces. But the omnipresent Thais were poised to take over these Tonkinese territories, considered by the French as theirs. This obliged Pavie to wait for six months in Bangkok to obtain the necessary passports from the Thai authorities. In addition to Siam's territorial claims, French interests in the region were being challenged by the incursions of Chinese bands, particularly the Black Flags—remnants of the Taiping rebellion, now addicted to opium, gambling and pillage—who had settled on the same territories. Pavie's progress upstream of the Mekong, and later of its Nam-Houa and its Nam-Ngoua tributaries, was interrupted by news of fighting upstream, disrupting his geographic observations and forcing him to return to Luang Prabang. The Thais burnt down the town; the population had fled, and the old king Oun Kham escaped capture or death only through the efforts of Pavie and his trusted assistant Keo. This later earned Pavie the consent of the king to accept the protectorate of France over his kingdom (Winichakul 1994, 109–110).

But security matters complicated Pavie's task. After a series of setbacks between October 1887 and March 1888, he resumed his exploration eastward to return to the Black River, which he decided to be the best route toward the Tonkin delta. In the region of Sip Song Chau Thais, considered by him to be part of Tonkin and therefore under French control, Pavie proceeded to enforce a program of administrative reorganization. But Chinese outlaws literally barred communications between Laotian and Tonkinese territories, isolating the French outpost at Lai. At a meeting in mid-April 1888 in the mountain town of Muong Son, Pavie obtained the Black Flags' cooperation in his mission and the release of the Lao prisoners taken during the Thai raid on Luang Prabang. Henceforth Pavie's narrative is full of such successes, for which he duly acknowledged the collaboration of such surrenderees as the famed Thai chief Deo van Tri on the one hand, and where any acts of brutality and violence committed in the course of the "pacification" were passed over in silence on the other hand (ibid., 269, 325–326). If Pavie's word is to believed, Colonel (later promoted to general) Pennequin, his second-in-command, simply gave the Black Flags a forceful ultimatum to quit Tonkin and return to China, even offering to supply their rations and porter service. By mid-March 1889, the bandits—with the exception of those already engaged in trade and farming and who were endorsed favorably by their canton chiefs—left for good. In 1893 Pennequin scored another success, this time against pirates operating in the Red River delta whom he convinced to remain in agreed-upon areas within which the French recognized their right to levy taxes and keep their armed troops. But this respite was only temporary; after the colonel's departure for France in late 1893, the policy changed and the pirates resumed their raids in Tonkin (ibid., 81–82).

The most arduous task assigned to Pavie was negotiating over territorial issues with his government's rivals: an "agent" of Siam, backed up by Siamese soldiers, had moved back the old boundary lines between Annam and the Mekong principalities, repositioning them far beyond the dividing limits on the Mekong's left bank. Moreover, the Siamese had settled down in Kamkeut and Kammon, considered by the French as Annamite cantons (ibid., 306–307). At the same time the British had begun to establish their presence in the upper Mekong valley and were perceived by the French to be backing the Siamese. So as to have a diplomatic officer with as high a rank as the others in Bangkok, the French government promoted Pavie to Consul in February 1892. In March, with a view to exerting pressure on Siam, the French gunboat Lutin arrived in the Siamese capital. The summer was a tense period as the French and other European fleets descended on Bangkok and Saigon, reaching a climax in a gun battle between Siamese and French forces on the Me-nam River on 13–14 July. On 19 July 1892 the French delivered an ultimatum, which Siam accepted only on 29 July and formally confirmed on 6 August.

Pavie's greatest accomplishment was the treaty of 3 October 1893 in which the Siamese court, notably, recognized as French possessions the left bank of the Mekong and the islands in the waterway; renounced all claims thereto; recognized a neutral zone of 25 kilometers together with the provinces of Battambang and Siem Reap on the right bank; and pledged to ban all traffic of Siamese boats or armed vessels on Tonle Sap, the Mekong and its affluents (ibid., 247–249). Siam's loss was France's gain of course, but by the mid-20th century, with its retreat from its Indochinese colonies France was the ultimate loser in regional terms. And unwittingly, Pavie rendered a great service to the notion of the Siamese "geo-body:" the map of the kingdom that he published in 1902—remarkable, as mentioned above, for having no territorial boundary lines, except that separating Siam and British Burma—served as the authority for all later maps of Siam for a long time, even down to the reign in 1910–1925 of Rama VI (Winichakul 1994, 128–129).

The Annamites as favored "race"

As the Bangkok stand-off demonstrated, the colonialist discourse professed to champion a 19th-century prototypical idea of "national liberation"; but the altruistic sentiments of the children of the Enlightenment were present in the colonial project from the very start. Much earlier, during his mission's sojourn in Laos, Garnier—who, as we saw, had expressed indignation over the slave market in Phnom Penh—wrote of his distress over the Siamese kingdom's "suffocating oppression" of the Laotians, described as an "intelligent and gentle race" (ibid., 81, 93). While regretting that "among the Cambodians all qualities have disappeared, and all [their] vitality seems to be extinguished," in contrast the Frenchman lavishly praised the Laotians' inquisitive spirit, their religious tolerance, and their physical beauty in general. But he could not banish the impression that Laotian males were very lazy, leaving the greatest share of daily chores to the women; moreover, they were a people "completely lacking" in "historical sense." In a word, Laos in Garnier's eyes was an ahistorical society, typified as it was by the "dreamy carelessness" of its "calm, pleasant and happy" people, who were alien to "turbulent or cruel passions." The historically unresolved essence of the Laotian "bon sauvage" moved the Frenchman to indulge in either simple whimsy: "How many times have I envied the carefree well-being and the unworried happiness of these tranquil people!" (ibid., 111), or naked irony: "What a contrast between the calm world of Laos and that in Europe, even the name of which was unknown to those around us! Ought we to pity them or congratulate them for their ignorance and wildness?" (ibid., 304).

Elsewhere in his account Garnier counseled against letting European settlers come into direct contact with the natives, for the simplicity and gentleness of the latter allegedly "encourage[d] their abuse" (ibid., 126). Yet his ardent wish was precisely to see France intervene more actively in this wondrous utopia, arguing that "[T]here exist among the Laotians numerous seeds of development and progress which only await a fertilizing impulse." Whereas the Cambodians were hopelessly apathetic, philistines and religious fanatics, their Laotian neighbors could "be revived with energy and richness amidst the beautiful regions that they inhabit under the civilizing influence of France" (ibid., 81). As if to soften his censoriousness, Garnier made a distinction between the northerners and the southerners of Laos: because of their hard existence the former maintained the "virility of their race," were hardworking and commercially oriented; whereas the latter had "lost all strength and energy due to their easy life" (ibid., 312). It is perhaps not coincidental that the lazy Lao southerners were geographically closer to the disfavored Cambodians; but the otherwise perspicacious Garnier was silent on this point.

For his part Pavie was bothered, at the start of his telegraphic-line project, by the absence of fraternizing between the laborers in his entourage: namely the "gay and boisterous" Annamites and the "taciturn" Cambodians. In early 1885, hardly had the section between Phnom Penh and Sambor been completed when Cambodian locals attacked a French detachment in the latter town. The fact that these were Annamite troops serving under the French flag on Cambodian territory complicated Khmer-French relations, to Pavie's chagrin. As he saw it, the Annamites had nothing but "aversion" for the Khmers, while the latter felt that they were treated with "contempt and disdain" by the former. Worse was to come when, after a quarrel between a local Khmer chief and the Annamite militiamen of the French resident official at Preyveng, the Cambodians killed fourteen of the Annamites who had accompanied the official to arrest the local chief. In retaliation the French-led troops razed temples and houses in Preyveng, causing the villagers to flee. These incidents were followed by uprisings elsewhere in the region, led by local chiefs who, Pavie ruefully noted, had otherwise "no personal reason for discontent." Khmer functionaries of the French administration were now objects of sarcasm or vengeful threats on the part of members of the Phnom Penh court. To alleviate the danger, he lobbied for the replacement of the Annamite militias by his own men, namely, those natives working on the telegraph line (Pavie 1901, 172–176).

For purposes of his exploration of parts of Siam and western Laos (March 1886–February 1887), Pavie recruited Cambodian assistants in preference over the other ethnic groups, knowing that

> I was going to simplify my task and increase my certitude of success, for on several occasions I had already had the occasion to appreciate the Khmers' virtues, their endurance and the courage with which they serve him whom they have chosen or accepted as their chief. (ibid., 200)

He was about the only Khmerophile, for most of his fellow colonialists openly favored the Annamites as settlers and/or colonial subjects over the Laotians and the Cambodians. A "highly intelligent and inflexible race" in Garnier's estimation, the Annamites had "remarkable colonizing capabilities and the gift of assimilation to the French race itself, which could be applied so well to these

gentle and timid populations of Laos" (Garnier 1996 I, 297). Several
decades later, Governor-General Doumer blithely assigned a status
of inferiority to the Cambodians and Laotians vis-à-vis their bigger
neighbor in these cavalier—and in the light of French expansionism,
highly sardonic—terms:

> [T]he two peoples along the Mekong's banks do not have and
> seem never to have had the force of expansion, the valor and the
> conqueror's temperament of the Annamites. They have, at different
> periods, allowed themselves to be defeated and dominated. Even
> today, one may note that they are very inferior to the Annamites in
> works of peace as they were in war. (Doumer 1930, 237–238)

French civil servants sent to Cambodia were the lazy incompetent
ones, and their subalterns there were Annamites. Cambodia's role,
according to an official report of the French Resident, "partly consists
of supplying the Saigon-Cholon market and secondarily the whole
of Indochina, with agricultural produce and raw materials which are
either exported or are returned to it in the form of finished or semi-
finished products." Cambodia thus seemed to be treated by France as
a granary, a mere hinterland of Indochina, and its people, a victim of
the stronger Franco-Vietnamese colonial bureaucracy (Pomonti and
Thion 1971, 12–13; Forest 1980, 442; Chanda 1986, 53–56).

In the early 20th century, as questions of "national identity" became
more acutely posed, official French policy vis-à-vis Indochina began
to boomerang. The Marxist-Leninist ideology which was taking
root in Indochina represented a new threat to the colonial system,
with its emphasis on "proletarian internationalism" and its readiness
to use radical means to "smash" so-called reactionary States. The
name "Indochinese Communist Party" (Dang Cong San Dong
Duong)—its original appellation, "Vietnamese Communist Party,"
was ordered changed by the Comintern—did not reflect the fact
that its membership was overwhelmingly Vietnamese (Duiker
1975, 19–20). But the unified-Indochina discourse finally suited
the Vietnamese well: it favored a wider theater of operations in the
conduct of a struggle "without borders," beyond or above the narrow
confines of nationalism. Since Vietnam, Cambodia and Laos were
all under the same French yoke, it made sense for them to act as if
they were one—and, implicitly, under a centralized leadership. The
objective consequence of the "Indochina revolution" paradigm was

thus to perpetuate the French policy of favoring the "Annamite race" as *primus inter pares*. As the party stated in 1931:

> Although the three countries are made of three different races, with different languages, different traditions, different behavior patterns, in reality they form only one country...It is not possible to make a revolution separately for Vietnam, Cambodia and Laos. In order to oppose the enemy of the revolution which has a united concentration of force in the entire Indochina, the communist party will have to concentrate the forces of the Indochinese proletariat in a united front, under the leadership of the Indochinese proletariat. (*Cong Nong Binh*, quoted in Huynh 1982, 129)

Conversely, as a postwar pro-Vietnamese pamphlet put it: if colonialism had succeeded in maintaining its divide-and-rule policy over the three peoples, it was because "their uprisings broke out separately, were not coordinated, and lacked a correct revolutionary line" (Ministry of Foreign Affairs 1984, 131), an explanation that broadly hinted at the desirability of a unitary revolutionary force. The fictitious concepts of "only one country" and "leadership of the Indochinese proletariat" were not overtly contested during the successive "Indochina Wars" (1945–54; then 1965–75), when militant unity was objectively indispensable for all anti-colonial, anti-imperialist protagonists of the region. It was as if being against French or American imperialism in Cambodia or Laos carried the obligation to approve of solidarity with the country spearheading the struggle against these Western powers and bearing the brunt of the conflict, namely Vietnam. Thus throughout the 1960s and 1970s did the "neutralist" Prince Sihanouk undergo untold stresses and strains as he negotiated Cambodia's way through the minefields of the war in its backyard.

But ideological tensions between the Cambodians and the Vietnamese, exacerbated by ancient grudges of the former against the French-backed "big brother" and complicated by divisions in the communist camp, eventually broke out in the open in mid-1975. The pro-Chinese Khmer Rouge line clashed with that of the pro-Soviet Vietnamese, providing a pretext for the Hanoi propagandists to reopen old wounds. For example, charges of Chinese merchants' collusion with French firms in the rice trade in the Mekong delta during the colonial era were revived. In addition, the French were accused of playing off ethnic Chinese settlers against the Vietnamese community (Ky 1978, 22). In another Vietnamese broadside, Zhou En-lai was revealed to have struck a deal with the French at the Geneva Conference of 1954 "in order to divide Vietnam and deny the Kampuchean resistance an area in which to regroup its forces" (Nguyen 1981, 91). Ironically, the rupture occurred just after both the Khmer Rouge (with the help of the Vietnamese) and the Vietnamese communists had defeated their respective enemies. In the showdown between a shared radical ideology—even of tenuously Western origin—and nationalism, the latter not surprisingly emerged triumphant.

What hath the French project wrought?

In the 19th century there was no universally accepted name for the whole length of the Mekong in the regions that it traversed: it was known as Song Lom in Vietnamese, Tonle Thom in Khmer, Me-nam Khong in Thai, and as Kieu-long Kiang in Chinese. Curiously, the French themselves referred to it as "the Cambodian river" (Garnier 1996 passim; Osborne 1975, 15; Pavie 1901, 79) as if it were commonly known as such by the Khmers (and much less by the Siamese, the Laotians, etc.). And yet France, whose "control" of the river was limited to the southern delta where it first gained a foothold, had the ambitious dream of federating the whole region into a unitary entity constituted around its main waterway. Beyond the epistemological aspect, engaging the physical essence of the Mekong was a politically charged exercise which shaped or inflected the course of history of the countries it irrigated: China or at least the Yunnan region; Thailand, Vietnam, Laos and Cambodia. And of course France, whose expansionism in a part of Asia she did not wish to lose by default to Great Britain ultimately led to her ill-fated reliance on the United States.

Along and around the Mekong, a European form of nationalism confronted Asian forms, or formal understandings, of nationalism. The outcome of the confrontation did not depend exclusively on internal (domestic) determinants: whether they liked it or not, and whether the borders they lived in were imaginary, arbitrary, disembodied constructs or not, the peoples of "French Indochina" were bound, as a matter of necessity and regardless of national resentments, to assist each other in the struggle against French colonialism (in any case, what leaders of the struggle perceived to be its negative manifestations). Of all the ex-"French Indochinese" parties involved, Cambodia in the 20th century seemed to have derived the least satisfaction from the rearrangement of "national" borders, hence its leaders' guarded or resentful attitudes vis-à-vis the more powerful Vietnam extending down to the 1970s. Laos seemed to have emerged relatively unscathed from the conflict, perhaps as a consequence of its official closeness to Vietnam and its manifestation of a less assertive nationalism. As for Vietnam, its ontological status as "real" nation-state has been put in doubt (Nepote 1985); and the official claim by Hanoi that since reunification the country has had one nationally expressed socialist will, from north to south, is belied by disjunctive manifestations of modernity in the south (Taylor 2001). Thus Vietnamese nationalism may appear problematic in that it is conceptually based either on an agreed-upon fiction or on a willful misreading of its historically constituted basis. But as countless examples in modern history bear out, tangible "reality" is finally inessential, unimportant, beside the point, where the construction and nurturing of the nationalist spirit are concerned. Without a sense of nation, collective efforts in the activity of so-called "nation-building" in the region would have amounted to naught; and yet, seemingly paradoxically, divergent or contradictory notions of respective national spaces have tended to abort expressions of larger solidarity. In the end it may very well be that the enduring legacy of the French attempts at regional integration was to have, unwittingly, made it harder for genuine integration in the Mekong region to be achieved.

Notes

1 The term's origin is rather controversial. The geographer Conrad Malte-Brun (a French rendition of his Danish name Malthe Conrad Bruun) is claimed by the editor of the French review, *Herodote*, to be the first to have used the hyphenated proper noun *Indo-Chine* in the 1820s (Lacoste 1981, 3). Another version has it that English missionaries and linguists had, as early as 1811, apparently referred to "Indo-China" to designate, "rather loosely, the Asia (sic) beyond India" (Goscha 1995, 15). For his part, the ethnologist Lucien Bernot contends that John Leyden was the first to use the term (see ibid., n15).

2 Translated from the original text of Garnier, *Voyage d'Exploration en Indochine* (1873), reproduced in Taboulet, in the interest of a more faithful rendition.

References

Bain, Chester. 1967. *Vietnam: the Roots of Conflict*. New Jersey: Prentice-Hall.

Chanda, Nayan. 1986. *Brother Enemy: The War After the War*. New York: Collier Books.

Chesneaux, Jean. 1955. *Contribution à l'Histoire de la Nation Vietnamienne*. Paris: Editions Sociales.

Condominas, Georges. 1980. *L'espace social: A propos de l'Asie du Sud-Est*. Paris: Flammarion.

Doumer, Paul. 1930. *L'Indochine française*. Paris: Librairie Vuibert.

Duiker, William. 1975. *The Comintern and Vietnamese Communism*. Ohio: Ohio University Center for International Studies.

Forest, Alain. 1980. *Le Cambodge et la Colonisation française: Histoire d'une Colonisation sans heurts*. Paris: L'Harmattan.

Ganiage, Jean. 1975. *L'expansion coloniale et les rivalités internationales*. Vol. I. Paris: Centre de Documentation Universitaire.

Garnier, Francis. 1996. *Travels in Cambodia and Parts of Laos. The Mekong Exploration Commission Report (1866–1868)*. Vol I. Bangkok: White Lotus.

———. 1996. *Further Travels in Laos and Yunnan. The Mekong Exploration Commission Report (1866–1868)*. Vol II. Bangkok: White Lotus.

Girardet, Raoul. 1972. *L'idée coloniale en France de 1871 à 1962*. Paris: La Table Ronde.

Goscha, Christopher E. 1995. *Vietnam or Indochina? Contesting Concepts of Space in Vietnamese Nationalism, 1887–1954*. Copenhagen: NIAS, Nordic Institute of Asian Studies Reports Series No. 28.

Huynh Kim Khanh. 1982. *Vietnamese Communism*. Ithaca: Cornell University Press.

Guérard, Albert. 1943. *Napoléon III*. Boston: Harvard University Press.

Ky Son. 1978. "The Hoa in Vietnam: Some Data". In *The Hoa in Vietnam: Dossier*, edited by Hoang Nguyen et al. Hanoi: Foreign Languages Publishing House.

Lach, Donald. 1968. *Southeast Asia in the Eyes of Europe: The 16th Century*. Chicago: University of Chicago Press.

Lacoste, Yves. 1981. "Mer de Chine ou Mer de l'Asie du Sud-Est?" *Herodote* 21 (April–June): 3–13.

Le Thanh Khoi. 1955. *Le Vietnam: Histoire et Civilisation*. Paris: Editions de Minuit.

———.1981. *Histoire du Vietnam: des origines à 1858*. Paris: Sudestasie.

Ministry of Foreign Affairs, People's Republic of Kampuchea. 1984. *The Chinese Rulers' Crimes against Kampuchea.*

Nepote, Jacques. 1985–86. "Quelle histoire? Pour quels Vietnamiens?" *Péninsule* 17, 11–12 (new series): 7–26.

Nguyen Khac Vien. 1993. *Vietnam: A Long History.* Hanoi: The Gioi Publishers.

Nguyen Minh Kien. 1981. *Understanding China.* Hanoi: Vietnam Courier.

Osborne, Milton. 1975. *River Road to China: the Mekong River Expedition 1866–1873.* London: George Allen & Unwin.

Pavie, Auguste. 1901. *Mission Pavie Indo-Chine 1879–1895*, vol. I. Paris: Ernest Leroux.

———. 1906. *Mission Pavie Indo-Chine 1879–1895*, vol. II. Paris: Ernest Leroux.

Pomonti, Jean Claude and Serge Thion. 1971. *Des Courtisans aux Partisans: Essais sur la Crise Cambodgienne.* Paris: Gallimard.

Said, Edward. 1979. *Orientalism.* New York: Vintage Books.

Taboulet, Georges. 1955. *La Geste Française en Indochine.* 2 vols. Paris: Adrien Maisonneuve.

Taylor, Philip. 2001. *Fragments of the Present: Searching for Modernity in Vietnam's South.* Honolulu: University of Hawaii Press.

Thompson, Virginia. 1937. *French Indo-China.* New York: Macmillan.

Tsuboi, Yoshiharu. 1987. *L'empire vietnamien face à la France et à la Chine.* Paris: L'Harmattan.

Winichakul, Thongchai. 1994. *Siam Mapped: A History of the Geo-Body of a Nation.* Hawaii: University of Hawaii Press.

2

FROM INDOCHINESE DREAMS TO POST-INDOCHINESE REALITIES

VATTHANA PHOLSENA

As the name suggests, the territory of Indochina was first perceived as a geographical space situated between India and China.[1] In the early days of conquest and pacification, Indochina was thus referred to as *Indo-Chine*, with a hyphen reflecting concomitantly its hybrid status and its lack of a specific identity. The French acquisition of these territories that would progressively form the entity eventually named *l'Indochine française*, was less the result of a planned and coherent *politique coloniale* than of an esoteric combination of individual actions, economic interests and imperial rivalry. The French presence in this region of Southeast Asia became, from the mid-nineteenth century, motivated by economic interests and commercial competition with Britain. Indeed, the French hoped that their foothold in Indochina would allow the penetration of the Chinese market via a region where the British were absent. Many expeditions were subsequently undertaken (including those by the renowned explorers, Ernest Doudart de Lagrée, Francis Garnier and Auguste Pavie) to assess trade routes and, in particular, the navigability of the Mekong River, into the interior of China. Opposition from local authorities, rapidly followed by armed conflicts led, however, to heated debates in the metropole, pitting politicians pushing for colonial expansion against those opposing further conquests in this area of Asia. Divided views in Paris were to be eventually subsumed by the end of the 19th century under a late conceptualization of French imperial policy, driven by a vision of France's grandeur and prestige, bolstered by territorial acquisitions abroad and achieved through military interventions.

A colonial invention

The political term *l'Indochine française* was formally adopted in France in 1887. By suppressing the hyphen and adding the suffix *française*, the Indian and Chinese political and cultural influences were somewhat played down (in a very limited linguistic sense), and the geographical space given a new and uniform identity under French ownership and guidance. The concept of *Indochine* was furthermore superimposed upon artificial political and administrative boundaries that formed *l'Union indochinoise* (widely referred to as French Indochina). The latter was composed of five entities: Laos, Cambodia, Tonkin, Annam and Cochinchina—the last three composing present-day Vietnam— governed by diverse regimes of control and administration: colonies (e.g., Cochinchina, Central and Southern Laos) and protectorates (e.g., Tonkin, Luang Prabang, Cambodia, Annam).

During their administration from 1887 until 1945, the French incessantly pursued the goal of filling the 'gap', that is, drawing together the disparate and culturally different peoples and kingdoms of what are today Cambodia, Laos and Vietnam. The act of constructing Indochina was at the same time carried out through concrete, though not entirely successful, policies (e.g., the policy of *mise en valeur* [2]), and also via more diffuse routes such as the publication and circulation of glowing articles and colourful reports by the metropolitan press (such as *Le Figaro, Le Petit Parisien, Le Tour du Monde, Le Petit Journal Illustré, L'Illustration*, etc.). These vivid accounts popularized the actions of French explorers and adventurers in Indochina and fed popular imagination.

The French authorities saw these territories as an empty space to colonize, but equally important, as a lost world once ruled by great civilizations and now pervaded by backwardness, for which they had to design a new and revitalized identity (as Panivong Norindr puts it, "one that would conjure up fantasies of colonial life and promote the benevolent role of enlightened France" (1996, 5). Christopher Goscha has also shown how the French colonial project in Indochina was guided by the ambition to make this wider political and geographical space a viable economic reality, with little consideration for local people and cultures. Vietnam was conceived as being the centerpiece of the French strategy of imperialism in Indochina, and the Vietnamese, as the indigenous backbone of this project (Goscha 1995). The French consequently encouraged a westward Vietnamese immigration into Laos and Cambodia in order to staff the administrative apparatus and to supply labor for the plantations and mines. The eruption of the Second World War in Europe and in Southeast Asia, however, dramatically changed the orientation of France's *mission civilisatrice* in her colonies. The country's military defeat by the German army and the subsequent establishment of the Vichy regime in 1940, along with the Japanese occupation of most of Southeast Asia, would pave the way for Pétain's National Revolution in the French colonies, including *l'Indochine française*.

After the fall of France in 1940 and the establishment of the French Vichy government by the German Nazi regime, French Indochina came under the control of Admiral Decoux's Vichy administration. The change of regime led to the development of a *politique indigène* ("indigenous policy"). This new orientation in French colonial policies was guided by an overall strategy, the dual objective of which was to counter the Japanese pan-Asian propaganda and to reinforce the loyalty of the constituent parts of Indochina to the metropolitan power (and hence to diminish the risk of implosion in the course of the Second World War) by enhancing their place within the framework of French Indochina, which would be recast as Federal Indochina under the Vichy regime. The new doctrine of federalism was a protective umbrella in name only for the different components of Indochina, as France retained full control of the colonial administration. Functional reasons aside, and at a deeper level, the underlying reason for the (selective) promotion of local cultures was a consequence of Vichy's traditionalist and anti-assimilationist ideology. In parallel with the metropole's discovery of a "True France" with the "Return to the Soil" and the "True Values" (*Famille, Travail, Patrie*), Vichy officials likewise encouraged the formation of local identities along regionalist lines (Vietnam, Laos and Cambodia). Thus, under the leadership of Admiral Decoux, Governor-General of Indochina from 1940 to 1945, a campaign for National Renovation was launched within each separate domain of French Indochina.

In reality, as Eric Jennings has argued, the restoration campaign of "local patriotisms", or *politique des égards*, while enthusiastically adopted by the conservative local elites (monarchists and nationalists alike) who shared to a great extent Pétainist values (such as patriarchy, hierarchy, authority and discipline), constructed and reified reductionist and essentialist identities defined by a "return to an ancient past", the 'discovery' of folkloric customs and 'true' traditions; in other words, by a search for authenticity and an aversion for *métissage* (in this context, the fusion between French and local cultures). Jennings writes:

> The National Revolution, resting at the crossroads of restoration and revolution, became, in Indochina, a concept laden with notions of national rediscovery. 'Pure' Viet, Lao, and Cambodian identities were constantly affirmed, emphasized, and ultimately reified in the French-language Indochinese press under Vichy—a press aimed at French and indigenous elite consumption. (2001, 157)

Vichy policy fuelled local nationalisms—Decoux was the first governor to use the word 'Vietnam'—but the French administration was careful to direct and monitor those nationalist sentiments by keeping the conservative elite on their side while articulating a new reductionist vision of what it meant to be Indochinese (ibid., 158). As Ivarsson notes for French Laos, "for Decoux and the French authorities to build up this specific Lao identity was not viewed as a goal in itself but as a means to integrate Laos further into the Indochinese Federation and make it a more viable member of this entity" (Ivarsson 1999, 64).

A series of social, economic, administrative and political reforms was therefore initiated, in tandem with the building of transport infrastructure, in order to make the Lao elite feel they had a future in French-Lao 'co-operation', and at the same time to counter the pan-Thai appeal of Bangkok, then under the military rule of Marshal Phibun Songkhram. With the rise of Thailand's pan-Thai movement and the apparent willingness of the Japanese to sacrifice French Laos to the expansionist aims of its Bangkok ally, the Vichy French government realized they needed to counter-attack if they wanted to prevent the loss of Laos from French Indochina. Greater financial resources from the general Indochinese budget were thus allocated to various spheres of Lao society. The reorganised École d'Administration in Vientiane now promoted the education of a Lao elite, at the expense of the Vietnamese students, so as to allow the newly trained Lao civil servants to play a greater role in the administration of their country. Meanwhile, new schools and health clinics were constructed, many in rural areas. As Jennings sums up, "France, as it was now argued, stood not as conqueror, assimilator, or even protector (a difficult claim, given the Japanese presence), but as arbiter, providing a supposedly indispensable cement for the Indochinese edifice" (Jennings 2001, 176). But that edifice was soon to collapse. On 9 March 1945, the Japanese interned what remained of the French colonial administration in Indochina and incited the rulers of Cambodia, Laos and Vietnam to proclaim their countries' independence under the Japanese patronage. These events signaled the beginning of the end for French Indochina. The planners and builders of a new Indochina were now the communists.

From colonial invention to communist project

The 1999 informal summit between the Cambodian, Lao and Vietnamese Prime Ministers in Vientiane, nine years after their last gathering, raised some eyebrows. Among ASEAN officials, some even interpreted this meeting as an early sign of the formation of an "Indochinese bloc". Ten years after the withdrawal of the Vietnamese troops from Cambodia, Cold War-like attitudes were swift to re-emerge. It would be a missed opportunity to wave aside these reactions as anachronistic, however. The present-day nation-states of Cambodia, Laos and Vietnam shared a common destiny over nearly a century from French colonization in the late 19th century to the Communists' victory in 1975. Above all, the key to the understanding of their enduring relationship remains rooted in the complex links built up in the wake of the Second World War between their guerrilla movements, and in particular in the Vietnamese Communist Party's highly influential role in the creation and the development of the Cambodian, and in particular, Lao revolutionary organizations (for further details, see Pholsena 2004, 149–170).

Communist effervescence in French Indochina was exclusively a Vietnamese affair in the late 1920s. At the creation of the Indochinese Communist Party (ICP) in October 1930, revolutionary activities in Cambodia and Laos were still undertaken almost entirely by their Vietnamese migrant communities, consisting of laborers in rubber plantations and mines (in Cambodia and Laos, respectively) and civil servants at all levels (save those lowest levels reserved for the locals) of the Indochinese colonial bureaucracy. In truth, the Vietnamese communists believed that the Lao and Cambodian populations were not ready, either politically or economically, for the development of revolutionary networks in their countries. It was indeed the the Russian-led 'Third', 'Communist' International (Comintern) designed to link communist parties and revolutionary organizations around the world—that persuaded the Vietnamese communists to

accept the inclusion of the Lao and the Cambodians in a resolution
at the October 1930 congress and, as such, into the struggle against
French imperialism. It was again the Comintern that initiated the
change in name from "Vietnamese Communist Party" (proposed
by Ho Chi Minh) to the "Indochinese Communist Party". The
1930 resolution unveiled the project of creating an "Indochinese
Federation" on the basis of free consent on the part of the three
peoples once they had triumphed over the imperialist forces via their
respective national revolutions. In May 1941, however, during the
ICP's eighth plenum that saw the creation of the Viet Minh (Viêt
Nam doc lap dong minh hoï, Independent League of Vietnam),
the Central Committee still noted the absence of a communist
organization in Laos and Cambodia with disappointment (Porter
1983, 62).

Despite the leading role of the Vietnamese communists in the
anti-colonial war against the French, it seemed that Ho Chi Minh
remained a reluctant participant in the Soviets' federation project.
For him, the space for revolutionary struggle was to be restricted
to Vietnam's modern frontiers. He considered French Indochina's
geographical boundaries unsuitable for carrying out revolutionary
activities that were essentially guided by Vietnamese nationalism.
Yet, the debates between these two spaces, "Vietnam" or "Indochina",
were not merely confined to the circles of power and initiated by
the Russians; French colonial policy, by attributing a greater role to
the Vietnamese (both in the colonial administration and the school
textbooks), encouraged the formation among some Vietnamese
nationalists of a nascent Indochinese space that they rapidly came to
imagine themselves leading against the French rulers. The French
colonial project in Indochina was guided by a will to transform
this vast heterogeneous geographical area into a coherent whole;
hence, some of the early Vietnamese nationalists, conservatives or
communists alike, re-appropriated this vision of an Indochinese
structure as the best edifice for developing and achieving Annamese,
then Vietnamese, nationalism (for a detailed analysis, see Goscha
1995).

Like France's imperial ambitions, the vision of an Indochinese
federation, whether imagined by the conservative nationalists or
assembled by the communists in their resolutions, would remain a
curtailed project. On 2 September 1945, the Vietnamese communist
leaders proclaimed the independence of *Vietnam*, thereby definitely
abandoning the Indochinese institutional frame. A few months

earlier, in August 1945, the ICP congress had already opted for the "Vietnamese line", less for ideological reasons than strategic imperatives. The choice of an Indochinese roadmap would indeed have compromised Thailand's support (then under the government of Pridi Banomyong, a left-wing sympathizer) and, above all, significantly annoyed China: neither of these two countries would have welcomed the emergence of such a vast geographical space and political structure dominated by Vietnam. Yet, where the internationalist communists failed, the Vietnamese military strategists would succeed: Indochinese unity would become a tragic reality on the battlefields.

As mentioned above, the Vietnamese did not pay much consideration to the development of revolutionary bases in Laos and Cambodia before the Second World War. The disruptive events of the 1940s forced them to change their approach, however. The French defeat by the Japanese forces in March 1945 indeed encouraged them to accelerate the revolution in Vietnam. But the preparation for a military offensive needed the crucial support of Lao and Cambodian communist allies in the rural zones, to protect them in the west against an attack from the French troops that had returned to their former colonial territories after the Japanese surrender in August 1945. From this moment to the fall of Saigon in April 1975, Vietnamese military and political strategy would not change again. The safety of, and access to, these retreat zones in Laos and Cambodia remained a constant imperative, a key to Vietnamese communist military survival and final victory. From this crucial turning point in Vietnamese communist policy vis-à-vis her neighbors, Indochina became "a strategic unity, a single military theatre of operations," in General Vo Nguyen Giap's own words. The fate of Laos and Cambodia was therefore sealed with the making of an Indochinese battlefield (Porter 1981, 88).

Beyond Indochina: old and new allies

Lao, Vietnamese and Cambodian governments have shared a heightened sense of what is required for their regimes' survival. It is in that sense that one must understand the so-called Indochinese summits: a gathering among three states that hold similar economic priorities (they are among the least developed countries in Southeast Asia) and a common political agenda, instead of an implausible resurrection of yet another Indochinese federation project (for more details, see Pholsena and Banomyong 2004). An association, though more symbolic than substantial, helps to consolidate a network of alliances against an external environment somehow perceived as unpredictable (economically) and prone to conflict (politically). In particular, Hanoi and Vientiane remain highly sensitive to criticisms annually formulated by Western countries (led by the United States) of their repression of religious freedom and political opposition, and more generally, their countries' lack of democracy and absence of civil society (*Vientiane Times*, 18 October 2002; Agence France Press, 11 November 2002). The rapprochement with China is therefore to be comprehended in this context. Laos and Vietnam (as well as Myanmar), in particular, have found in China a very good ally against Western countries' and non-governmental organizations' demands regarding human rights and democratization. The support is mutual: the former Indochinese countries (and Myanmar) defend the One China policy. Some analysts have argued that this newfound solidarity gives to the countries involved a sense of systemic and ideological security that had vanished with the disintegration of the former Soviet Union (Muni 2002, 127). Furthermore, aside from sharing the same political priority (i.e., non-regime change), Vientiane and Hanoi also pursue the Chinese development model, namely, economic liberalization under the Communist Party's control.

China proves to be a valuable ally financially, too. Cambodia received in 1999 a no-interest loan from China amounting to more than US$220 million. The normalization of the relationship between China and Cambodia began in the second half of the 1990s when Beijing stopped supporting the Khmer Rouge guerilla movement. Since then, relations between the two countries have been improving continuously. The giant neighbor is now among the top ten investors in the country. What is more, in November 2002, during the visit to Phnom Penh by the Chinese Prime Minister Zhu Rongji, Sihanouk emphatically declared that "China [was] Cambodia's most important and reliable friend" and reiterated his support for the One China policy in "all circumstances". Likewise, Zhu Rongji repeated China's wish to keep on helping her "close friend" in her socio-economic and cultural development. As proof of China's goodwill, he announced the cancellation of Cambodia's debts to China, accumulated since the 1950s (*South China Morning Post*, 12 November 2002).

Similarly, Chinese aid and investment has dramatically increased over the past few years in Laos, although Thailand remains Laos'

primary trade and economic partner. The 1997 regional financial crisis
sent a brutal signal to the Lao leadership on their over-dependence on
the Thai economy, then badly shaken by the financial turmoil. The
impact was severe on the Lao economy, and the government found
itself suddenly in need of other economic partners. This reorientation
in international economic strategy favored China, which welcomed
this rapprochement very positively. Vientiane may regard China
less as a potential rival to Thailand's economic supremacy than as a
protection against economic instability in the region, though. Having
learnt from the lessons of 1997, Laos in reality no longer wants to
depend too heavily on one single economic partner.[3]

At the opening of the third millennium, the spectre of an
Indochinese entity (either in the form of an empire or a Vietnamese-
dominated federation) while it may still be haunting some analysts'
minds (de Tréglodé 2000, 1–33), belongs to the history of French
colonialism, the anti-colonial struggle and Cold War conflicts in
Southeast Asia. Each of the three countries pursues at present a
multilateral foreign policy combined with bilateral diplomacy,
the prime objectives of which are the continuation of economic
development and the safeguarding of political stability. In 1988,
Vietnam officially reoriented her foreign policy so as to become
based on diversified relations and "friendship with every country"
(Thayer 1999, 1–24). The socialist standpoint on international
relations guided by the theory of the "two camps" (that is, a world
divided between the socialist and imperialist forces) was being
replaced by a pragmatic and less Manichean vision. The end of
ideological antagonisms in the region (helped by the disintegration
of the former Soviet Union and the semi-retreat of the United States
from the region, at least until the events of September 11, 2001), the
higher priority afforded to economic development and liberalization,
regional commitment through the Association of Southeast Asian
Nations (ASEAN) combined with a more autonomous foreign
policy on the part of Laos, and especially of Cambodia, vis-à-vis
Vietnam: all these factors have progressively rendered obsolete the
project of an Indochinese structure founded on a system of strategic,
political and institutional alliances between Hanoi, Phnom Penh
and Vientiane. Their ASEAN membership (in 1995, 1997 and
1999 for Vietnam, Laos and Cambodia, respectively) further shows
their readiness to rejoin the international community as well as the
willingness of the other Southeast Asian states to welcome them back
after years, if not decades, of diplomatic isolation. Only the "special

relationship" between Laos and Vietnam has been persisting in a fashion noteworthy for its longevity and constancy—a legacy from the post-Second World War era which has refused to die out.

Laos and Vietnam: a "special relationship"

In 2000, two official delegations of Lao high-ranking military officers paid a visit to Vietnam. The first visit led to a declaration by the then Vietnamese prime minister Phan Van Khai, who called for "the two countries' armed forces to closely coordinate the training of their personnel, track down drug traffickers and counter-revolutionaries, so as to contribute to build up a peaceful and prosperous Vietnam-Laos boundary line."[4] This warning was well timed. On 26 October 1999, a small group of students organized the first ever anti-government protest in front of the presidential palace in the town center of Vientiane. The protesters were rapidly arrested and jailed; nevertheless both Lao and Vietnamese leaders took the incident very seriously (de Tréglodé 2000, 9–10). The second visit by a Lao military delegation, in June 2000, was not fortuitous either. Over the preceding few months, Vientiane had been the target of a series of bomb attacks whose origins remain a mystery for most people even today.

Meanwhile, rumors of gun battles in the province of Xieng Khouang (in northeastern Laos) were circulating. Foreign newspapers and development workers mentioned an uprising led by members of the Hmong ethnic minority group and an intervention by Vietnamese troops to assist the Lao army in their repression of the allegedly ethnic rebellion. Both Lao and Vietnamese authorities vigorously denied these reports. Again both governments accused the media abroad as well as external forces of plotting against the Lao regime and attempting to damage the "special relationship" between the two countries. Whatever the truth, these events clearly demonstrate that Laos' internal affairs are still closely monitored by Hanoi. In other words, for the Vietnamese communist leadership, Laos remains a strategically crucial state that must be kept in the fold. But the sociological reality at the local level in Laos shows that the people of Laos, as opposed to their leaders, have moved on to the post-Indochinese era.

Looking to the West

The first ever attempt to conduct a sociological survey in post-war Laos was carried out in 1997, when 2,003 households were surveyed in six districts of Vientiane Municipality.[5] Despite its limitations, the report gives precious information for a better understanding of the people's perceptions of some of the issues that have been the focus of official concerns lately. Especially instructive are two questions concerning the respondents' views of the world. First, they were asked to name the country they would most like to visit, given the opportunity. The most popular choice was clearly the United States (32 percent), followed by Japan (14.4 percent); Thailand came in third place (10 percent), preceding the socialist regimes of China (7.1 percent) and Vietnam (5.9 percent). The former Soviet Union was not even mentioned, and neither was France.

If you were able to choose a country to go and visit, which one would you like to visit the most?

Country	Frequency	Percentage
Not go anywhere	17	9.2
Anywhere	218	11.4
America	612	32.0
Japan	275	14.4
Thailand	191	10.0
China	136	7.1
Vietnam	113	1.5
Australia	64	3.4
Canada	27	1.4
England	25	1.3
Switzerland	24	1.3
Singapore	23	1.2
Germany	18	0.9
India	7	0.4
Hungary	1	0.1

Source: 1997–1998 Vientiane Social Survey Project (question 42).

But the following question, complementary to the previous one, saw a dramatic change, not only in the order of the list but also in its content. People were asked which modern societies they would most like as a model for Laos. More than a third (37 or 2 percent) answered their own country, Laos. Japan came second (26.3 percent), followed by Singapore (19.9 percent). The rest of the countries (including the United States and the "developed modern" countries) collected fewer than 5 percent of the answers; these included Thailand and Vietnam, both of them being barely quoted (0.1 percent). As for China, it disappeared from the list, while France appeared in it.

Which modern society would you like the most to be a model for Laos?

Country	Frequency	Percent
Lao	695	37.2
Japan	491	26.3
Singapore	372	19.9
Developed modern countries	107	5.7
America	67	3.6
France	64	3.4
Russia	52	2.8
Hungary	13	0.7
Thailand	2	0.1
Cambodia	2	0.1
Vietnam	2	0.1

Source: *1997–1998 Vientiane Social Survey Project*, Institute for Cultural Research, Ministry of Information and Culture, Vientiane (question 43).

These results suggest that overall, Lao people seem to hold a relatively positive image of their society as a third of the respondents list their own country as the model to follow, despite its very weak socio-economic indicators. Japan and Singapore's presence as second and third choices, respectively, can be explained by their positive representation abroad, through the fact that they have successfully managed to combine images of an efficient capitalist economy and respect for 'traditional values'. Accordingly, there is no rejection of the capitalist system as such; rather, it is the socialist model which has long since lost its appeal: Vietnam is hardly listed, and China not all. On the other hand, the respondents' choices also show the limited influence of Western countries, confirmed by the low scores attained by the United States and France. The lack of enthusiasm manifested vis-à-vis Thailand is also interesting, and yet not surprising. Being the closest country to Laos culturally and linguistically, one might have expected a higher score. The relationship between the two countries is traditionally described as being like that between older and younger brothers—the age hierarchy oscillating between the two depending on the interlocutors.[6] Their sharing of Buddhist-based cultural values, as a matter of fact, has been overshadowed and their differences heightened by the leaderships' opposing ideologies over the past 25 years.

Since the early 1990s, Laos has increasingly become integrated into the capitalist world market. To be sure, the openness of its economy is not at all comparable to other states in Southeast Asia that have inscribed the culture of capitalism in their societies. Nevertheless, the country still has to confront the harsh reality of the effects of its (slow) economic integration into the global market. It is important to bear in mind that Laos remains very dependent on foreign assistance. Since 1990, financial aid from bilateral donors and multilateral funding organizations has amounted to more than US$250 million per year. The author of a recently published book (2002), entitled *Laos within the International Community* (in Lao), is unequivocal with regard to the country's new challenges; he acknowledges, thus:

> Isolation is no longer possible. Such coexistence is saturated by intellectual competition, though: a country that possesses a better education system, hence more competent people, will have the capacity to economically and socially develop and strengthen, to become prosperous and to build up an international reputation. To the contrary, an incompetent country will be downgraded to the group of poor and backward countries. It is the situation with which Laos is confronted today, and we believe that no Lao feels happy about his or her nation's humiliating position…But we have to accept it, at least temporarily, so as to avoid being removed from the assistance list, in which case we would become even poorer…Let's accept this position, let's not prolong it to the point whereby it would become an endless habit and make us become permanent aid seekers. (Soukhavath 2002, 157)

The country may have recovered her full membership within the international community, but the growing exposure of the population to the outside world has stimulated the perception among ordinary

Lao that their society is "backward" compared to others in the region and in the world; the discrepancy between the regime and the population has never been so great. Since the end of the socialist economy, development has become the government's national obsession and catchcry, while the dominant view among ordinary Lao about their society today may be its "backwardness". Their leaders lean towards Vietnam for political (and perhaps military) backing, while their citizens, especially the younger generations, look to Thailand for cultural consumption and economic gain.

Laos and Thailand: ambivalent relations

Few studies shed much light on the phenomenon of migration from Laos to Thailand. In any case, it is hardly a matter of speculation to argue that since the opening of the country in the early 1990s, the number of illegal labor migrants from Laos to Thailand has significantly increased. A recent assessment of illegal labor migration and trafficking in Laos, for instance, shows the rapid rise in illegal labor migrants in its three target provinces—among the most populated in Laos—Khammouane (central Laos), Savannakhet and Champassak (both in southern Laos), with an increase of nearly 40 percent (from 32,789 to 45,215 people) over a period of just one year (between 1999 and 2000). According to Thai Immigration Police reports, the majority of these illegal migrant workers were aged between 15 and 24 years, half of whom were under the age of 18 (ILO/IPEC 2003, 19). The socio-economic factors of this migration are familiar. On the one hand, Thailand's economy is in need of cheap labor in industries such as fishing, fruit-growing, entertainment and manufacturing, while on the other, Laos offers few job opportunities other than subsistence farming to young people for whom schooling often does not constitute a long-term alternative.[7]

Outward migration in Laos is to a significant degree structural. A small-scale research study focusing on two districts in Saravane (southeastern Laos) and in Sainyabuli (northwestern Laos) has observed: "Movements are so widespread in the villages of Khongxedon [in Saravane province] and in Paklai [Saiynabuli province] that it is reasonable to define work in Thailand as an phenomenon fully integrated into these villages' lifestyle" (Chazée 2002). Its authors further argue that these cross-border migrations, with their share of risk and hope for adventure, find their origins in cultural practices and are comparable with a rite of passage (similar to that performed by young people of Khmer origin in the south of northeastern Thailand). A report on illegal migration and child trafficking on the Lao-Thai and Myanmar-Thai borders confirms the 'spontaneous' nature of this migration: while 36.5 percent of the young Lao interviewed took their decision to go to Thailand with their parents or had informed them, half of the interviewees left without telling them. More important, 96.6 percent of these young migrants said they left for Thailand because others had gone across the Mekong before them. The study notes that the majority of those who migrated collected information beforehand from people in their village (friends or relatives). By contrast, very few teenagers (9 out of 103 respondents) had asked foreigners (Wille 2000, 27–29).

In fact, some studies have shown that migration in some communities and districts of Laos is well organized thanks to their long-established links with employers in Thailand; they observe, thus: "Even though well-established trafficking networks facilitate the illegal border crossing and onward migration, migrants often know exactly where they are headed and the terms of employment they can expect" (ILO/IPEC 2003, xi). Over time this type of migration acquires its own autonomy upon which contingent factors (e.g., financial gain, family survival strategy, and desire for adventure) that had set off the movements in the first place have lesser impact. It is migration based on a network of interpersonal relations that link the actual migrants, the former migrants and the non-migrants residing in the place of departure and of destination. When the migration reaches a certain level, the expansion of these networks reduces the costs and the risks, which logically leads to an increase in the number of migrants and therefore maintains their flow.

"Differences between the Thai and Lao identities are exacerbated during conflicts and periods of tensions, because they boost patriotic feelings. In peaceful times, however, Lao youngsters follow the Thai, because they don't have any idols in the country," a Lao journalist explained.[8] It is now well known that the influence of Thai mass media is a matter of great concern for the Lao authorities. The Lao Women's Union, for instance, has criticized Thai television programmes for encouraging incorrect dress and manners at the expense of traditional clothing such as the *pha sin* (the Lao sarong). Similarly, some officials have accused the media of playing a significant role in the rise of consumerism, or worse, of crime in Laos (Vipha 2001). These official statements often lack substantiation, however.

In any case, the presence of Thai media is ubiquitous in all sectors (television, radio, newspapers and magazines) and at every level of society, including the country's leadership, who indeed keep a close eye on Thai television broadcasts and radio programmes. There is no competition between the latter and the local media: 70 percent to 75 percent of the population in Laos watch Thai television programmes, compared to 20 percent to 25 percent who watch Lao broadcasting (ibid., 179).

Yet, despite the strong appeal of Thai cultural products, their consumption and appropriation nevertheless have their limits. In a late 1990s survey of Lao youth living in urban areas, a large proportion of positive opinions were expressed by interviewees craving for their neighboring country's modernity. However, a few respondents, especially female adolescents, gave a much bleaker perception of Thai society. Here are some excerpts of their statements: "We're not going with them [those who go and find work in Thailand]. We're scared that they would take our eyes."; "They have a bad society, with no laws, and people do whatever they want."; "They will sell us as prostitutes, and then the police will catch us and we'll go to prison, and we're scared that someone may rape us" (UNICEF 1998). Thailand's cultural and economic ascendancy over Laos generates ambiguous and deviating effects, oscillating between attraction and repulsion. Thailand is what Laos should never become for some Lao, including the Lao authorities. The Friendship Bridge paradoxically exemplifies this hazy relation whereby proximity functions like an antithesis. Yet, in 1994, the year of its inauguration, there were hopes that the bridge would boost the rapprochement between the two countries and their peoples via the development of trade and tourism. It has become instead, according to a recent study, the symbol of consumerism and materialism in the eyes of some in Laos. The weekend shopping enjoyed by the small, but growing, Lao urban middle class is specially targeted, denounced as "antipatriotic" and those who practice it as "corrupted by Thai capitalism."[9]

In spite of their cultural, linguistic and geographical proximity, the two peoples on the opposite banks of the Mekong River retain this peculiar combination of *closeness* and *strangeness* toward one another, as if the relationships between the two countries were mediated through a distorting glass. "The Lao and the Thai peoples share similar culture and traditions, but Laos has managed to preserve her culture", is a comment one frequently hears from Thai tourists returning from Vientiane and Luang Prabang (their favourite destinations in Laos), upholding an image of Laos imbued with nostalgia and bemoaning thereafter the 'lost authenticity' of their own country. In the eyes of these Thai, Lao society and culture thus appear like the Thailand "before" (the "genuine" Thailand), that is, before the double effects of modernization and globalization (Reynolds 1998, 115–145). Their visit to the other side of the Mekong river is not merely a trip through space but also, and perhaps above all, a journey through time.

The picture is further complicated when one adopts a localized perspective. In those micro-contexts identity boundaries are becoming blurred, so much so that national belonging appears to be superseded to some degree by a more pervasive sense of community. Along the Mekong banks that border the town of Savannakhet (120,000 inhabitants) in southern Laos, it is possible to discern the houses and buildings of the city of Mukdahan (113,000 people), located on the other side of the river in northeastern Thailand. Movements between the two banks occur on a daily basis. These activities are not solely motivated by local trade, though; they possess their own dynamic, built upon a shared history between the populations of the twin cities. After all, their inhabitants used to belong to the same political entity until Siam was forced to cede the eastern banks of the Mekong to France in 1893. However, this switch of sovereignty did not bring to an end the development of family and socio-economic ties through the decades, although the Vietnam and Cold War periods considerably reduced these interactions.

The Mekong, far from being a mighty obstacle to overcome, has constituted an awesome link between the two communities. It is therefore not so much the geographical proximity that accounts for these daily travels between Savannakhet and Mukdahan as a sense of shared ethnic origins (the inhabitants of Savannakhet and Mukdahan would say that they share to some degree the same ethnic identity, i.e. Lao) as well as linguistic and cultural closeness. These populations indeed follow the same Buddhist calendar and celebrate the same Buddhist festivals. Consequently, the people of Savannakhet and Mukdahan go back and forth across the river in the most informal way for work, business, trade, shopping, family visits, participation in festivals, and so on. The concept of international frontiers seems to be less enforced in this part of the region.

From a sense of shared ethnic origins to forming one community of identity would not be, however, an accurate description of the relations between the peoples of Savannakhet and Mukdahan. The sharing of cultural, religious and family ties does not erase economic inequality and dissimilar social realities, nor does it obliterate people's sense of national belonging. Prostitution and AIDS are phenomena that reveal best the two faces of the links that tie the "sister cities". The opening of frontiers and the development of commercial trade between the two countries appear to have led to an increase in the number of Lao women prostitutes in Savannakhet (CARE International 1998). Approximately 900 women were reported to be involved in commercial sexual activity in the province of Savannakhet against about 300 in the province of Mukdahan in 1999 (Lyttleton and Amarapibal 2002, 515). A number of Thai men now increasingly pursue commercial sex across the border in Savannakhet. In their eyes, Lao women possess two characteristics that make them unique objects of desire. They are different from Thai women, as they are perceived as "exotic" and "new"; they are "from the other side". Novelty is the oft-repeated attraction. Yet, this difference is counter-balanced by the very cultural and linguistic proximity which provides a sense of security and intimacy—hence, the illusion of a "safe" relationship—to these men in their relations with these Lao women, which they cannot seem to find with the Thai prostitutes with whom interactions are more openly commercial. In other words, Lao women are the "Other in terms of erotic appeal; they are non-Other in terms of prohibitive HIV threat, they can be trusted, they are kin, they are part of the same community" (ibid.). But it is precisely this kind of immediacy that forms the most favourable environment for less vigilant sexual intercourse, and constitutes one of the causes of the upsurge of HIV infections in these border areas.

Further developments?

As Christopher Goscha has shown elsewhere (Goscha 2004, 141–185), after the Second World War the Vietnamese communists began to form and consolidate revolutionary bases, structures and cadres in Laos and Cambodia, whereas before 1945 their efforts to build up and run revolutionary networks in western Indochina relied almost entirely on Vietnamese migrants. Goscha gives a fascinating account of how the Vietnamese went about spreading the revolutionary word in villages throughout Laos, both in the north and in the south. These "revolutionary missionaries" learnt not only Lao but upland minority languages as well; sometimes they even lived with the local population, learning their customs but also teaching them 'modern' hygiene and agricultural techniques. In short, the Vietnamese gave 'civilizing' lessons alongside the ideological ones, the two types feeding a discourse of modernity among the 'backward' minority peoples, in the process attempting, and sometimes succeeding, to win over local hearts and minds. Although much research still remains to be done in this area (which needs to combine both archival study and oral history), it is not a matter of speculation to argue that the Lao communist leadership and army depended to a great extent on their Vietnamese counterparts for both their military and political training and organization, as well as for manpower, matériel and logistics. But what has remained almost entirely unstudied is the social and cultural impact of war on the population, especially in eastern Laos. While the notion of 'Indochina' may be irrelevant for many in Laos today, the present day consequences of its political, ideological and strategic uses among these populations should not be underestimated.

Notes

1   The distinguished French scholar, Georges Coedès, referred to the geographical
    space as "Inde au-delà du Gange" in his seminal book, *Les États hindouisés
    d'Indochine et d'Indonésie*.
2   Two contradictory principles underpinned the French administration of Indochina:
    on the one hand, colonization had to be 'cheap'; on the other, reaping profits from
    colonies was an equally strong imperative, a strategy known in French as *mise en
    valeur*, which required substantial financial investments (Brocheux and Hémery
    1994, 74). These objectives reflected, in effect, two radically different perspectives
    in terms of political rule. The 'cheap domination' perspective would merely require
    a type of indirect rule, following the British model in India. Conversely, the *mise
    en valeur* postulated a strongly interventionist administration (ibid., 75). The latter
    view eventually prevailed when Paul Doumer took up his position as Governor-
    General of Indochina in 1897.
3   Interview with Lao official, Ministry of Foreign Affairs, April 2002.
4   *Voice of Viêt-nam*, 24 February 2000, cited in BBC *Summary of World Broadcasts*
    (Part Three, Far East, 28 February 2000).
5   *1997–1998 Vientiane Social Survey Project*, Institute for Cultural Research, Ministry
    of Information and Culture, Vientiane.
6   See, from a Lao perspective, the study of Lao-Thai relations by Mayoury and
    Pheuiphanh Ngaosyvathn (1994). Their intention, expressed in the introductory
    chapter, says it all about the challenging task: "this book is aimed at exploring the
    intricacies of the Lao-Thai saga of love and loathing. It is a story both tragic and
    comic, with abrasive sentimentality and explosive emotion sometimes substituting
    for the facts facing the two countries."
7   Less than 60 percent of children were enrolled in school (primary, secondary and
    tertiary levels) in Laos in 2000–2001 (UNDP 2003, 239).
8   Interview in Vientiane, March 2002.
9   "Friendship Bridge in Name Only." *The Nation*, 19 January 2002; and interview
    with a Lao journalist, March 2002.

References

Brocheux, Pierre and Daniel Hémery. 1994. *Indochine, la colonisation ambiguë*. Paris:
        Éditions La Découverte.
Chazée, Laurent. 2002. Executive Summary: Smallholder Development Project, Rural
        Sociology. Unpublished report, Vientiane.
Clutterbuck, Martin. 1993. "Official Enemy: Thai Culture." *Far Eastern Economic
        Review*, 11 February.
Coedès, Georges. 1989. *Les États hindouisés d'Indochine et d'Indonésie*. Paris: De
        Boccard.
Cooperative for Assistance and Relief Everywhere (CARE International). 1998.
        Potential for Spread of HIV/AIDS on the Lao-Vietnamese Border, Sepon
        District, Savannakhet Province. Unpublished report, Vientiane.
de Tréglodé, Benoît. 2000. "Un théâtre d'ombres: le Viêt-nam entre la Chine et
        l'ASEAN au lendemain de la crise asiatique." *Les Etudes du CERI* 68: 1–33.

Goscha, Christopher E. 2004. "Vietnam and the World Outside: The Case of Vietnamese Communist Advisors in Laos (1948–1962)." *South East Asia Research* 12, 2 (July): 141–185.

———. 1995. *Viêt-Nam or Indochina? Contesting Concepts of Space in Vietnamese Nationalism, 1887–1954.* Copenhagen: Nordic Institute of Asian Studies Reports Series No. 28.

ILO/IPEC (International Programme on the Elimination of Child Labour). 2003. *Lao PDR: Preliminary Assessment of Illegal Labour Migration and Trafficking in Children and Women for Labour Exploitation.* Bangkok: International Labour Organization.

Institute for Cultural Research, Ministry of Information and Culture. *1997–1998 Vientiane Social Survey Project.* Vientiane: Institute for Cultural Research.

Ivarsson, Søren. 1999. "Towards a New Laos: *Lao Nhay* and the Campaign for National "Reawakening." In *Laos: Culture and Society*, edited by Grant Evans, pp. 61–78. Chiang Mai: Silkworm Books.

Jennings, Eric T. 2001. *Vichy in the Tropics: Pétain's National Revolution in Madagascar, Guadeloupe, and Indochina, 1940–1944.* Stanford: Stanford University Press.

Lyttleton, Chris and Amorntip Amarapibal. 2002. "Sister Cities and Easy Passage: HIV, Mobility and Economies of Desire in a Thai/Lao Border Zone". *Social Science and Medicine* 54: 505–518.

Muni, S.D. 2002. *China's Strategic Engagement with the New Asean: An Exploratory Study of China's Post-Cold War Political, Strategic and Economic Relations with Myanmar, Laos, Cambodia and Viêt-nam.* Singapore: Institute of Defence and Strategic Studies, Monograph No. 2.

Ngaosyvathn, Mayoury and Pheuiphanh. 1994. *Kith and Kin Politics: The Relationship between Laos and Thailand.* Manila: Journal of Contemporary Asia Publishers.

Panivong, Norindr. 1996. *Phantasmatic Indochina: French Colonial Ideology in Architecture, Film, and Literature.* Durham: Duke University Press.

Pholsena, Vatthana. 2004. "Le Viêt Nam et ses voisins de l'ex-Indochine." In *Viêt-Nam Contemporain*, edited by Stéphane Dovert and Benoît de Tréglodé, pp. 149–170. Bangkok: IRASEC; Paris: Les Indes Savantes.

Pholsena, Vatthana and Ruth Banomyong. 2004. *Le Laos au XXIème siècle: Les défis de l'intégration régionale.* Bangkok: Research Institute on Contemporary Southeast Asia (IRASEC).

Porter, Gareth. 1983. "Vietnamese Communist Policy toward Kampuchea, 1930–1970." In *Revolution and its Aftermath in Kampuchea: Eight Essays*, edited by David P. Chandler and Ben Kiernan. New Haven: Yale University Southeast Asia Studies Monograph Series No. 25.

———. 1981. "Vietnamese Policy and the Indochina Crisis." In *The Third Indochina Conflict*, edited by David W. P. Elliott. Boulder: Westview Press.

Reynolds, Craig J. 1998. "Globalization and Cultural Nationalism in Modern Thailand." In *Southeast Asian Identities: Culture and the Politics of Representation in Indonesia, Malaysia, Singapore, and Thailand*, edited by Joel S. Kahn, pp. 115–145. London: I.B. Tauris; Singapore: Institute of Southeast Asian Studies.

———. 1999. "Vietnamese Foreign Policy: Multilateralism and the Threat of Peaceful Evolution." In *Vietnamese Foreign Policy in Transition*, edited by Carlyle A. Thayer and Ramses Amer, pp. 1–24. Singapore: Institute of Southeast Asian Studies.

Soukhavath, Bounkhong. 2002. *Pathet Lao nay sangkhom nanasat* (Laos Within the International Community). Vientiane.

UNICEF. 1998. *Listening to the Voice of Young People*. Vientiane: UNICEF, in collaboration with Lao Youth Union, Lao Women's Union, Department of Education Vientiane Municipality, and Save the Children (UK).

United Nations Development Programme (UNDP). 2003. *Human Development Report 2003*. New York: Oxford University Press.

Vipha Utamachant. 2001. *Phonkratopkhongsanyawitanyoulaethorathatkhamphromdaenra wangthailao* (The Impacts of the Radio and Television Signals Across the Thai-Lao Border). Bangkok: Chulalongkorn University Press.

Wille, Christina. 2000. *Trafficking in Children in the Worst Forms of Child Labour in Thailand: Rapid Assessment Findings from Four Research Sites along the Thailand-Lao PDR and Thailand-Myanmar Border Areas*. Bangkok: ILO/IPEC.

3

GEOPOLITICS AND DEVELOPMENT COOPERATION IN THE MEKONG REGION

NGUYEN PHUONG BINH

Flowing through China and mainland Southeast Asia, the Mekong River is cherished by the millions who share its waters. The river is not only economically but also geopolitically vital to these countries since it is a source of good harvests, fish, hydropower, and provides the basis and rationale for greater integration among peoples in the area. As the main artery of Mekong culture, the river has been witness to the region's history, through war and peace, conflict and cooperation. Among other things, colonial power struggles, the Second World War, and the Cold War, kept peace and development away from the region for a long time.

The end of the Cold War has seen growing trade and investment links between Laos, Vietnam, Cambodia, Myanmar, Thailand and China, with improved economic opportunities for all. But the old battlefields have not been completely transformed into marketplaces. There are conflicts over the use of the Mekong's resources, for example, with repercussions for the environment as well as relations between the countries concerned.

Beginning with a survey of the Mekong region's development in the 20th and the beginning of the 21st centuries, this chapter looks at how geopolitics has propelled or shaped each countries' responses to more recent regional initiatives. In conclusion, it is argued that despite the existence of regional groupings such as the Greater Mekong Subregion (GMS)—Cambodia, Laos, Myanmar, Thailand and Vietnam—and the various avenues for working together as part of the Association of Southeast Asian Nations (ASEAN), there are few effective mechanisms for solving regional disputes.

Beginning in conflict, ending in cooperation

The Mekong River is a gateway to China and connects the region not only with northeast but also South Asia, providing access to the Indian and Pacific Oceans. The geostrategic significance of the region attracted colonial powers in the past and continues to be a factor in major power involvement in the region in the present. Today, a foothold in this region is seen as advantageous for a number of reasons: the region is rich in natural resources; it provides access to the huge markets of China and India; access to the region has maritime security and transport implications; and last, but not least, the region serves as a security belt around China.

In the 19th century when colonial wars expanded to all of Southeast Asia, the Mekong region was the subject of a struggle for primacy between France and Britain. Over the course of the century this struggle involved, at various periods, China, Siam (independent), Cambodia, Laos, Vietnam (the latter three under French colonialism), Myanmar (under British colonialism), France, Great Britain, Japan, the United States, and Russia. Colonial invasion and expansion came to an end close to the turn of the 19th century with the 1896 Anglo-French Agreement, which defined each power's area of influence and domination. Independent Siam (Thailand) served as a buffer between these areas. Subsequent agreements between France, Britain and Siam shaped the boundaries of three of the present-day Mekong countries: Laos, Cambodia, Vietnam. But without national independence, these countries served the bidding of their colonial masters. The ensuing anti-colonial and anti-imperialist struggle was waged over a stretch of time, resulting in the victory of the revolutionary forces by the end of the Second World War. The 1940s and 1950s were a time of national celebration: the Democratic Republic of Vietnam gained its independence in 1945; Myanmar, in 1948; China, 1949; and Laos and Cambodia, in 1953. Peace was, however, elusive as war sparked off again in Indochina. The Geneva Conference on Indochina convened after the French defeat at Dien Bien Phu in 1954 and attended by France, the United Kingdom, the United States, China, and the former Soviet Union, provided for a two-year deadline for ending the division of Vietnam (North and South). But the division was to last for two decades.

Laos and especially Cambodia have had similarly complicated histories of regaining independence and national construction because of the influence of the major powers. The end of the Vietnam War in 1975 did not give the Mekong countries an opportunity to enjoy peace and development because the Cambodian conflict lasted up to 1991. Myanmar, for its part, has had a different historical trajectory. After independence from the British in 1948, the country had to deal with armed ethnic opposition, which was, to a large extent, the legacy of the "divide and rule" policy of the colonialists. Domestic instability largely arising from military rule has cost the country tremendous time and resources that could have otherwise been used for national development. Among the Southeast Asian Mekong countries, Thailand is the only one to have enjoyed independence and relative peace, and hence the ability to formulate its own policies, which has been to its benefit: it has the most developed economy in the region.

Thus, it could be said that the Mekong region is left with unhappy memories of three Indochina wars, which involved major powers like France, the United Kingdom, Japan, the United States, China, and the former Soviet Union, and conflicts among the Mekong countries themselves. These wars caused enormous destruction in Laos, Cambodia and Vietnam in particular and deprived them of decades of national and regional capacity-building and development. It is understandable that right after the Second World War, the newly independent states could not pay due attention to the development of the Mekong River as they had to focus on the consolidation of new regimes and the protection of their countries' independence. The nation-state building process in these countries was saddled with difficulties, partly rooted in history and also arising from a new strategic environment shaped by the Cold War. An illustration of the dificulties was the failure of the Mekong River Committee in 1957, which included Thailand, Laos, Cambodia and (South) Vietnam. Initiated by the United States, the formation of the Committee was an attempt to prevent communist influence in the region by promoting economic development in the Mekong basin. In Cold War terms, the Mekong basin was the "iron curtain" that separated the communist states from the "free" world.

Since the mid-1980s and especially after the end of the Cold War, however, an understanding of a shared regional destiny and the possibility of prosperity began to evolve. First of all, the collapse of the bipolar system paved the way for dialogue and cooperation among countries with different political regimes. Furthermore, the disintegration of the Soviet Union and the transition of Eastern European countries in the late 1980s signified the failure of centrally planned economies and encouraged countries like Vietnam, Laos, and

Cambodia to adopt economic reforms and new security concepts. In addition, the Cambodian conflict, the last obstacle to good relations among neighbors in the region, ended in 1991. After a long period of tension and conflict, the Mekong countries realized that in many ways, they shared the same fate and that only cooperation and integration could ensure peace and development in the region. In the context of greater globalization, the need for cooperation has become even more imperative as new transnational challenges require joint, innovative responses. In the changing international environment after the Cold War, where not only military but economic strength decided national might, the world's major powers also saw that they, too, have a stake in the stability and prosperity of the region.

As a result, a new outlook on security and development has emerged. China's economic reforms since 1978 and its enhanced relations with the ASEAN countries since the 1990s are strong demonstrations of this new perspective. So are Vietnam's "renovation" (*Doi Moi*) policy adopted in 1986, Laos' "new economic mechanism" also adopted in 1986, and Thailand's often-quoted motto of "turning Indochina from the battlefield into the marketplace", as declared in 1988.

Thus, although the history of the Mekong region in the 20th century was marked by the intervention of world powers and various struggles for national sovereignty, with more episodes of confrontation than dialogue, the century came to a close in a new environment more conducive to cooperation and the promise of development in a region finally at peace.

Internal dynamics of regional peace and development

External factors undoubtedly left their mark on inter-state relations within the Mekong area. When countries get along well with each other, the issue of history does not matter much, but when they are not on good terms, history can be exploited for various purposes, which in turn hampers the course of development cooperation. Since the countries in the Mekong basin had to struggle to gain and defend their national independence and are still, in some ways, weak states, the issues of sovereignty and integrity remain sensitive. Consequently, multilateral cooperation has not been easy. Suspicion and mistrust rooted in past problems left unresolved, the consequences of divisive colonial policy, and the remnants of a Cold War mentality have all influenced the thinking of these countries; indeed, the habit of cooperation has been difficult to cultivate.

For example, bilateral and multilateral agreements relating to the use of the Mekong resources do exist, but the sharing of water resources is still complicated and not easily managed. Left unchecked, differences of opinion over water use could escalate into disputes, particularly since the region lacks an effective mechanism for conflict resolution. The fact that the two upstream states of China and Myanmar are not members of the Mekong River Commission (MRC) and therefore cannot be signatories to regional agreements also affects the development of the Mekong basin. That the Mekong region consists of mostly less developed states is also another factor that impedes cooperation. Finance and capacity-building are necessary to realize cooperation targets and projects, and their varying levels of economic development affect the degree of commitment and contribution that member states in the region can make.

Conversely, the need for coordination over the exploitation of the river's resources for irrigation, hydropower generation, fisheries, etc, encourages regional development cooperation. The adoption by the Mekong states of various important documents such as the Asian Development Bank's (ADB) Program on Economic Cooperation in the Greater Mekong Subregion (GMS 1992), the Agreement on the Cooperation for the Sustainable Development of the Mekong River Basin signed by Vietnam, Laos, Cambodia, and Thailand (1995), the ASEAN-Mekong Basin Development Cooperation (1995), and the UN Convention on the Law on Non-Navigational Uses of International Watercourses (1997) may provide the bases for coordination and cooperation on the development of the Mekong River.

Furthermore, the process of regional reconciliation in Southeast Asia—after 1975 when the war ended in all three Indochinese countries, and after 1995 when Vietnam first joined the ASEAN, with Laos and Cambodia following suit—has had a positive impact on regional rapprochement and the establishment of mutual benefits. ASEAN's increased interest in the Mekong region have strengthened initiatives for cooperation such as the above mentioned ASEAN-Mekong Basin Development Cooperation.

The need to coordinate the various national development policies vis-à-vis the Mekong River itself, however, remains. Since the river flows through six countries, the actions and policies of each one directly or indirectly affects the others, and competition over resource access and use is inevitable. Moreover, increasing interdependence and population mobility among the countries in the region has given rise to transnational problems which require collective responses.

Geopolitics of Mekong development policies viewed from upstream China

Laos has the greatest share of the Mekong River, with the largest amount of water flows (35 percent of the total) and where it occupies a larger basin area (26 percent) than any other riparian state. Similar indicators for Myanmar are 2 and 2 percent, respectively; for Thailand, 18 and 23 percent, respectively; Cambodia, 18 and 20 percent, respectively; Vietnam, 11 and 8 percent, respectively; and China, 16 and 12 percent, respectively (Goh 2001, 471). However, it is geopolitics and not just geographical control over the Mekong alone which determines the degree of influence each of these countries has on the region.

Let us begin with China, the largest country in the region. For the other Mekong countries, China's size and critical position as the upstream country, its economic and political clout, and active involvement in global and regional affairs mean that it is a major geostrategic player in the region.

In turn, China attaches growing importance to the promotion of mutually beneficial economic cooperation with ASEAN as well as with each of its riparian neighbors. The exploration of the Mekong's potential for water-borne transportation, irrigation, and hydroelectric power are priorities of the country. China's rapid economic growth (double digits in the 1980s and 1990s, and from 8 to 9 percent recently) requires tremendous energy resources and Yunnan's capacity to generate electricity—1,500 megawatts (Osborne 2000, 229), (mainly from the Mekong River)—accounts for 15.2 percent of the country's total electricity capacity.

China's policy toward the Mekong region reflects both internal and external considerations. The Western Region Development Strategy,[1] launched in March 2000, is China's effort to reduce the increasing disproportion between coastal provinces and hinterland provinces, lessen internal migration pressures, and solve social issues caused by underdevelopment. The program aims to develop eleven administrative regions (Xinjiang, Ningxia, Quinghai, Sichuan, Gansu, Guizhau, Shanxi, Yunnan and Xizang [Tibet], the Guangxi Zhuang Autonomous Region, and Chongqing Municipality) that jointly represent 56.8 percent of the country's total area and 23 percent of its population (Chen Luosheng n.d.). Yunnan plays a central role in the implementation of this strategy. This development policy, notably, is not merely oriented inward; it also fits neatly into the development plans of the GMS. By joining the GMS cooperation projects, Yunnan will enjoy a shortcut to the sea through the port of Haiphong in Vietnam, for instance. Networks of roads, railways, and waterways could also connect Yunnan and nearby areas of China with their neighbors in the south, thus enabling inland provinces to integrate more closely with the region and the world. National economic development, social and political stability, and good relations with Southeast Asian countries are the best guarantees for the country's security. As a member of the GMS, China also has access to substantial amounts of capital for infrastructure development from international funding agencies such as the ADB and the United Nations Development Program (UNDP).

Addressing the First Greater Mekong Subregion Economic Cooperation Summit in 2002, Chinese Prime Minister Zhu Rongji stressed his country's strong commitment to regional cooperation by being an active participant in the GMS. He also stressed that the development of China would have positive impact on regional cooperation; that China's accession to the World Trade Organization promises an even broader scope for its cooperation with other subregional countries; and that the development of its western region will create more opportunities and favorable conditions for economic cooperation with the GMS countries.[2]

In fact, China has actively participated in many major GMS projects. Pursuant to discussions between China, Laos, Thailand and the ADB, initial preparations were completed for the construction of the Kunming-Bangkok Road. Also, China will provide US$30 million in the form of interest-free loans and grants for the sections of the Road Improvement Project in Lao PDR. At the first GMS Summit, China acceded to and signed the Agreement for the Facilitation of Cross-Border Movement of People and Goods in the GMS and the Intergovernmental Agreement on Power Trade. China, furthermore, has undertaken cooperation projects with other riparian countries in navigation, agriculture, customs procedures, trade facilitation, and disaster relief (ibid.). China has also contributed US$5 million to clear away rocks and sandbars in the Mekong River to aid river-borne transport.

Meanwhile, China's relations with ASEAN have also rapidly developed. China's Mekong development plans lie within its policy toward Southeast Asia in general and China's enhanced relations with ASEAN has facilitated the implementation of China's domestic development policies. The volume of trade between China and ASEAN increased by 40 percent in 2003 compared to 2002 and reached US$78.352 trillion—the highest recorded (*The People*, 2 October 2004).

In 2002 leaders of ASEAN and China signed the Framework Agreement on ASEAN-China Economic Cooperation, which serves as the fulcrum for establishing a free trade area by 2010 for the older ASEAN members and by 2015 for the newer members with flexibility on sensitive commodities. In this connection, China granted special and preferential tariff treatment to the three newest ASEAN members, Cambodia, Laos and Myanmar. Moreover, China and ASEAN signed the Declaration on the Conduct of Parties in the South China Sea, which provides for confidence-building activities between ASEAN and China. China also adopted the Joint Declaration of ASEAN and China on Cooperation in the Field of Non-Traditional Security Issues. A Joint Declaration of ASEAN and China on Strategic Partnership for Peace and Prosperity was signed in 2003 at the ASEAN+China Summit. China subsequently acceded to the ASEAN Treaty of Amity and Cooperation and its leaders have expressed the country's intention to accede to the Protocol of the Treaty on the Southeast Asia Nuclear Weapons-Free Zone. These dynamic measures by China are clear proof of deepening political trust between China and its regional partners and a sign of greater cooperation in the years to come.[3]

Geopolitics from the perspective of Southeast Asian Mekong countries

The main areas of potential of the Mekong River for Myanmar— another upstream country—are hydroelectric power and forestry. Yet Myanmar seems to pay less attention to the development of the Mekong basin in part because its share of the river basin and water volume is minimal (2 percent) and also because of pressing domestic concerns. Until 1988, the country still relied on basic colonial infrastructure, some of which was destroyed because of internal strife (Kyaw 2004, 1). Myanmar's isolation from the international community is another factor that limits its involvement in regional cooperation despite its shift in status from ASEAN observer in 1995 to full member two years later. As a full member, Myanmar has taken part in the ASEAN-Mekong Basin Development Cooperation, some GMS projects, the ASEAN+3, ASEAN+China as well as other projects of the so-called growth triangles and quadrangles in the subregion. Included here is the Bagan Declaration on Economic Cooperation among Cambodia, Laos, Myanmar, and Thailand (2003). But international pressure on the Myanmar military regime to democratize and uphold human rights remains firm. In August 2003, the country announced a roadmap for transition to a disciplined and modern democratic state to meet this outside pressure, but the international community still awaits action on this plan.

The Mekong River plays a significant role in the socio-economic development of Laos since the river contributes the largest part of its water resource to this country. Timber and electricity exports account for more than half of the country's annual export revenue. Furthermore, as the only state which borders all five other riparian countries, Laos is critically located in the central Mekong basin. Because of this important location, Laos has advantages in attracting grants from international organizations and donors in building dams for generating hydropower. However, because it is landlocked and is less populated and less developed than the other riverine countries, Laos' access to international commerce and integration is still limited. By participating in ASEAN and Mekong River development cooperation, Laos hopes to gain access to the sea and obtain the financial and technical assistance it needs to reduce poverty.

Thailand accounts for 22 percent of the total Mekong basin, one-third of its land and 38 percent of the population (Vu 2001, 132). The Mekong, therefore, is economically important to the country. Thailand's advanced economic, human resource and technical capacities enhance its participation in the subregion's development and enable the country to take a leading role in promoting regional collaboration. Moreover, domestic demand for Mekong River development is also strong. The northeast of Thailand, which forms part of the Mekong basin, is one of the poorest and driest in the country. In the wake of the Asian crisis, the need for sustainable development became more urgent for Thailand, and although its economy is more developed than others in the region, agriculture is still important domestically. Water from the Mekong's tributaries is essential for agricultural development as well as for the growing industrial and service sectors. However, Thailand's plans to divert water from the Mekong and its tributaries for these purposes are a source of tension as they conflict with the regional policy.

The Mekong plays a vital role in Cambodia's socio-economic development as most of the country's territory is located in the river basin. The river, and especially the Great Lake-Tonle Sap, is an essential source of food supply for the Cambodian people. But wars, conflict, and unstable internal politics have constrained Cambodia from concentrating on the development of the basin. A shortage of capital and of human resources also adversely affect the country's development and cooperation programs. After the 1993 UN-sponsored election, Cambodia quickly joined the regional integration process by becoming an ASEAN observer in 1995 and full member in 1999. The accession of Cambodia to ASEAN was guided by political and economic considerations as clarified by the country's leaders (Kao 2002, 59–68) and through ASEAN, Cambodia has become more involved in the Mekong region's development.

In Vietnam, the last of the lower Mekong countries, the river basin area accounts for one-fifth of the country's territory, equivalent to 9 percent of the total basin area and about 35 percent of the basin's total population. Water from the Mekong is a vital source of the delta's irrigation and the hydropower potential of the central highlands (Vu 2001, 132). The river basin is also essential to the Vietnamese economy. The Mekong Delta produces over 14 million tons of rice annually (out of the country's total of more than 29 million tons), or about 25–27 percent of its GDP (Nguyen and Kieu 2001, 131; *The Nation*, 3 September 2004). Vietnam is thus greatly affected by the actions of its upstream neighbours. Changes in the river's water level and ecosystem, for example, directly affect the Mekong Delta. Over the past few years, widespread flooding in central and southern Vietnam and the penetration of saline water into the southern coast have been the cause of much distress. Vietnam's interest is to reduce the negative impact on the Mekong water level and ecology brought about by the exploitation of sand and the river's resources.

In turn, the central highlands and provinces of Vietnam are geographically strategic as they constitute a gateway between the entire region and the South China Sea, especially for landlocked Laos. Its deep-water seaports are located near international sea lanes and roads connect these seaports to neighboring countries. A network of railways and land roads linking Yunnan to Vietnam provides a direct gateway to the sea for Yunnan. Vietnam also lies on the proposed trans-Asian railway that is to run from Singapore to Turkey with segments running through Thailand, Cambodia, Vietnam, and China. The location of Vietnam as the center of transcontinental and pan-oceanic transportation is an important consideration in the country's efforts at subregional cooperation. However, the central highlands and provinces are still underdeveloped areas with poverty rates higher than the national average. Participation in regional cooperation will help the country cultivate its natural advantages by tapping these provinces' economic resources and accelerating poverty reduction, both of which will ensure national economic development and security. Experience shows that economic difficulties and backwardness can be the main causes of social instability.

International country actors

Apart from the Mekong riverine nations, other significant players in the region's development are international organizations such as the United Nations Economic and Social Commission for Asia and the Pacific (UN-ESCAP), UNDP, ADB, and countries like the United States and Japan. This section focuses on the role of the latter two nations.

As part of its anti-communist drive in the region, the United States pushed for the establishment of the Mekong Committee in 1957. After the Vietnam War, despite its long and heavy involvement in the region, the US government was noticeably noncommittal with regard to the development of the Mekong, leaving the initiative to the countries in the region and to regional institutions like the ADB and ASEAN (Nguyen 1999, 223). But in recent times the United States has begun to show greater visibility in regional development, for example, funding the activities of the MRC, foremost of which is flood mitigation. Flood measurement posts are beginning to be installed in Cambodian villages along the Mekong River to provide early warning to downstream communities at risk from flooding. The MRC, the American Red Cross in Cambodia, and the Cambodian Red Cross are carrying out the flood post-project, with US$1.24 million in funding from the US Foreign Disaster Assistance over a five-year period. The program was developed after floods swept the region in 2000, killing 347 Cambodians, more than 500 in Vietnam, and destroying 10 percent of the wet season production in Laos. Damage was estimated at US$285 million in Vietnam alone and US$161 million in Cambodia. The project is part of a wider, US$20 million MRC water management plan, covering Cambodia, Thailand, Laos, and Vietnam (*Vietnam News*, 31 March 2004).

Japan began to pay greater attention to the Mekong since the proclamation of the Fukuda Doctrine in Manila in August 1977. At the time Japan was searching for a bigger political role in Asia to reflect its status as the world's second largest economy. Prime Minister Takeo Fukuda thus announced a three-point policy toward Southeast Asia: that Japan was firmly committed to peace and was determined not to become a military power; that it would establish a relationship of mutual trust not only in political and economic areas but also in the social and cultural realms; and that Japan would cooperate actively with the Indochinese states on the basis of mutual understanding, thereby contributing to peace and prosperity in all of Southeast Asia (Soeya 1993, 99). Economic, and specifically, overseas development aid (ODA) became the most important tool of Japanese policy toward the region, shaped by its postwar constitution and the need to counterbalance memories of Japanese militarism during the Second World War in many countries of the region.

In nurturing a new image for itself, Japan actively sought a resolution to the Cambodian conflict and the restructuring of Indochina. In 1993 Japan initiated the Forum for Indochina's Comprehensive Development and three years later, its Foreign Ministry established a task force to research GMS development strategies. Japan's invigorated policy was guided by its relations with ASEAN, which had improved over the last thirty years, especially in economic and development cooperation. Japan is one of the largest ODA donors to ASEAN, and ASEAN has become Japan's second biggest trading partner. Japan's direct investment in ASEAN, for instance, has exceeded US$100 billion. In the past decade alone, Japan's ODA provision to ASEAN amounted to over US$2 billion. The major recipients of Japanese assistance are the GMS countries—China, Thailand, Vietnam, Cambodia, and Laos. Together with its active and effective contribution to the Initiative for ASEAN Integration and the Mekong Subregional Development, Japan's ODA constitutes an important resource for ASEAN member countries striving to promote economic growth and reduce the development gaps among themselves (*VNA Daily Bulletin*, 12 December 2003).

At various regional forums like the ASEAN+3 and ASEAN+Japan meetings, high-ranking Japanese officials spoke highly of the Mekong Basin Cooperation Development as an example of cooperation between Japan and ASEAN. The prospect of a free trade area between Japan and ASEAN, and the accession of Japan to the Southeast Asian Agency for Regional Transport and Communications Development in 2003, have furthered this cooperation. Addressing the ASEAN-Japan Memorial Summit in Tokyo in December 2003, where leaders of the ASEAN countries and Japan signed the Tokyo Declaration for the Dynamic and Enduring ASEAN-Japan Partnership in the New Millennium and adopted the ASEAN-Japan Action Plan, Prime Minister Koizumi stressed that ASEAN was Japan's major partner in economic, political and security cooperation. Japan then pledged US$1.5 billion to cooperation projects with Vietnam, Cambodia, Thailand, Laos, and Myanmar, focusing on infrastructure development, poverty alleviation and human resource development (ibid.).

Real and prospective cooperation, failures and successes

The first postwar attempt to harness the Mekong River's potential for development was the establishment of the Bureau of Flood Control and Water Resources Development in 1949 by the UN Economic Commission for Asia and the Far East (ECAFE, later renamed ESCAP). The aim of the bureau was to investigate the potential of the river for irrigation and hydropower. However, this activity was not fruitful because of financial and technical difficulties and the lack of support from the riverine countries. In 1957 the first cooperative institution in the Mekong region was set up—the Committee for Coordination of Investigations of the Lower Mekong Basin (Mekong Committee)—with Thailand, Laos, Cambodia, and (Southern) Vietnam as members. Initiated by the US Bureau of Reclamation and sponsored by the UN-ECAFE, the Mekong Committee was, however, considered a product of Cold War superpower politics. The United States, France and Japan committed themselves to assisting this organization. The "investigations" concerned hydropower and irrigation projects, flood control and the regulation of water supply, navigation and fisheries, but actually aimed "to 'develop' the region as a bulwark against communism" (Goh 2001, 477).

In 1970, the Committee formulated medium- (1970–1980) and long-term (1981–2000) plans to develop the water resource of the lower Mekong basin (Tran 1999, 8). But when the Indochina War ended and Khmer Rouge-led Cambodia was withdrawn from the Mekong Committee in 1975, development plans for the Mekong were suspended. The Mekong Committee, nevertheless, continued to exist with a secretariat in Bangkok. The remaining members then set up the Mekong Provisional Committee (also known as the Interim Mekong Committee) in 1978 to continue collecting data and plan for the development of the Mekong. Reconsidering the plans proposed in the 1970s, the Interim Committee put forward "The Mekong Perspectives" in 1987, with investigations of investment capacities for the period up to 2000 and beyond (ibid.).

Realizing the need for economic development cooperation in the Mekong, the ADB initiated the GMS in 1992. The initiative was warmly welcomed by states in the region also interested in extending development cooperation at the bilateral, trilateral, and multilateral levels within the framework of the GMS. The economies of the area hope to benefit from the subregion's massive projects ranging from transportation to tourism.

Meanwhile, a parallel effort was made by Southeast Asian countries in the Mekong basin to reconstitute the defunct Mekong Committee as the Mekong River Commission. This action was made possible by the Paris Agreement on Comprehensive Peace in Cambodia in 1991, which enabled Cambodia to rejoin the group. In April 1995 the members of the Commission, Cambodia, Laos, Thailand, and Vietnam, signed the Agreement on Cooperation for Sustainable Development of the Mekong River Basin.

Furthermore, the enlargement of ASEAN in the 1990s with the addition of GMS members Cambodia, Laos, Myanmar and Vietnam have opened new channels for cooperation on development projects in the Mekong region. The West-East Corridor[4], for instance, which is actually a route established a century ago by Vietnamese traders in Thakhek and Savannakhet in Laos, has created more opportunities to increase economic ties especially for Thailand, Laos, Cambodia, and Vietnam. However, the 1997–1998 Asian financial crisis and its immediate aftermath adversely impacted on the ASEAN economies and plans for Mekong development. Today, ASEAN is once again stepping up efforts to upgrade infrastructure, develop human resources and reduce poverty in the region.

In practice, these various networks intertwine and work closely with one another because they span the same region and espouse similar goals. In November 2001 the ASEAN Summit in Brunei approved the GMS project on the Singapore-Kunming railway project. The railway will link Singapore with Kuala Lumpur in Malaysia, Hat Yai, Bangkok and Sa Kaew in Thailand, Poipet and Phnom Penh in Cambodia, Ho Chi Minh City and Da Nang in Vietnam, and Kunming in China. The railway will form part of the infrastructure of an important transport route similar to that developed in the South-North economic corridor. The railway project will also supplement other transport corridors in the GMS (such as the trans-Asian highway), thus creating a diverse transport network in Southeast and East Asia (*VNA Daily Bulletin*, 2 April 2002). In addition, the railway will beef up trade exchanges and transnational tourism between the ASEAN countries and China and between these countries and the outside world.

The First Summit of the GMS (2002) set the tone for Mekong development cooperation, which was affirmed by the 8th ASEAN Summit. Aimed at the promotion of economic and social development, poverty reduction and environmental protection, the GMS Summit focused on transport building initiatives, simplified cross-border trade and investment procedures, a transnational telecommunications network, coordinated implementation of an agreement on energy purchase, private sector involvement and competitiveness, an environmental protection strategy, human resource development, flood mitigation and management of water resources, and tourism. The leaders of the GMS then adopted the Ten-Year Strategic Framework for the GMS Program and eleven flagship programs in order to achieve closer economic cooperation and attain prosperity for the region (Joint GMS Summit Declaration, 3 November 2002). The discussions also included concerns raised by downstream countries over major development projects upstream, especially China's dam projects which affect the flow of the Mekong River.

Apart from ASEAN and the GMS, another network was formed, expanding the scope of cooperation in the larger Asian region. The ASEAN+China network aims primarily to establish a free trade area (FTA). With a combined population of 1.7 billion, the ASEAN+China FTA will have a total combined GDP of US$2 trillion and two-way trade amounting to about US$1.23 trillion (www.rieto.go.jp). ASEAN and China further agreed to launch an initial package of tariff reductions to pave the way for the FTA. The aim of the so-called "early harvest" package is to cut down tariffs to zero percent in three years for the six most economically advanced ASEAN members—Singapore, Malaysia, Indonesia, the Philippines, Thailand, and Brunei. The Framework Agreement on ASEAN-China Comprehensive Economic Cooperation, signed by these countries in 2002, set 2010 as the deadline for the establishment of the FTA for the six original ASEAN members, and 2015 for the new and less developed ASEAN members. Article 6 of the Agreement lists the categories of farm products included in the package, such as live animals, meat and edible meat, fish, dairy products, other animal products, live trees, edible vegetables, and edible fruits and nuts. The inclusion of non-farm products will be the subject of subsequent bilateral negotiations between China and the ASEAN.

Development cooperation in the Mekong region can also be seen in the form of growth quadrangles or triangles among the member countries. The Quadripartite Economic Cooperation Plan (1994), composed of Myanmar, Thailand, China, and Laos, contains guidelines on the navigation of the upper reaches of the Mekong River in an effort to foster transportation and tourism within the region (Smith and Gross 2000, 24). The "development triangle" of Vietnam, Laos, and Cambodia—the new and less-developed countries of the ASEAN—was adopted at the informal Prime Ministers' meeting in Vientiane in 1999, and encompasses seven provinces: Rattanakiri and Stung Treng (Cambodia), Attapeu and Sekong (Laos), and Kontum, Gia Lai and Dac Lac (Vietnam). Cooperation within the triangle is aimed at optimizing each country's internal strength while accessing external aid. Apart from projects on agriculture, tourism and so on, the development triangle program also covers tariffs, tax reduction and exemption, and other measures to facilitate a smooth flow of commodities and people among the three countries (*Vietnam News*, 28 January 2002).

There are also separate agreements entered into by certain member countries of the ASEAN and the GMS, such as the navigation agreement signed by China, Myanmar, Laos, and Thailand in 2000 (*The Nation*, 21 April 2000). In October 2002 Laos, Thailand, and China signed a agreement on building a road from Thailand's province of Chiang Rai through the Bokeo and Luang Namtha provinces of Laos to Kunming in China's Yunnan province. The road is a link to the planned Singapore-Beijing trans-Asia highway running through northern Laos. Once completed the road will facilitate commercial cooperation among Laos, Thailand, and China (*VNA Daily Bulletin*, 13 and 14 October 2002), and promote the development of the poorer areas of these countries. Furthermore, in 2003 Thailand put forward the Initiative on Economic Cooperation Strategy between Thailand, Myanmar, Laos, and Cambodia (known as the Bagan Declaration), aimed at increasing competitiveness, generating economic growth in border areas, creating jobs, and reducing income disparity among these countries. Thailand subsequently initiated a separate cooperation framework with Laos and Cambodia.

In the process of building these networks and mechanisms of development cooperation, bilateral relations in the region have been strengthened. The Thailand-China FTA, the Vietnam-Laos agreement on tariff cuts, trade cooperation between Thailand and Vietnam, and even the daily bus service between Thailand and Laos are all vivid examples of thriving bilateral relations between neighboring states.

Upstream vs downstream interests

However, despite the visible improvements and achievements in the realm of economic cooperation, numerous issues continue to challenge development cooperation efforts. Among these are the lack of coordination among the various national development programs relating to the Mekong River, given each country's geopolitical perspective and interest; insufficient coordination, too, among the various international agencies and donor countries amid growing competition among the Mekong countries for foreign assistance; an overlap among international networks and projects concerning the Mekong River; lingering negative effects of the Asian financial crisis in 1997; and the inadequacy of the MRC arising largely from the fact that its members do not represent the entire Mekong region but only the lower basin.

It should be noted that the GMS countries belong to and support several development cooperation frameworks that tend to disperse the focus of cooperation, sometimes making the cooperation effort selective rather than all-inclusive. Joining the MRC as an observer, China, for example, has focused more on cooperation with upstream countries as evidenced by the Quadripartite Economic Cooperation and the Agreement on Transportation Cooperation involving China, Myanmar, Laos, and Thailand. These agreements leave out the two lower stream countries of Cambodia and Vietnam, which are more vulnerable to the development activities of the upstream countries. Similarly, Vietnam was not considered in the Economic Cooperation Strategy (which includes Thailand, Cambodia, Laos, and Myanmar). Formed at the initiative of Thailand in 2003, the strategy excluded Vietnam on the grounds that Thailand has no common border with it (*The Nation*, 31 July 2003 and 8–14 December 2003; *Bangkok Post*, 21 December 2003).

The expansion of cooperation in the ACMECS (Ayeyawady-Chao Phraya-Mekong Economic Cooperation Strategy), which now includes Cambodia, Laos, Myanmar, Thailand and Vietnam, seems to meet the needs of the Southeast Asian mainland countries (the Mekong ASEAN members) and to harmonize their interests by utilizing member countries' diverse strengths to foster the development of the subregion. The first ACMECS Summit (12 November 2003) produced the "Bagan Declaration", which established the ACMECS framework and action plan covering five sectors of cooperation, namely, trade and investment facilitation, agricultural and industrial cooperation, transport linkages, tourism cooperation and human resource development. The plan lists 46 common and 224 bilateral projects for implementation over the next ten years. In 2005 public health was admitted as the sixth sector of ACMECS cooperation as a response to the rising danger of transborder diseases, especially avian influenza (http://www.mfa.go.th).

While the GMS countries recognize the need to cooperate with each other in order to promote the sustainable development of the region, national policies are shaped by a range of factors, starting with geography all the way up to notions of national gain. National interest is most evident in the issue of water resource development and allocation, which serves diverse, sometimes conflicting, national purposes: for China and Vietnam, it would be to meet the energy gap; for Laos and Myanmar, to gain foreign revenue; and for Thailand, to satisfy the growing demand for water including irrigation (Kaosaard and Dore 2003, 11). The Mekong River Commission noted, for instance, that,

> Water is diverted from the river by tens of thousands of local dams, mostly in Thailand and China, which divert water from the Mekong for agricultural land irrigation and power generation. But the dams cause fluctuations in water levels on the river, upsetting the livelihoods of the people who have for years organized their lives around

predictable high levels in rainy season and low levels in the dry season. (*Vietnam News*, 2 December 2003)

Kim Geheb, the Commission's research coordinator and head of the Challenge Programme on Water and Food, in his article "Managing the Mekong's Future Cooperatively" (*The Nation*, 9 March 2004), warns that an estimated 750,000 hectares of Vietnamese farmland in the delta are annually affected by saline water, and changes in flow patterns could affect the rich Mekong fishery—worth an estimated US$1.4 billion—and drastically reduce fish catches in Cambodia. Thailand's own experience clearly shows the impact of dams on fishery. Pointing out that upstream nations are responsible for the downstream consequences of their actions, Geheb concludes that it is necessary to manage the Mekong River basin as an integrated area and not as an amalgam of six separate nations.

The issues of river tributaries (of which there are a hundred), hydropower, and water diversion are also very acute and there is no coordinated mechanism for all the states in the region to manage them and resolve differences inevitable in any enterprise involving shared resources. Though disputes among nations over freshwater resources are not likely to spark violent conflicts, water security can have a destabilizing effect on regional and international security (Smith and Gross 2000, 18).

In order to partly tackle these issues, delegates of the MRC members signed two cooperation documents during their 10th annual meeting (2003): the Regulations on Prior Notification and Consultation, and the Agreement and the Regulations on Supervision of the Use of the Mekong River Water. The agreements provide for a monitoring system on the use of water from the river and its tributaries, including provisions for environmental assessments. These agreements, however, do not bind the upstream countries (they do not belong to the MRC) whose projects on the river affect the countries in the lower basin. Water use, and its extraction and management are contentious issues in the region as dams and hydropower stations continue to sprout along the river.

It is obvious that a single country alone cannot solve the problems that beset the region as whole. Even Cambodia, whose participation in the MRC was interrupted by internal violence and conflict with neighboring Vietnam, accepts that close cooperation is crucial to prevent minor conflicts and better living conditions (Prime Minister's address before the MRC, *VNA Daily Bulletin*, 1 December 2003).

The increasing interdependence of nations also means greater potential for the spillover of transnational problems, such as water and ecological destruction, illicit migration, drug trade, HIV/AIDS, human trafficking, and so on. These issues present the other side of development and integration that can only be effectively addressed by joint efforts.

The post-Cold War climate of peace has, no doubt, provided the environment for intensive and long-term regional cooperation. The expansion of ASEAN and ongoing cooperation with its dialogue partners in the Asian region and the international community are the fruit of this new environment. Rid of wars and conflicts that once destroyed and divided countries in the Mekong region, the 21st century is a time of deliberate cooperation, and the driving force in designing the region's development can only be the member countries themselves, individually *and* collectively. The MRC represents one such effort, particularly by nations that were once engaged in combat.

Table 3.1: Time Line of Geopolitical Events and GMS Development Cooperation Initiatives

Year	Geopolitics	GMS Development Cooperation
1945	Proclamation of Democratic Republic of Vietnam	
1948	Independence of Burma (now Myanmar) from Britain	
1949	Establishment of People's Republic of China	Establishment of Bureau of Flood Control and Water Resources Development by UN-ECAFE
1953	Independence of Laos and Cambodia	
1954	Fall of Dien Bien Phu; Geneva conference on Indochina; independence of North Vietnam	
1957		Formation of UN-sponsored Mekong Committee, consisting of Thailand, Laos, Cambodia and South Vietnam
1959		Establishment of Mekong Committee secretariat in Bangkok
1967		Establishment of ASEAN
1970	End of Cambodia's neutrality	Indicative Mekong Basin Plan
1971		Nam Ngum Dam completed
1973	Conclusion of Paris Conference on Vietnam, withdrawal of US troops	

1975	Takeover by communist regimes in Cambodia, Laos, and Vietnam	Mekong Committee's Joint Declaration of Principles on the Use of the Lower Mekong Basin Water; withdrawal of Cambodia from Mekong Committee
1978		Interim Mekong Committee established
1979	Collapse of the Khmer Rouge; border war between Vietnam and China	
1986	Launch of Vietnam's *Doi Moi*	
1987		Revised Indicative Basin Plan
1988	Thai declaration to "turn Indochina "from battlefield to marketplace"; border conflict between Laos and Thailand	
1991	Paris Peace Accord on Cambodia	
1992		ADB-initiated Greater Mekong Subregion (GMS) Cooperation, consisting of Vietnam, Laos, Cambodia, Myanmar, Thailand, and Yunnan province (China)
1993	UN-sponsored elections in Cambodia	
1994		Quadripartite Economic Cooperation Plan, composed of China, Myanmar, Laos, and Thailand
1995	Vietnam joins ASEAN	MRC established; Japan-initiated Forum for Comprehensive Development in Indochina; Working Group on economic development cooperation of Cambodia, Laos, and Myanmar; Mekong Basin Development Cooperation (MBDC) initiated by Malaysia and Singapore
1996		MRC Revised work plan; ASEAN approval of Basic Framework of Mekong Basin Development Cooperation
1997	Laos and Myanmar join ASEAN	Cessation of several projects owing to regional financial crisis
1998		Renewed initiative by ASEAN on Mekong basin development cooperation; approval of Hanoi Plan of Action and West-East Corridor; talks between MRC and donor states and organizations
1999	Cambodia joins ASEAN	Cross-border agreement between Laos, Thailand and Vietnam; triangle development area established by Vietnam, Laos and Cambodia

2001		Cross-border agreement signed by Cambodia; agreement to establish ASEAN-China free trade area
2002		Cross-border agreement signed by China; Framework Agreement on ASEAN+1; 1st GMS Summit in Phnom Penh results in agreements on power, trade and cross-border movements
2003		ASEAN+3 Summit; ten years of the MRC; ASEAN-Japan Commemorative Summit; China, later Japan signs ASEAN Treaty of Amity and Cooperation; Myanmar signs cross-border agreement

Source: Philip Hirsch, Gerard Cheong, et al., "Natural Resource Management in the Mekong River Basin: Perspectives for Australian Development Cooperation," University of Sydney, 1996, with updated information by Mya Than and the author.

Notes

1 This is referred to by He Shengda (chapter 4) as the West Development Program.
2 Zhu Rongji, Address at the First Greater Mekong Subregion Economic Cooperation Summit, Phnom Penh, 3 November 2002.
3 Press Statements: ASEAN+China Summit, ASEAN+Japan Summit, ASEAN+ Republic of Korea Summit, and ASEAN-India Summit, Bali, Indonesia, 8 October Press Statements. 2003.
4 The ADB uses the term East-West Corridor to describe the geographical areas covered, but from the Vietnamese perspective, West-East is the appropriate geographical term. As explained by Viet (2000), the West-East cooperation "is not separate from the GMS cooperation but supplements and does not duplicate the existing projects in the Mekong Subregion."

References

Chen Luosheng. n.d. "Some Thoughts on China"s Western Region Development Strategy." http://www.54479.com/study/shownews.asp.

Geheb, Kim. 2004. "Managing the Mekong"s Future Cooperatively." *The Nation*, 9 March.

Goh, Evelyn. 2001. "The Hydro-Politics of the Mekong River Basin: Regional Cooperation and Environmental Security." In *Non-Traditional Security Issues in Southeast Asia*, edited by Andrew T.H. Tan and J.D. Kenneth Boutin, pp. 468–506. Singapore: Select Publishing for Institute of Defence and Strategic Studies.

Hirsch, Philip and Gerard Cheong. 1996. "Natural Resource Management in the Mekong River Basin: Perspectives for Australian Development Cooperation." Final overview report to AusAID. University of Sydney. http://www.usyd.edu.au/su/geography/hirsch/index.htm.

Kao Kim Hourn. 2002. *Cambodia's Foreign Policy and ASEAN*. Phnom Penh: Cambodian Institute for Cooperation and Peace.

Kaosa-ard, Mingsarn and John Dore, eds. 2003. *Social Challenges in the Mekong Region*. Chiang Mai: Chiang Mai University Social Research Institute.

Kyaw Thein. 2004. "Efforts for the Prevalence of Peace and Stability." Paper presented at seminar, Understanding Myanmar, Yangon, 27–28 January.

"Making it Happen: A Common Strategy on Cooperation for Growth, Equity and Prosperity in the Greater Mekong Subregion." Joint GMS Summit Declaration. 2002. Phnom Penh, Cambodia, 3 November.

Nguyen Thi Dieu. 1999. *The Mekong River and the Struggle for Indochina*. London: Praeger.

Nguyen Tran Que and Kieu Van Trung. 2001. *Song va tieu vung Mekong. Tiem nang va hop tac phat trien quoc te* (The Mekong River and the Greater Mekong Subregion: Potential for International Development Cooperation). Hanoi: Khoa hoc Xa hoi.

Osborne, Milton. 2000. *The Mekong: Turbulent Past, Uncertain Future*. Sydney: Allen & Unwin.

Smith, Paul J. and Charles H. Gross. 2000. "Water and Conflict in Asia." Paper presented at the Asia-Pacific Center for Security Studies Seminar Series, Honolulu, February.

Soeya, Yoshihide. 1993. "Japan's Policy towards Southeast Asia: Anatomy of 'Autonomous Diplomacy' and the American Factor." In *China, India, Japan and the Security of Southeast Asia*, edited by Chandran Jeshurun, pp. 93–113. Singapore: Institute of Southeast Asian Studies.

Tran Cao Thanh. 1999. "Programs and Perspectives of International Cooperation on the Economic Development of the Mekong Sub-region." *Southeast Asian Studies* 3, 36: 8–17.

Viet Chung. 2000. "West-East Corridor." http://www.mofa.gov.vn/quocte/2000_asean/28.htm.

Vu Xuan Truong. 2001. "Vietnam and Thailand in Multilateral Programs on the Mekong Development." Paper presented at the workshop, Vietnam-Thailand Relations: Looking into the Future. Institute for International Relations, Hanoi.

4

"FRIENDLY AND WEALTHY NEIGHBORS, STABLE NATION": YUNNAN'S PARTICIPATION IN THE GMS

HE SHENGDA

The Greater Mekong basin is, as World Trade Organization Director-General Supachai Panitchpakdi asserts, an area with extremely high potential for cooperation between China (particularly southwest China's Yunnan province) and its neighboring countries (Supachai and Clifford 2001, 129). Spurred by the Asian Development Bank (ADB) in the early 1990s, economic cooperation in the Lancang-Mekong Basin involves the six riparian countries collectively called the Greater Mekong Subregion (GMS), namely: Cambodia, China (Yunnan), Lao PDR, Myanmar, Thailand and Vietnam. The most obvious feature of GMS cooperation is the wide variety of fields of endeavor across various countries, with each country playing its own role under the cooperation mechanism. While the six members exhibit some commonalities, they pursue different development paths arising from varying economic growth levels, domestic demand and capacity to engage in cooperation projects. Coordination and consultation are thus crucial to the success of the GMS and current mechanisms could be improved to enhance progress. A comprehensive analysis of the strategic objectives of all parties to the GMS and the implications of these goals on cooperation should also be made for, in the final analysis, "GMS cooperation initiatives show the challenges that the world is facing, especially in these remote areas of diversity and destitution..." (ibid., 130). This chapter examines the framework of China's regional economic development, the advantages of and obstacles to promoting subregional cooperation, and recommendations for enhancing China's role in the GMS.

China as neighbor to the Mekong

China's participation in GMS cooperation is in line with its domestic policy of fostering social well-being and its diplomatic objective of promoting world peace and regional development. Its participation in regional cooperation focuses on two strategic objectives. The first is to secure regional peace and stability and further consolidate friendly relations with neighboring countries, thereby creating a peaceful regional environment for China's domestic development. The second is to promote regional cooperation and accelerate regional development and prosperity through bilateral/multilateral cooperation so that new economic opportunities for neighboring countries are created, in turn assisting in the opening up and development of China's less developed provinces and regions.

To attain these objectives, China is guided by the maxim, "being friendly to neighbors and making neighbors partners." The overall report of the Communist Party of China's 16th Congress stressed that China has and will continue to develop friendly relations and cooperate with its neighbors at a higher level than the past (Jiang Zemin 2002, 43). In his speech at the ASEAN-China Summit in Bali in October 2003, Chinese Premier Wen Jiabao summarized China's regional policies as "friendly neighbors, stable nation and wealthy neighbors" (*Beijing Review*, 25 December 2003).

GMS cooperation is of strategic significance to China for several reasons. The Mekong region is, first of all, the geographic hub that links China, Southeast Asia and South Asia. It is for this reason that a key element of regional cooperation in the GMS is transportation infrastructure not just by sea but land and air as well. Second, as Table 4.1 shows, the region abounds in natural resources and still possesses fairly substantial forest cover. The Mekong region's basic socio-economic indicators (Table 4.2) further suggest a huge potential for economic growth that is the object of present day regional development efforts. Third, history and culture bind ethnic communities across the region, bringing about a sense of affinity upon which collaboration could be anchored.

Table 4.1: Major Resources and Industries of GMS Members

Member	Resources	Forest Cover	Major Agro-Products	Major Industries and Minerals
Myanmar	Forest, farmland and aquatic products, petroleum and gas, tin, gemstones, tungsten, copper	50%	Rice, wheat, sugarcane, peanuts, beans	Rice milling, timber processing, nonferrous metals
Thailand	Tropical fruits, rice, aquatic products, tin, tungsten, lignite, iron	38%	Rice, maize, cassava, natural rubber, cotton	Mineral smelting, construction materials, petrochemicals, textiles, food processing, automobiles
Cambodia	Manganese, lead, phosphorus, zinc, gold	40%	Rice, maize, natural rubber	Food processing, light industry
Lao PDR	Forest, farmland, tin, lead, coal	58%	Rice, maize, tobacco	Power generation, cement, cigarette, cotton spinning
Vietnam	Coal, iron, chrome, petroleum and gas, tin	30%	Aquatic products rice, coffee maize, coconut, pineapple, sugarcane, rubber,	Mineral smelting, electric power, machinery, chemicals, building materials, food processing
Yunnan	Forest, metal minerals coal, water power	25%	Rice, tobacco, tea, sugar, rubber, fruits and vegetables of temperate zone	Tobacco, nonferrous metals, steel, phosphate chemicals, electric power, machinery, high technology

Source: He Shengda and Wang Xuhong, 2003, *The Construction of the ASEAN-China Free Trade Area and Yunnan's Opening to Southeast Asia*, p. 387.

Table 4.2: Key Indicators of the GMS, 2002

Member	Population (million)	Total Area (thousand sq km)	GDP (US$ billion)	1997/98 GDP as % of SEA	Per Capita GDP (US$)	Export-Import (US$ billion)
Myanmar	52.00	676	16.0	2.1	300	5.20
Thailand	63.08	513	125.0	23.8	1,990	125.24
Cambodia	12.30	181	3.2	0.5	260	3.10
Lao PDR	5.38	236	1.7	0.3	326	0.84
Vietnam	78.69	329	34.8	4.5	436	33.31
Yunnan	43.33	394	25.12	n.a.	586	2.23
Total	254.78	2,329	205.82	31.2	n.a.	169.92

Sources: Data from Economic Intelligence Unit 2002; *Yunnan Yearbook* 2002; World Bank, *World Development* Report 2002.

China's participation in the GMS therefore entails three elements: the further consolidation of China's relations with mainland Southeast Asian countries to create a better external environment for China, especially for its southwest provinces; the promotion of the China-ASEAN Free Trade Area (FTA) for accelerated regional prosperity; and the full participation of Yunnan province as China's principal player in the region, which in turn will speed up the development of southwestern China.

Contexts of China's Mekong policy

China is a country with worldwide influence but its focal points are primarily directed at the Asian region. As Southeast Asia is China's most crucial neighbor, relations with the region are of great importance. From China's standpoint, cooperation with the GMS can only logically be situated within the larger context of China's relations with the ASEAN. GMS cooperation constitutes a major component of the China-ASEAN economic cooperation and is one of the five priorities in the China-ASEAN FTA agreement. Established in 2001, the China-ASEAN FTA reflects a common desire to enhance trade and economic ties between the two entities. The Framework Agreement on Comprehensive Economic Cooperation between ASEAN and China (2002) gives substance to economic cooperation beyond a rather limited statement of trade cooperation. Taking the construction of a free trade area as its core task, the Framework Agreement details multiple fields of cooperation, from industry, agriculture, tourism and finance, to environment, infrastructure and human resource development. The agreement also identifies GMS cooperation as one of the FTA's five priorities. In 2002 Premier Zhu Rongji and the five leaders of the Mekong riparian countries attended the First GMS Summit and signed a Joint Declaration[1] and two other documents on cross-border movement of goods and people and on electricity procurement in the region.

Given this framework, GMS economic cooperation is essential to the successful establishment of the China-ASEAN FTA. As former premier Zhu Rongji explained at the first GMS Summit, regional cooperation of GMS countries meets the newly emerged situation of world integration and regionalization. GMS cooperation is being undertaken at the right time, in the right location, with friendly partners, and for new opportunities. Further promotion of regional cooperation will speed up the economic development of parties concerned and will create advantages for ASEAN 10+3 [ASEAN+China, Japan and Korea] or ASEAN 10+1 [ASEAN+China] cooperation (*People's Daily*. 4 November 2002).

In similar vein, addressing the 5th ASEAN Ministerial Meeting on GMS Cooperation and Development in August 2003 in Kunming, Vice Premier Zeng Peiyan stated: "The ASEAN-GMS cooperation mechanism is a major part of economic cooperation between China and each of the ASEAN members, and is also a substantial action in constructing the China-ASEAN FTA" (*Economic Daily*, 8 January 2003).

Domestically, China's Mekong policy is shaped by conditions in Yunnan, the country's central player in the Mekong subregion, whose economy relative to the eastern provinces has been shrinking over the past twenty years. The backwardness of western China can be explained by a variety of factors but its geographical isolation from the outside world is particularly crucial to explaining its present condition. A major reason for the rapid economic development of China's eastern provinces is their greater openness to the outside world. In Yunnan province, which accounts for 3.4 percent the country's total population, the GDP is only 2.2 percent of the country's total, with a per capita GDP at 63 percent of China's average. The province accounts for only 1.8 percent of the nation's industrial sector, 2.3 percent of the service sector, and only 0.4 percent of foreign direct investment in China. While Yunnan's export/import trade value reached its historically highest point of US$2.67 billion in 2003, it still accounts for a mere 0.32 percent of China's total export/import value. From 1984–2003, Yunnan received foreign direct investment amounting to no more than US$1.4 billion, or less than the amount of a single county of the eastern provinces.[2]

The western part of China, however, possesses plentiful natural and human resources and great potential. The huge West Development Program,[3] one of China's long-term development strategies, is regarded as an important engine of economic reform and development. "China has reached high economic growth over the past two decades through economic reform and opening," writes Feng Zhaokui, "while it will secure a new round of rapid growth, mostly depending on the development of the western part of the country" (2000, 11). At the same time, the Chinese central government stresses coordinated development so as to reduce disparities between the eastern and western sides. The CPC 16th Congress announcement that China will steadily "reinforce regional cooperation and promote exchanges and cooperation with the neighbors to a higher level," would only be achievable for the western provinces by opening up more, primarily to the neighboring countries. Yunnan province, says Feng Zhaokui, should "make full use of its geographic advantages, linking with Southeast Asia and South Asia, especially the GMS as the hub of Euro-Asian traffic network" (ibid.). China's Commission on Development and Planning (2002) places Yunnan as the economic and trade passage between GMS and Southeast Asia. Over the years Yunnan has strengthened its relations with its neighbors. Today the governments of Vietnam, Lao PDR, Thailand, Myanmar and Cambodia all have consulates in the provincial capital, Kunming.

GMS, the cord to Yunnan

The strategy and objective of Yunnan's participation in GMS cooperation is in conformity with that of China. But because of China's vast interests in the broader world, its participation in the GMS is only part of the country's macro strategy, and upgrading GMS cooperation to a larger scale seems to require more time. Yunnan, on the other hand, is heavily affected by movements from the countries on its border in the GMS. These Mekong countries, in fact, are Yunnan's most important economic partners. The sense of urgency, therefore, is more strongly felt on the ground (in the province of Yunnan) than by the central government or any other part of China. Moreover, through GMS cooperation, Yunnan has improved its infrastructure and accelerated economic exchanges with its neighbors, giving the province crucial access to external markets and resources. In the process, Yunnan has been able to readjust its economic structure, reallocate its resources and shift to a market orientation. For Yunnan, then, GMS cooperation is a strategic step toward opening up the province further and hastening its economic and social development in the early 21st century.

For this reason, Yunnan has stressed the importance of GMS cooperation. Early in 1992, it established the Office of ADB's GMS Program and, two years later, the Provincial Coordination Office, in response to the National Coordination Office of the Lancang-Mekong Basin Pro-phase Research and Development. In the 6th Ministers Meeting of GMS Cooperation in 1996, Yunnan representatives put forward ten areas of cooperation, namely: aviation, navigation, highways, railways, postal systems, electricity networks, tourism, trade, finance and human resources. In addition, Yunnan proposed the development of the following resources: human resources, water resources, tourism, land, biotechnology and mining; and identified four areas as obstacles to cooperation: environmental degradation, illegal migration, drug production, and the spread of AIDS and other social maladies.

Among the areas of GMS cooperation, transportation, energy, environmental protection and sustainable development stand out as priorities. By the end of 2003, the ADB had injected more than US$450 million into Yunnan to cover existing programs such as the Chuxiong-Dali Expressway (US$150 million), Yuanjiang-Mohei Expressway (US$250 million), Dachaoshan Power Transmission Project, and Simao Afforestation Project, as well as others to be implemented, such as the Baoshan-Longling Expressway and Dali-Lijiang Railway. By the year 2007, the transportation connection between Yunnan and the GMS countries by road, waterway (Lancang-Mekong River) and by air should be well in place.

Accompanying improvements in the transport sector is the growth in trade. Yunnan's bilateral export/import trade value with the GMS countries reached US$631 million in 2002, of which US$479 are exports from Yunnan. These exports represent 33.5 percent of the total export value of the province. In 2003 the trade value with the five GMS countries increased to US$830 million—an impressive

30 percent growth rate compared to the previous year. As for trade items, manufactured products account for 80 percent of the total export value (He and Wang 2003, 225). With economic development and an improved trade environment in all the GMS countries, the volume of bilateral trade is increasing. The export/import trade value between Yunnan and the GMS countries is expected to reach US$160–200 million in 2020. In turn, the rapid growth of the export/ import trade with GMS countries will accelerate the readjustment of Yunnan's economy.

The value of Yunnan's projects and labor contracts in the GMS has also expanded. From 1995–2002 the total value of projects and labor contracts between Yunnan province and the five GMS countries amounted to US$1.1 billion, of which US$600 million went to projects with a good track record. Over the past decade, the Yunnan International Economic and Technical Cooperation has contracted dozens of construction projects in Lao PDR, among which the Vang Rong Cement Plant is regarded as a model of Yunnan's outbound strategy. The Banglang hydrostation in Myanmar is now under construction by the Yunnan Machinery Equipment Export/Import Company. This project is believed to be the largest construction project undertaken by a Yunnan enterprise in a Southeast Asian country. Other significant projects contracted by Yunnan enterprises in GMS countries include the Na Hang Power Station and a lead mine (both in Vietnam), Yunnan-Cambodia Jincheng Medicine Company (Cambodia), North Thailand Technological and Economic Trade Area (Thailand), and a chloride project (Laos).

Furthermore, to reduce dependence on opium as a cash crop, the GMS devised agricultural cooperation and alternative crop programs that aim to bring about new economic opportunities to the inhabitants in border areas where opium is grown. For its part, the provincial government of Yunnan assists the six prefectures of Simao, Xishuangbana, Lincang, Baoshan, Dehong and Nujiang in order to develop alternative crops to supplant opium plantations in northern Myanmar and northern Laos, by means of financial and technical assistance, infrastructure construction, tourism development, and promotion of border trade. The replacement plantations cover a total area of 30,000 hectares.

In all of these, Yunnan province is expected to experience accelerated growth. The province's participation in GMS cooperation spans a broad range of economic and social sectors such as manufacturing, agriculture, transportation, energy, communication, environmental protection, tourism, human resource development, export/import trade, mutual investment, and drug control, of which more than a hundred projects are and will be covered by ADB assistance. All these projects will help Yunnan improve its infrastructure, protect the environment, and more generally upgrade its economic and social conditions. If these projects are successful, by 2020 the total amount of the province's fixed assets will accumulate to approximately US$60 billion, with the annual growth of fixed assets estimated at US$3.75 billion. This surely is an important factor for the economic development of the province.

The process of urbanization in Yunnan is also expected to hasten with the progress of GMS cooperation and the establishment of north-south economic corridors. The construction of a new modernized Kunming city and the Ge-Kai-Meng city cluster, among others, are expected to usher in the development of cities and towns along these corridors. As a result, the urbanization rate of the province will increase from 23 percent in the year 2000 to 46 percent by 2020. In addition, the telecommunications industry will prosper with the construction by China Telecom of the GMS International Telecommunications Center in Yunnan. A connection with Singapore's International Center is also envisioned to extend coverage as well as to provide cheaper service. Finally, tourism will be another beneficiary of GMS cooperation, with the promotion of tourism in the subregion.

Drinking water from the same river: Yunnan's overriding objective

Yunnan's participation in GMS cooperation is guided by the concept of "drinking water from the same river and co-building a nice homestead". Specifically, Yunnan has six goals in sight.

First, the province aims to beef up international traffic by linking the road, rail, air and water networks in the GMS. Its strategic vision is to use the road system as the basic backbone, with the airlines as accessory, the waterways as a complement, and railways as the medium to long-term means of transportation. At the moment, the focus is on road (Kunming-Vientiane-Bangkok highway, Kunming-Hanoi highway, and Kunming-Myanmar highway) and waterway construction (Lancang-Mekong international shipping route) and, to a limited extent, railway reconstruction (Kunming-Hanoi railway) and air transportation linking Yunnan with the GMS and other Southeast Asian countries.

Second, Yunnan hopes to cooperate with other GMS countries in building three north-south economic corridors that would connect the GMS market to China's and develop the economy along the corridors, namely, Kunming-Mandalay-Rangoon, Kunming-Hanoi-Hai Phong, and Kunming-Vientiane-Bangkok. Apart from trade along these corridors, other beneficiary sectors would be tourism, energy, minerals and agriculture.

Third, GMS cooperation will become a pioneer of the ASEAN-China FTA. Operating under the framework of ASEAN 10+1, GMS cooperation should strengthen networking between Cambodia, Lao PDR, Myanmar, Thailand and Vietnam plus China based on rational systems of access to trade and investment, eventually leading to the creation of a GMS common market.

Fourth, Yunnan seeks to improve the ecosystem and protect the environment in the interests of sustainable development of the entire subregion. The rational use of GMS resources is to be guided by this principle. Forest protection projects which will preserve rare species should therefore be established along the Lancang-Mekong, the Red River, and the Irrawaddy and Nujiang-Salween Rivers.

Fifth, the province intends to implement plans for cooperation in ten areas: transportation and traffic passage, trade, industrial infrastructure, electric power, energy and mining, agriculture, tourism, a regional telecommunications system, ecosystem, human resources, and drug control and alternative crop plantations.

Finally, Yunnan aims to develop Kunming as the economic center of the GMS, which would heighten Yunnan's role and status in the subregion. Although Yunnan has some advantages over other GMS countries in terms of its economic structure and technological capacity, it is backward compared to other provinces in China and some ASEAN countries. The province's role in GMS cooperation is thus circumscribed by its economic capacity.

To achieve these objectives, therefore, Yunnan province must maximize the opportunities created by China's West Development Program and the construction of the China-ASEAN FTA, to reinforce and mobilize its domestic resources for participating in GMS cooperation schemes, to improve technologies, and to further the process of economic restructuring.

Diverse, multi-level cooperation

Although the GMS is small compared to China's other regional undertakings, the scope of cooperation is nevertheless extensive and the participants, diverse. The cooperation mechanisms of the GMS overlap, operate simultaneously and at multiple levels: internationally, where the ADB acts as the principal institution; at the regional level, where China and the ASEAN are major actors; and the subregional level, in which a province of China and its neighbors in the Mekong are the main players. While the coexistence of diverse, multi-level cooperation mechanisms in a single subregion indicates the GMS's ability to attract worldwide support, the varied nature of these mechanisms also reflects different pursuits, emphases and target beneficiaries and, to a certain extent, a lack of general planning and coordination.

The ADB is the major player at the international level and the GMS ministerial meetings serve as the main venue for discussions. Twelve meetings were held from 1992 to 2003, tackling such areas of cooperation as transportation, energy, communication, and tourism. For each of these sectors a forum or working group has been formed to work out the mechanics of various proposals. The ADB-supported program is huge, requiring considerable financial and human resources, and is project-oriented, guided by a common set of general principles and managed by mutually agreed upon institutional arrangements.

Regional cooperation in the Mekong between the ten-member ASEAN and China formally began in 1996, when their respective ministers met in Kuala Lumpur and approved the Basic Framework of Mekong Basin Development and Cooperation. Infrastructure, investment and trade, agriculture, mining, industry and small enterprises, and human resource development were identified as the areas of cooperation. But in fact, the Framework Agreement of ASEAN-China Comprehensive Economic Cooperation (2001) is the origin of subregional cooperation, for the 2001 framework not only stipulated all-around economic cooperation between China and the ASEAN in the coming decade, but also ascertained GMS cooperation as one of the priorities of bilateral cooperation. Annex 4 of the document, for instance, deals with the acceleration of the Singapore-Kunming rail link and the Bangkok-Kunming highway projects, and the implementation of the mid- and long-term development plans of the GMS that were mapped out in the first GMS summit in Cambodia.

At the subregional level, two types of cooperation mechanism exist: one that involves selected countries in the subregion, and another that involves all the GMS countries. The first type deals more with growth zones and therefore specifies development targets. Such selective arrangements may be bilateral, such as the Yunnan-Northern Thailand cooperation, which held its first workshop in April 2004, but the bulk are multilateral. Examples of selective multilateral arrangements are the North-South Corridor discussed earlier; the East-West Corridor (1998), linking central Vietnam with central Laos and northeast Thailand; the Development Triangle (1999), involving two provinces of Cambodia (Rattanakiri and Stung Treng), two provinces of Laos (Attapeu and Sekong), and three provinces of Vietnam (Kun Tom, Gia Lai and Dac Lac; the Golden Quandrangle (1994), which includes Xishuangbanna and Simao prefectures of Yunnan province, seven provinces of northern Laos, Kengtung and Tachilek in east Myanmar, and Chiang Mai and Chiang Rai provinces of Thailand; and the Ayeyawady-Chao Phraya-Mekong Economic Cooperation Strategy (ACMECS 2003), which brings together comparatively developed Thailand and the less developed countries of Laos, Cambodia and Myanmar.

Each of these selective arrangements has a specific purpose. The triangular scheme of Vietnam, Laos and Cambodia, for instance, aims for cooperation in agriculture, forestry, trade, transportation, energy, education and tourism. The core tasks of the East-West Corridor, on the other hand, are to reduce travel time from northeast Thailand to the seaport of central Vietnam and develop particular areas of the participating economies along the corridor: cash crops, forestry, mining and sea products in central Vietnam; agriculture, forestry, mining and hydropower resources in central Laos; and agriculture and cottage industries in northeast Thailand. The development of the border areas shared by Yunnan, Laos, Myanmar and Thailand is the primary concern of the Golden Quadrangle. The funding sources of these growth zones vary. The ADB, UNDP and Japan, for example, support the development of the East-West Corridor, while the ACMECS was conceived under the auspices of Thailand.

The second type of subregional mechanism is all-inclusive, although over the years the scope of GMS cooperation has evolved from limited to larger groupings. The first mechanism was the MRC set up in 1995 and consisting of the four downstream countries (Cambodia, Lao PDR, Thailand and Vietnam). The Agreement of Sustainable Development and Cooperation of the Mekong

River Subregion laid down the plans for water and other resource development and management. In 1996 Myanmar and China became dialogue partners of the Commission. The all-inclusive subregional arrangement is the GMS, formed upon the initiative of the ADB.

GMS and larger Asia

The GMS countries also have cooperation mechanisms with countries outside the subregion such as India and Japan. Early in the 1990s, India put forward its "East-oriented strategy" to develop its relations with Southeast Asian countries and the ASEAN as a whole. Mainland Southeast Asia eventually became the center of India's attention. Soon India, Bangladesh, Sri Lanka and Thailand initiated a cooperation venture encircling the Bay of Bengal. When Myanmar joined the organization in 1998, it was renamed BIMSTEC. BIMSTEC has a total population of 1.3 billion, with a total GDP value reaching US$550 billion. As a result of this effort, the economic relationship between India, Myanmar and Thailand—the latter two in the drainage area of the Mekong River—has been strengthened, particularly in trade and investment as well as transportation, tourism, fishery and energy. The ultimate goal of BIMSTEC is a free trade area. In 2004 senior officials met to discuss, among other matters, reciprocal visas for businessmen and other measures preparatory to the establishment of a free trade area. Two days later they were joined by Nepal and Bhutan. All except Bangladesh subsequently signed a framework agreement on a free trade zone that would reduce tariff from 2005 and initially encompass India, Thailand and Sri Lanka until 2012 and the other countries until 2017. Should BIMSTEC come into being as a free trade area, it will be the first to involve not only South Asia but also two members of the ASEAN and the GMS—Thailand and Myanmar.

Furthermore, in 2000 India, Cambodia, Myanmar, Thailand, Laos and Vietnam initiated the Ganges-Mekong Linkage Project and the following year, the relationship between India and the ASEAN was elevated to the summit level. The first ASEAN-India summit took place in November 2002, the occasion for India's public expression of its commitment to assist the development of Myanmar, Vietnam, Cambodia and Laos. Meanwhile, concrete cooperation projects were taking shape. Seven months prior to the summit, India, Myanmar and Thailand decided to build a highway from Tamu in Manipur, India, through Bagan in central Myanmar, down to Mae Sot in the extreme southwest of Thailand. In September 2003 Prime Minister Vajpayee, speaking at the 2nd ASEAN-India Business Summit, announced India's plan to invest in a railway from New Delhi to Hanoi, via Myanmar, Thailand, Laos and Cambodia. All these moves by India prompted Singapore's President S.R. Nathan to remark that Southeast Asia was witnessing the emergence of a "New India".[4]

Another Asian participant in GMS cooperation from outside the subregion is Japan, a long-time investor in Southeast Asia. From the late 1960s to the late 1990s, Japan invested more than US$80 billion in the region, and although investments slowed down at the end of the period, since 2002 Japan has reinvigorated its efforts at cooperation with Southeast Asia. In November that year, Japan and ASEAN agreed on the principles of an ASEAN-Japan free trade zone, the framework for which was signed in Bali a year later. By this agreement, Japan and ASEAN will build the free trade zone in 2010. Japan also promised US$3 billion to develop the Mekong Basin over the next three years (*Lianhezaobao*, 15 December 2003). The special summit between Japan and ASEAN in 2003 resulted in Japan's formal declaration that it would support the Southeast Asian Agency for Regional Transport and Communications Development. Leaders of both sides also signed the ASEAN-Japan Action Plan and the Tokyo Declaration for the Dynamic and Enduring ASEAN-Japan Partnership in the New Millennium. In a subsequent conference involving the Japanese government, the Japan International Development Bank, ADB and officials from the ASEAN member countries, Japan committed ¥8.1 billion to build the multinational bridge connecting Mukdahan on the Thai side of the Mekong riverbank and Savannakhet (Laos) across it, and to open the road from central Vietnam to Moulmein in Myanmar via Laos and Thailand. As a result, Japan-ASEAN cooperation in GMS especially in transportation and the development of the economic corridors has been strengthened markedly.

Japan is also heavily involved in the Forum for Indochina's Comprehensive Development and the Working Group on Industrial Cooperation for Cambodia, Laos and Myanmar (founded in 1994). These two cooperation mechanisms are expected to play an important role in the aid project that Japan offers to GMS countries amounting to some US$3 billion.

Apart from governmental participation in various agreements on trade, aid and cooperation, non- or semi-official participation by international and regional organizations is also evident in the GMS. These bodies include the ASEAN Human Rights Working Group, the Asia-Pacific Economic Cooperation (APEC), UN-ESCAP-led GMS Commerce Forum, Asia-Europe Meeting (ASEM) Society Forum, ADB-NGO Network, United Nations, ADB Environment Program and the Regional Dialogue of Southeast Asian Water Management. Non-governmental organizations, global (such as the Dialogue between Water, Foodstuff and Environment) and regional (such as Toward Ecological Recovery, Regional Alliance and the Southeast Asia River Network), tend to focus on the ecology, environment and local inhabitants of the GMS, and the need to balance ecological needs and environmental protection with the welfare especially of indigenous communities. These organizations are gaining ground as their influence over development schemes in the Mekong heightens.

Conditions favorable to China's participation

Against this backdrop of development cooperation mechanisms, one must consider the positive and difficult aspects of cooperation. A serious appreciation of these factors is necessary not only in the decision-making process but also in planning and implementation. In the case of the GMS, conditions that encourage China's participation are the probability of better and stable political relations between China and countries in the subregion, the enthusiasm and willingness of the GMS countries, the larger framework of ASEAN—in particular, the China-ASEAN FTA, China's relatively strong economic power, and support from international communities for cooperation.

Solid political relations between China and the Mekong countries are no doubt the most important foundation for regional cooperation. All five GMS countries are members of ASEAN. The process of cooperation with these five will therefore be influenced not only by the relations between China and these countries but also by the relations between China and ASEAN as a whole. The normalization of China's relations with ASEAN, which commenced in the early 1990s, has produced statements of cooperation and several treaties on trade, investment and technology transfer, thereby laying the overall basis for cooperation and development in the region. In October 2003, China signed the Treaty of Amity and Cooperation with Southeast Asia, which was followed by a joint statement to establish a strategic partnership toward peace and prosperity (*People's Daily*, 8 October 2003). This was a milestone that inaugurated a new era in China-ASEAN relations.

Internal developments in the GMS member countries have also enhanced the stability of political relations in the region. China's West Developmental Program, for example, and the rapidly developing economy of its southwest provinces have provided receptive conditions for cooperation. The economic reforms of Vietnam, Lao PDR and Cambodia also indicate their earnestness in creating a political and social environment conducive to cooperation. Although some issues still afflict countries in the region, such as domestic politics in Myanmar, these problems have not set back cooperation in the GMS. (The 10th ministers' meeting of GMS cooperation was in fact held in 2001 in Yangon.)

The openness of GMS member countries to cooperation is not to be taken lightly for their attitudes are important factors in determining the process and outcome of cooperation. The Chinese central government has been supportive of GMS cooperation since 1992, when China attended the GMS economic cooperation meeting sponsored by the ADB. Kunming hosted two ministerial meetings (the 6th and the 12th in 1996 and 2003, respectively). In July 1994 China established the Office of Lancang-Mekong River Development Pro-phase Research and Coordination consisting of representatives from 19 departments of the central government (including the Ministries of Science and Technology, Foreign Affairs, National Commission of Development and Reform, and People's Bank of China) and members of the Yunnan provincial government. Yunnan itself also set up a counterpart office at the provincial level.

Chinese leaders have repeatedly articulated the country's commitment to regional cooperation. In 1993 then Chinese President Jiang Zemin spoke of progress on the upstream Mekong River when he met Thailand's Prime Minister Chuan Leekpai. Four years later he and the ASEAN leaders jointly declared that China and ASEAN have a shared interest in the development of the Mekong basin, and promised to support the GMS through trade, tourism and transportation activities (*People's Daily*, 17 December 1997). At the first summit meeting for GMS cooperation in 2002, Zhu Rongji declared: "We hope to participate in GMS cooperation in a larger scope and with a more vigorous attitude" (*People's Daily*, 14 November 2002). The following year Premier Wen Jiabao explained China's policy toward its neighbors as a win-win strategy that would deepen regional and subregional cooperation, pushing regional economic integration and realize co-development in Asia.

Leaders of Southeast Asia have also publicly declared their support for regional cooperation. Early in 1989, Thai Prime Minister Chatichai Choonhavan put forward the idea of transforming Indochina from "the battlefield to the market" and turning mainland Southeast Asian into an "economic circle". The Thai government subsequently suggested the creation of the "Golden Quadrangle" (see earlier section), which solicited positive feedback from the governments of China, Myanmar and Laos. The GMS Sustainable Development Agreement was signed in Chiang Rai in 1995 by the governments of Thailand, Vietnam, Lao PDR and Cambodia, and the MRC established officially thereafter, with China later coming in as a dialogue partner. After the financial crisis of the 1990s, Southeast Asian countries became more aware of the importance of GMS cooperation. In recent years, senior leaders from these countries have visited one another to discuss GMS cooperation activities and mechanisms for regional growth.

As stated earlier, China situates the GMS within the larger context of ASEAN. Without the sustained affirmation and support of ASEAN as a whole, GMS cooperation will not move forward. After Vietnam joined ASEAN in 1996, the then seven member countries of ASEAN along with China, Cambodia, Lao PDR, and Myanmar approved the Framework of ASEAN-GMS Development and Cooperation, the tenet of which is to reinforce economic cooperation among the signatory countries. Since then five ministerial meetings have taken place between these intersecting regional bodies. Between China and ASEAN, the overarching framework from China's perspective is the China-ASEAN Comprehensive Economic Cooperation Agreement (2002), which centers on the construction of the China-ASEAN FTA. In this free trade area, southwest China, especially Yunnan, will serve as the link between the Chinese and ASEAN markets.

China's economy has been growing rapidly since 1978. The National Statistical Bureau reported in 2003 that GNP rose by 9.1 percent, the total value amounting to US$1,400 billion. Per capita GPD is US$1,090; the foreign exchange reserves stands at US$403.3 billion; the value of international trade is US$851.2 billion; and the actual utilization of foreign investments amounts to US$53.5 billion (*People's Daily*, 27 February 2004). China has not only entered the heavy and chemical industrial phase but also embarked on a new phase of high technology industries accompanied by structural adjustments in industry. In the 21st century China aims to exert an even greater economic presence in the region, which will also benefit its neighbors.

Cooperation in the GMS is further emboldened by the international support the region enjoys. Here the ADB, UNDP and World Bank are major pillars. The ADB, in particular, not only initiated the GMS ministerial conference in 1992 but has also participated in and promoted cooperation in the Mekong with the requisite capital and strength. Such support is not inconsequential, considering that the majority of the Mekong countries are economically underdeveloped.

Factors that constrict cooperation

On the other hand, certain conditions limit the possibilities for cooperation. Differences in the levels of economic development constitute the first challenge to cooperation. Laos, Myanmar and Cambodia are among the world's least developed countries; Yunnan is also an economic laggard relative to other regions in China. The per capita GDP of Vietnam is lower than that of Yunnan. Only the Thai economy has developed to a higher level. Poor infrastructure, an immature market economy and the drug trade in the Golden Triangle are some of the economic factors that restrict GMS cooperation.

Present road infrastructure, for example, hardly meets the demand of contemporary economic cooperation despite recent efforts to upgrade transport facilities and infrastructure. In the past five years the province of Yunnan has infused RMB10 billion a year in highway construction; the Yunnan expressway is over 1,000 kilometers. In addition, flights have opened from Kumming to Singapore, Kuala Lumpur, Bangkok, Chiang Mai, Yangon, Mandalay, Vientiane, Hanoi, Ho Chi Minh City, Siem Reap and so on. But these measures still do not meet the needs of economic and technological cooperation and economic exchange between China and the ASEAN markets. Currently, there is only a low-grade highway linking Yunnan with the GMS countries. There is waterway passage on the Lancang-Mekong but ships have to dock at Houayxay in northern Laos and carry no more than 250 tons. Land-to-water transportation from Kunming to Yangon is non-existent. Highways in northern Myanmar are rough, especially north of Mandalay: they are open on fine days and blocked when it rains. Infrastructure in northern Laos is similarly constrained. The Yunnan-Vietnam railway is narrow (it was built about a hundred years ago), and its annual freight capacity is a mere 0.45 millionth of a ton. Regional cooperation requires an interconnecting modern network of highways and railways, which needs massive investment.

Furthermore, the scale of bilateral economic and trade cooperation has been restricted by the industrial and production infrastructures of the Mekong countries. With their vast terrain and abundant river resources, each country, especially Cambodia, Laos, Myanmar and Vietnam, will need to adjust its economy and raise consumption levels. At present the volume of trade is low. The total trade value between China and the five GMS countries, for example, is US$13 billion, representing only 2.4 percent of China's total trade value and only 24 percent of China's trade value with the other ASEAN members (US$54.8 billion) in 2002. A large chunk of the China-GMS trade is between China and Thailand (US$8.56 billion in 2002), accounting for about 65 percent of China's total trade with the GMS countries. Juxtaposed against China's trade with the rest of the ASEAN countries, the China-GMS trade pales by comparison. It is difficult to improve these trade balances in the short run unless there is a lot of economic and technological cooperation, especially for the exploitation of natural resources.

Table 4.3. China-Southeast Asian Trade, 2001–2002 (US$ million)

Region	Country	2001			2002		
		Export	Import	Total	Export	Import	Total
GMS	Thailand	2,337.45	4,712.85	7,050.30	2,958.40	5,602.30	8,560.70
	Vietnam	1,804.45	1,011.75	2,816.20	2,148.90	1,115.30	3,264.20
	Myanmar	497.35	134.19	631.54	724.80	136.90	861.70
	Cambodia	205.61	34.08	239.69	251.60	24.50	276.10
	Lao PDR	54.41	7.46	61.87	54.30	9.70	64.00
	Total	4,899.27	5,900.33	10,799.60	6,138.00	6,888.70	13,026.70
Other ASEAN	Singapore	5,791.88	5,142.52	10,934.40	6,965.70	7,052.40	14,018.10
	Malaysia	3,220.26	6,205.21	9,425.47	4,974.50	9,296.00	14,270.50
	Indonesia	2,836.54	3,888.07	6,724.61	3,426.90	4,501.40	7,928.30
	Philippines	1,620.31	1,945.22	3,565.53	2,042.30	3,217.20	5,259.50
	Brunei	17.15	148.24	165.39	21.10	241.80	262.90
	Total	13,486.14	17,329.26	30,815.40	17,430.50	24,308.80	41,739.30
	Total	18,385.41	23,299.31	41,615.00	23,568.50	31,197.50	54,766.00

Source: *China Statistical Yearbook, 2002*, Beijing: China Statistics Press, 2003.

Another negative factor is the severe shortage of capital input owing to the region's low-income economies, except Thailand, whose per capita GDP is over US$2,000. China and Thailand have taken vigorous steps to promote cooperation, but their investment capacities are themselves limited in scope. Although the economy of China has advanced, its level still cannot be compared with that of the United States, which has a GDP of more than US$10 trillion or Japan, whose GDP is nearly US$5 trillion. China has a population of 1.3 billion, with a per capita GDP far less than that of many other countries. In a word, China is a developing country with a middle-to-low income level. Moreover, as the world's largest developing country, after posting high economic growth in the past twenty years, China nonetheless faces serious domestic problems such as the gap between coastal and inland areas, between east and west, and between urban and rural areas. China needs massive funds to carry out a continuous development program. Yet China occupies a place in the community of nations that compels it to also assist developing countries. Although GMS cooperation is a focal point in China's border diplomacy, its impact on China's overall economy and external trade balance remains rather limited. Even in the trade between China and Southeast Asia, the GMS is but a small part (less than 25 percent). Therefore, although the Chinese central government has and will increase its support for GMS cooperation, China's investment in the GMS is still small. As for other countries in the region, Thailand possesses the strongest economy, but its investment capacity is also not very large.

Geography, nation and region

Mechanisms for cooperation in the GMS pose another challenge. As shown in the previous section, many kinds co-exist, affecting different aspects of cooperation. Moreover, openness to cooperation operates in the context of globalization and regional integration as well as the individual, bilateral and multilateral relations in the region. While all the participating parties have committed themselves to strengthening cooperation with each other, they have also had to take into account their domestic situation. The fact is that even as they share common interests as GMS members, they have different aims and needs. Consider, for instance, the bases for GMS cooperation cited by the ADB and how these bases operate on the ground. According to the ADB (1993), GMS cooperation is premised on the following:

- The Mekong River has great impact on the economic life of the six member countries.
- All but Thailand belong to a transition economy.
- All six countries need to and are likely to cooperate on the Mekong drainage.
- Complementary, mutual economic cooperation of the six countries can promote their domestic economy.
- The border trade is growing and exceeds formal commerce in some areas.
- Infrastructure lags behind and badly hampers the commodity trade.
- With its shortage of development capital, the subregion thirsts for foreign investment.
- The member countries have a common cultural heritage.

Ten years of development have no doubt ushered in rapid changes in the GMS. Vietnam's GDP, for example, is twice that of ten years ago and so is Yunnan's. Moreover, the possibility of cooperation has become a reality for members of the GMS. Notwithstanding their commonalities, however, the GMS members have different backgrounds, are at different stages of development, run on different economic systems, have uneven resource capacities and, with respect to the Mekong River, do not enjoy the same access to the water or possess the same drainage proportion. The Greater Mekong River basin is located in the middle of the GMS, but it is *not* the GMS. The latter embraces China's Yunnan, Cambodia, Laos, Myanmar, Vietnam and Thailand, covering 2.32 million square kilometers, while the Greater Mekong River basin is merely the area along the river and its tributaries, which takes up 0.81 million square kilometers, of which Yunnan occupies 12 percent of the basin area and 16 percent of the water flow; Laos, 26 and 35 percent, respectively; Myanmar, 2 and 2 percent, respectively; Thailand, 23 and 18 percent, respectively; Cambodia, 20 and 18 percent, respectively; and Vietnam, 8 and 11 percent, respectively (Goh 2001, 471). Because of these differences, tension is inevitable especially over water resource usage.

Laos takes up a third of all the water energy resources and nearly half the length of the river. Hence the national aspiration that Laos become the "center" of water energy resource development, given that its neighbors require a huge volume of power (*Lianhezaobao*, 15 December 2003). With assistance from Japan, Laos could become the energy base of mainland Southeast Asia. Situated at the center of the

Mekong River and the only inland country in the GMS, Laos also hopes that transportation facilities and networks within the subregion are improved and that trade and tourism are pushed forward. But Laos is the poorest country in the GMS and needs support from the outside world.

Thailand, in contrast, is the biggest Southeast Asian country in the GMS and the most developed. It requires tremendous electricity to fuel its economic development but suffers a shortage of water resources or pays a high price for water usage. Thus it benefits Thailand to import low cost electricity from Yunnan and Laos. Moreover, Thailand has 8.5 million hectares of land in the northeast that account for half of all farmland in the country. But only 500,000 hectares have access to irrigation. Inducing water from the Mekong River is therefore crucial to agricultural growth in the northeast. But because Thailand lies upstream, utilizing water from the river would arouse the opposition of Cambodia and Vietnam.

Myanmar's share is share of the basin area and volume of water flow from the Mekong River are the smallest (a mere two percent) in the region. Myanmar, therefore, hardly runs into any conflict with its neighbors over water use. Nonetheless GMS cooperation influences Myanmar's economic growth, particularly in the areas of trade and tourism. Close to Myanmar's interests is the East-West Economic Corridor, which links it to Thailand, Laos and Vietnam. The country's participation in GMS cooperation is also marked by a regional need to address the drug trade in the Golden Triangle.

The GMS is an important agricultural development zone for Cambodia. Cooperation projects that reduce flood and drought can help transform the formerly war-torn country into the granary of the GMS. Electric power supply in Cambodia is also gravely insufficient and hydropower projects could eliminate this heavy burden. But its location downstream makes the country sensitive to water resource exploitation and use by countries upstream. Vietnam, too, lies in the lower reaches of the Mekong River and its delta is Vietnam's rice bowl. Flood control during the rainy season and the prevention of land salinization are the country's foremost agricultural challenges. Therefore Vietnam is deeply concerned about the impact of upstream water use on the Mekong delta.

Situated upstream, Yunnan province has a major interest in hydropower exploitation and navigation along the Mekong. The province occupies 20.7 percent of the river's drainage area and takes in 14.5 percent of the total water flow. But the potential for access and development is far greater: as much as 36.56 million kilowatts of hydropower could be developed theoretically, of which 27.37 million kilowatts could be exploited. Also, the cost of constructing hydropower stations in Yunnan is relatively cheap. Presently two such stations, Manwan and Dachaoshan, produce 2.6 million kilowatts; combined with the eight hydroelectric stations being planned, a total capacity of 15.7 million kilowatts is anticipated. These stations would satisfy the power requirements of Yunnan and provide excellent conditions for cooperation with neighboring countries like Thailand. As the Chinese government's country report on China's participation additionally points out (2002), the construction of power stations on the river would reduce flooding in the rainy season and increase the rate of water flow during the dry season. The policy declaration of the 6th GMS forum on electricity in 1999 expressed the desire to increase electricity supply in the subregion, but also raised the concerns of downstream countries over the impact of hydropower projects upstream. In terms of navigation, the Lancang-Mekong River is the "golden channel" to Southeast Asia, and the construction of the navigation lane would benefit all the GMS countries and boost bilateral trade.

"Becoming a prosperous neighbor"

As a partner in GMS cooperation, Yunnan still needs to strengthen its economic capabilities so that it can meet cooperation targets. Yunnan is just one province of China, and one of the least developed at that, while other countries in the subregion participate in cooperation schemes at a national level. Yunnan thus participates on a different legal footing compared with its neighboring countries. Furthermore, the economic power of Yunnan is still rather limited, with its 2003 GDP at US$30 billion, lower than that of Vietnam and about 13 percent of the combined GDP of the other GMS countries (US$220 billion). Although Yunnan enjoys some technological advantage in certain fields, it needs greater support for GMS cooperation from the central government in order to attain the status of " rich neighbor" and "wealthy border". A sense of urgency thus moves the province for it is a major stakeholder and beneficiary of subregional cooperation.

Among the concrete measures China can take are the following. First, make GMS cooperation a key component of China's strategy to open up to the outside world and an essential element of China's diplomatic endeavors in East Asia. One way to do this would be to meld China's West Development Program with its policy of "friendly neighbors, stable nation and wealthy neighbor" in Southeast Asia. The consolidation of domestic and regional concerns would then help China to assign an important place to GMS cooperation.

Second, improve the system for China's participation in the GMS so as to ensure more vigorous participation in bilateral and multilateral cooperation and closer coordination between China and the five GMS countries. As most GMS countries are still at the developing stage, cooperation depends heavily on external capital, technologies and markets, while diverse politics, economies, societies, ethnic groups and cultures place regional cooperation in a more complex context. As the ADB observed in its evaluation of the first decade of GMS cooperation, notwithstanding the numerous bilateral and multilateral agreements signed throughout the period, progress was slowed down by poor coordination and implementation of projects. Rather than have all these agreements, and since most projects have their own operating frameworks, the report suggested a more flexible ("non-institutional") system that would be able to address common concerns of the member countries. The report concluded that "patience and long-term commitment" are needed for GMS cooperation (2002, 3).

With further development plans in the making and in view of the various and diverse mechanisms of cooperation, each with its role and scope, consultation and coordination among the member countries are more imperative in the next phase of GMS cooperation. As recommended by the ADB in its 2nd Ten-Year Strategic Framework of GMS Cooperation (ADB 2002), "strategic alliance and partnership" should be established among all the partners and among the various cooperation mechanisms. However, while multiple mechanisms indicate that all sides of GMS cooperation have common interests, they also highlight different requirements of each party. Thus no single mechanism can be expected to cover all the areas of cooperation. For some time more, then, a strategic alliance should be established in which the leadership of the GMS is not vested in any one country but rather, in a genuine partnership among all member countries. Existing mechanisms can continue to play their respective roles while the strategic alliance is being built up, and the economically strong powers may play a larger role only to secure a positive outcome for all the parties concerned.

From the standpoint of Yunnan, China should act at the highest level of government to promote GMS cooperation and fulfill its concomitant requirements. It is proposed that the central government upgrade the Office of Lancang-Mekong Basin Prophase Research and Coordination to a state-level China Coordination Office or China Committee for GMS Cooperation. As the lead group, this body will address emerging issues in GMS cooperation. Under its leadership, a branch office should be set up in Yunnan province given the latter's direct stake in GMS cooperation. To remove the awkwardness arising from China's participation as a state and Yunnan's provincial participation in the GMS, the central government should act as the decision-maker with respect to the counterpart governments of the GMS, while Yunnan plays its role as the actual implementor of projects approved by the central government and assists in securing solutions to issues in bilateral and multilateral cooperation within the subregion.

Third, reinforce environmental protection and pollution control in the Greater Mekong basin for the long-term development of the entire subregion. With the further expansion of GMS cooperation initiatives, environmental issues in the area attract growing attention from foreign governments, international institutions and non-governmental organizations. Environmental protection will become a focal point of international relations in the greater Mekong basin, with water use and management as the most contentious issue. Water resources—hydropower, flood control, irrigation, water supply, water transportation, and aquaculture—are and will remain enduring concerns. Considering that hydropower is a kind of renewable "green" energy and further, that the GMS members—most of whom have low-income economies—nevertheless have a gigantic demand for electric power, differences over water resource development, access, usage, management and maintenance become inevitable. While dam construction upstream may have an impact on the environment of the river basin, the excessive exploitation of coal and petroleum for equivalent energy will create even greater damage to the ecosystem. Hydropower is a friendlier and more viable alternative and opinions that it is bad for the environment may not actually serve the purpose of the area's development in the long run. Some experts like Gu Hongbin argue that "thousands of dams have been and are still being constructed in the world while few cases resulted in obvious and serious environmental damage. The best resolution should be to secure remedial measures in accordance with each respective case" (2003, 56).

Because the ecosystem of the river is integrated, environmental protection and sustainable development should take into account the entire river basin and not just parts of it. In forthcoming projects, China has been advised to "closely work with other GMS countries over the issues of water resource development and environment protection. The same importance should be attached to both resource development and environment protection" (Zhang 2003, 318). Toward this objective China should continue to exchange information on the environment with the GMS countries.

Fourth, maximize Yunnan's role as China's major actor in the GMS with full support of the central government. In his address before the ASEAN ministers in 2003, Chinese Vice Premier Zeng Peiyan cited Yunnan's special role in the GMS. But as a local authority of China, the Yunnan provincial government is unable to act as a state partner in GMS cooperation. It needs the central government's leadership, institutional and financial support, and backing for research and development on potential cooperation projects. With such support, Yunnan should be able to make full use of its geographic advantage and make itself the bridge connecting China with the GMS.

Concrete measures, concrete gains

To attain the objectives of cooperation in the various sectors, the following concrete measures are further recommended.

1. Make Kunming the liaison center between China and the ASEAN countries. Annex 4 of the "10+1" Agreement identifies Kunming as the bridge between the two. Some GMS institutions, for example, can be stationed permanently in Kunming, and conference-exhibition centers and commercial sites can also be set up in the capital city of Yunnan. Bilateral cooperation mechanisms such as the Working Group of Yunnan-North Thailand Cooperation could also be located in Kunming.

2. Based on the plans prepared by the relevant provincial departments of Yunnan for 2004–2008 and 2003–2015, incorporate the large international passageway connecting Yunnan with Southeast Asia and its corresponding infrastructure into the China-ASEAN FTA framework as an essential element of bilateral economic and technological cooperation and a major program of bilateral cooperation in the construction of the economic corridors.

3. To establish a legal and policy assistance system and create an environment conducive to cooperation, and abolish or amend regulations and policies not in conformity with the China-ASEAN FTA Agreement and GMS cooperation mechanisms. Furthermore, existing preferential treatments of investment and trade must be fulfilled and with new or improved incentives to boost trade.

4. Build cross-border infrastructure in order to facilitate international passenger and cargo traffic connecting China/Yunnan with Southeast Asia, including key projects such as the Kunming-Bangkok Highway, Pan-Asia Railway, and Lancang-Mekong River Waterway. Yunnan and Myanmar should take cooperative action to connect the Kunming-Rangoon road with the Irrawaddy River. The East Line of the Pan-Asia Railway in Yunnan province (Yuxi-Hekou section) should be constructed as soon as possible. The pre-construction phase of the middle line of the Kunming-Bangkok and the western line of the Kunming-Dali-Baoshan-Mandalay Railways should be completed. Further improvements of the Lancang-Mekong waterway should also be undertaken and direct flights from Kunming to each of ASEAN countries started soon. Meanwhile, the higher-level road network of Yunnan province should be linked with its peripheral countries in 2007. Cross-border infrastructure also requires the full implementation of the Agreement on the Facilitation of Cross-border Movement of Goods and People, which not only covers the GMS transportation network but also "software" requirements described below. In the process, Kunming would be transformed into a modernized international center of trade, investment and tourism.

5. Expand the volume of trade by encouraging Yunnan enterprises to go out into the region and set up commodity centers or international wholesale markets in the main cities of the GMS. The Kunming Hi-tech Development Co. should be encouraged to establish development zones and commodity centers in north Thailand's Chiang Rai province. Furthermore, trade procedures should be simplified by rationalizing customs and visa procedures, adopting joint customs and quarantine inspections, and streamlining procedures for the movement of goods and people so as to reduce transport costs and create a better environment for border trade. These "software" measures should be accompanied by "hardware" projects relating to the comprehensive infrastructure that needs to be set up in major cities and ports (Kunming, Mohan, Ruili)

where regional commodity fairs and trade negotiations can take place. Investments should be attracted by setting up new financial institutions for multi-channel approaches and inviting international investors in creative ways. For instance, Yunnan could issue bonds for GMS economic development and cooperation in order to mobilize private resources.

6. Establish a finance platform. Laos, Myanmar and Cambodia have relatively low foreign exchange reserves and little capacity to pay. Research should thus be conducted to work out a new system of bank settlement and smooth and reciprocal capital flows between Yunnan and the ASEAN countries. Research on currency should also be conducted, such as the regionalization of the renminbi. A financial settlement network should be set up to cover all the 25 border-crossing cities and counties of the province, with key settlement centers in Kunming and other border cities of Jinghong, Hekou and Ruili.

7. Actively take part in telecommunications development and establish an information hub for the subregion. This would include the establishment of the Kunming International Communication Supplementary Process Center to conduct e-commerce, tourism and provide a comprehensive information service system, and better improve the existing GMS International Cooperation Information Center website.

8. Strengthen GMS tourism cooperation. GMS countries should negotiate the implementation of the proposed joint visa system and develop the Lancang-Mekong Basin as the "golden line" of tourism in order to create a tourist corridor.

9. Promote electric power trade and energy in accordance with the Inter-governmental Agreement on Electricity Procurement in the Greater Mekong Sub-region. Based on this agreement, an electric power trade coordination council should be formed with Yunnan province as its core actor. The implementation of the agreement will enable Yunnan to become China's largest export base of electric power. At the same time, Yunnan should strive to promote and participate in the petroleum and gas projects linking southwestern China and the mainland Southeast Asia (from Kunming to Myanmar or Thailand).

10. Boost the development of minerals. Yunnan should exploit its advantage in technology processing to develop the abundant supply of minerals in the province as well as in the GMS countries, and encourage domestic enterprises to take part in regional energy

and resource development so as to turn the resource advantage into an economic benefit not just for Yunnan but for all other GMS countries.

11. Push agricultural cooperation by participating in the implementation of the Memorandum of Understanding on Agricultural Cooperation between ASEAN and China's Ministry of Agriculture. Bilateral/multilateral agreements should be reached over land tenancy and the duration of land leases in the GMS countries. Yunnan should secure the support of the central government in building export bases of agro-products. A livestock market should be established in the border cities and later expanded into an agro-product trade center between southwest China and the GMS countries.

12. Protect the ecosystem in the interest of sustainable development. With central government support, Yunnan province should play an important role in GMS environmental cooperation and be part of the ADB's environment projects in the region. In addition, a shelterbelt along the Lancang River, Red River and Nujiang River should be constructed, and a nature protection network set up. The eco-corridors along the international rivers should protect rare species in cooperation with partners in the GMS.

13. Promote cooperation in human resource development. Yunnan should secure assistance from the China-ASEAN Fund for GMS Cooperation to attract talents from Southeast Asia. Education resources should be restructured to establish a China-ASEAN Human Resource Development Center in Kunming and a Mekong Institute in the Kunming campus. Scholarships should be established for students from the GMS.

14. Develop cooperation in the field of science and technology. The Ministry of Science and Technology should enter into long-term agreements with the GMS countries and establish a China-GMS National Technology Cooperation Program to support the establishment of the National Lancang-Mekong River Subregional Science and Technology Center and a Science and Technology Development Cooperation Foundation in Kunming.

15. Consider health care as an important sector of cooperation. The Mekong River Basin Disease Monitoring Program calls for an infectious disease control and monitoring system in the GMS. Yunnan should not only take part in the program but also offer Chinese traditional medicine, academic exchanges and joint access to clinical examinations as part of its cooperation effort with the

GMS. Kunming should be developed as the center of cooperation in Chinese traditional medicine.

16. Also develop Kunming as an important conference and meeting site in keeping with China's public service platform for the China-ASEAN FTA and GMS cooperation. Yunnan province should therefore expand its contacts with business circles both at home and abroad.

17. Strengthen cooperation with the GMS countries and related international institutions over drug control. Yunnan should further develop alternative crop plantations in the Golden Triangle area and take more vigorous action against drug processing and trafficking.

18. Establish a Center for Lancang-Mekong Subregional Cooperation Studies to enhance strategic planning, conduct comprehensive research on subregional cooperation and related issues such as environmental protection, propose forward-looking policies and measures on regional cooperation, and strengthen contacts with related foreign research institutions.

Notes

1   "Making it Happen: A Common Strategy on Cooperation for Growth, Equity and Prosperity in the Greater Mekong Subregion." Joint GMS Summit Declaration. 2002. Phnom Penh, Cambodia, 3 November.
2   Calculated from statistics issued by the Yunnan Foreign Trade and Economic Cooperation Bureau, February 2004.
3   In Chapter 3, Nguyen Phuong Binh calls this program the Western Region Development Strategy.
4   President S.R. Nathan's comment was made during a State visit to India, 3 January 2003.

References

ASEAN-China. 2002. "Framework Agreement on Comprehensive Economic Cooperation between the Association of Southeast Asian Nations and the People's Republic of China." Phnom Penh, Cambodia, 5 November.

Asian Development Bank (ADB). 1993. *Subregional Economic Cooperation: Initial Possibilities for Cambodia, Lao PDR, Myanmar, Thailand, Vietnam and Yunnan Province of the People's Republic of China*. Manila: ADB.

———. 1994. "Subregional Economic Cooperation among Cambodia, People's Republic of China, Lao People's Democratic Republic, Myanmar, Thailand, and Vietnam: Proceedings of the Fourth Conference." Chiang Mai, 15–16 September.

———. 1995. "Sub-regional Infrastructure Projects in Indochina and the Greater Mekong Area: A Compendium of Project Profiles." Tokyo, February.

———. 2000. *Economic Cooperation in the Greater Mekong Subregion: An Overview*. Manila: ADB.

———. 2002. *Building on Success: A Strategic Framework for the Next Ten Years of the Greater Mekong Subregion Economic Cooperation Program*. Manila: ADB.

———. 2003. *Annual Report* (2002). Manila: ADB.

China Statistical Yearbook (2002). 2003. Beijing: China Statistics Press.

Commission of Development and Planning, Government of the People's Republic of China. 2002. "Country Report on China's Participation in GMS Cooperation." Beijing.

Economist Intelligence Unit. 2002. *Country Report (Cambodia, Laos, Myanmar, Thailand, Vietnam)*. London: The Economist Group.

Feng Zhaokui. 2001. "China in the New Century: Three Engines." *World Knowledge* (in Chinese) 1 (January): 10–11.

Goh, Evelyn. 2001. "The Hydro-Politics of the Mekong River Basin: Regional Cooperation and Environmental Security." In *Non-Traditional Security Issues in Southeast Asia*, edited by Andrew T.H. Tan and J.D. Kenneth Boutin, pp. 468–506. Singapore: Select Publishing for Institute of Defence and Strategic Studies,

Gu Hongbin. 2003. "Dams in Nujiang and World Natural Heritage: Not in Conflict." *China National Geography* (in Chinese) 10 (October): 56–58.

He Shengda. 1997. *Southeast Asia toward the 21st Century and its Relations with China*. Kunming: Publishing House of Yunnan University.

He Shengda and Chen Minhua. 2001. *ASEAN and China at the Turn of the Century*. Kunming: Publishing House of Yunnan Nationality.

He Shengda and Wang Xuhong. 2003. *The Construction of the ASEAN-China Free Trade Area and Yunnan's Opening to Southeast Asia*. Kunming: People's Publishing House of Yunnan.

Jiang Zemin. 2002. "Build a Well-off Society in All-around Way and Create a New Situation in Building Socialism with Chinese Characteristics." Report to the 16th National Congress of the Communist Party of China. Beijing: People's Publishing House.

Li Yigang. 2001. *The Development of Southwestern China and Lancang-Mekong Subregional Cooperation*. Kunming: Publishing House of Young Sciences and Technology.

Ma Shuheng. 1995. *The Orient Danube: A Research on the Lancang-Mekong River*. Kunming: Publishing House of Yunnan Nationality.

Ministry of Foreign Affairs. 1997. *Japan and ASEAN for the 21st Century*. Tokyo: Ministry of Foreign Affairs.

Sarma, Atut. 2002. *Exploring Indo-ASEAN Economic Partnership in a Globalising World*. New Delhi: Blackwell.

Supachai Panitchpakdi and Mark Cllifford. 2001. *China and the WTO: Changing China, Changing World Trade* (Chinese edition). Beijing: China Machine Press.

Yunnan Yearbook (2001). 2002. Kunming: People's Publishing House of Yunnan.

Yunnan Yearbook (2002). 2003. Kunming: People's Publishing House of Yunnan.

Zhang Yunling. 2003. *Asian-Pacific International Environment Facing China in the Next 10–15 Years*. Beijing: China Social Sciences Press.

Zhou Xiaojun. 2003. "What will the Bridgehead of China-ASEAN FTA be?" *Economic Daily*, 8 January.

5

REGION WITHIN A REGION: THE MEKONG AND ASEAN

DOUNG CHANTO SISOWATH

The Mekong region was for too long home to political and ideological warfare. Efforts at conflict resolution often failed perhaps because they were largely spearheaded by external powers in collusion with local allies in the region. Even the Southeast Asia Treaty Organization, founded in 1954 with US support to counter communism in Indochina, failed to prevent the escalation of conflict for the treaty did not bind member countries to help each other in case of military threat. The Indochina wars are over, but some of their effects linger and the task of addressing poverty, economic deprivation and social insecurity remains a daunting imperative.

The Mekong countries are trying to rebuild their way of life. Independence and nation-building entail financial and political responsibility and sharing limited resources among neighbor states within the subregion. But with social and financial institutions destroyed by decades of conflict and growing dependence on external assistance, some of the Mekong countries are becoming more and more vulnerable to the international political economy and global geopolitics as well as to regional pressure.

The entry of the former Indochinese countries into ASEAN signals a new attempt at reconstruction, this time within the immediate context of Southeast Asia. As with any association of sovereign states, the spirit and substance of cooperation require certain concessions of national sovereignty, without however compromising sovereignty itself. ASEAN protects this sovereignty through the principle of non-intervention in the internal affairs of member-states. Yet competition over shared resources—in this case, the Mekong River and basin—and disputes arising from contested access and use, require a certain degree and modality of intervention, lest the disputes escalate into open conflict. This chapter addresses how ASEAN and other regional bodies such as the Mekong River Commission (MRC) and the Greater Mekong Subregion (GMS) have responded to the social and political challenges of the Mekong from two angles: the standpoint of conflict resolution with respect to the region's most vital environmental and livelihood resource, the Mekong basin; and the economic and political recovery of the GMS member countries. The larger context of the discussion is the "community of caring societies" declared in the ASEAN Vision 2020.

The Mekong turns toward the region

The historical legacy of the Mekong region is characterized by the struggle for independence and ideological conflict, with the vision of transforming the region from colonialism to independence, collectivism, and today, regionalism. The failure of communism worldwide has compelled the Mekong countries to adapt to the free market economy in place of the centralized economy of the past. Economic liberalization is the most visible sign of change in the region while political and social fairness continues to demand extensive attention. Economic liberalization has enabled member-states to learn from their failed economic policies and use these lessons to strengthen a regional mechanism that would promote tighter cooperation for conflict prevention and increase the space for development and economic interaction.

Antagonistic attitudes toward capitalism and so-called western values have given way to new perspectives and policy reforms. For instance, in the realm of economic policy, Vietnam launched Doi Moi in 1986; in foreign relations and security, it implemented an exit strategy out of Cambodia, which it invaded in 1979, completing its withdrawal in 1991. Similarly, Cambodia started to liberalize its economy in 1986. For the first time since coming to power in 1979, the Heng Samrin government began collecting rent and utility fees. The government also amended the constitution to allow small-scale private enterprise and increased the taxes on private shopkeepers. At a more moderate pace, Laos has also experienced economic change following a party decision at the end of 1979 to liberalize its economy. Most independent observers believe that by 1986, Laos had achieved near self-sufficiency in rice production, albeit at a low level of consumption. Per capita income has increased since 1975 but remains pitifully low, with estimates ranging from US$120 to

US$150 per year. Health problems are severe; the infant mortality rate in 2004, for example, was 65 per 1,000 babies born (www.unicef.org/infobycountry/laopdr_statistics.html). Even Thailand, with the strongest economy in mainland Southeast Asia, perhaps because it was deeply affected by the 1997 Asian crisis, now emphasizes financial discipline and governance to reduce dependence on international lending institutions' concept and model of development.[‡] Myanmar, whose military junta has been trying to convince the international community of the legitimacy of its regime, officially endorses ASEAN's economic and political initiatives.

On the other hand, internal problems have international ramifications and exert an impact upon regional cooperation. Cambodia, for instance, is trying to practice the rule of law and respect for human rights but struggles to improve its legal infrastructure in consonance with the government's "Rectangular Strategy" (2004), which emphasizes governance reform and strengthens the legal infrastructure. But Cambodia's domestic situation obviously limits its capacity to take part in regional cooperation projects. Myanmar is another example. Military rule complicates the country's political relations with ASEAN's trading partners, mainly European countries and the United States. Hence ASEAN has been pressured by the European Union to find a solution to the "Myanmar situation". ASEAN's ability (or inability) to do so creates an international perception that the Association is a club with little political commitment to human rights. Bound by the principle of non-intervention in the domestic affairs of its member countries, ASEAN tends to appear as a soft institution, unable to enforce universally accepted doctrines.

On the other hand, the Mekong countries are in a state of transition and given the region's history of conflict and struggle, difficulties are inevitable. In all these transitional measures, what could being part of ASEAN contribute and how might it improve the political, economic and cultural space of the Mekong states?

In many ways, ASEAN as a regional institution has made economic and political transition in the Mekong possible, helping the region achieve fair results in a number of areas, mainly, political dialogue and cooperation. For example, Indonesia played a constructive and leading role in the Jakarta Informal Meetings I and II that ultimately led to the United Nations Security Council resolution on the Cambodian conflict. The meetings brought antagonists in the Cambodian conflict to the negotiating table, eventually resulting in the 1991 Paris Peace Agreement for a Comprehensive Political

Settlement of the Cambodian Conflict. Endorsed by the UN Security
Council, the agreement paved the way for a national election in 1993.
As a mechanism for ushering change, one of the most outstanding
features of ASEAN is its ability to provide opportunities to the least
developing member-states to engage in international economic
and political dialogue with other governments and institutions.
Through ASEAN, all members, including developed and developing
countries, are able to articulate their respective national interests
while considering regional interests in investment, trade and related
concerns.

The 'down' side of upstream projects

While opening economic cooperation in the Mekong region creates
opportunities for the growth of the riparian communities, on
the ground, however, the assumption of economic interaction
or interdependency is more rhetorical than real. Consequently,
in the long term, the struggle for access to natural resources,
market competition, territorial exploitation and unresolved damages
by upstream-downstream development to the environment and
livelihood of downstream inhabitants could, if not properly addressed,
increase the level of inter-state conflict (Baird et al. 2002). Indeed, of
all the disputes in the Mekong region, transboundary projects with
downstream effects are the most contentious. Downstream effects,
for one, require immediate attention because of their impact on
the ecosystem. Cambodia has suffered irregular water flows caused
by Vietnam's dams on the Se San and at the Yali Falls, for example.
According to a study by Oxfam America, the irregular flows in turn
have adversely affected the livelihood of downstream communities
in Cambodia's Rattanakiri and Stung Treng provinces. The study
further found that the economic impact on Rattanakiri alone was
severe. Assuming the total land area was flooded, approximately
1,500 kg of unmilled rice and 10,048,800 kg of unmilled paddy rice
would be lost. At 500 riel/kg, the total value of these losses would be
over four billion riel or US$1,281,735 (ibid., 46–48), an astounding
burden on the local people.

Another risk to the region is China's plan to continue building
dams—to help alleviate its energy shortage—at fourteen different
points along the upper reaches of the Mekong River in Yunnan
province. The dams are also meant to control the flooding that creates

havoc downstream but could also have wide-ranging affects on the river's ecology and numerous fisheries (ibid., 49–51). Furthermore, human activities are reducing the basin's forest cover, which leaves open the possibility that the soil located around the river source will gradually lose its water retention capacity. Another major concern is the polluting effect of effluent flowing into the Mekong itself, which could reach serious proportions.

From the standpoint of sustainable development, the MRC studies on environmental problems along the Mekong find the following to be the most pressing issues: flood; drought and damage from salination in the delta; and large flow fluctuations between the wet and dry seasons, which cause large differences in water levels and a deterioration of water quality during parts of the year (Stensholt 1997). Still, the greatest problem is that governments in the region have not adopted the environmental measures necessary to preserve the ecosystem as their economies develop. River pollution already exists and will probably be aggravated as industrialization proceeds in different areas unless preventative measures are taken.

Transboundary issues complicate social relations among peoples in the region as well as between people and their governments. When information on cross-border projects is not transparent, that is to say, the relevant facts and figures are not made available to all the stakeholders concerned, the negative consequences can be extensive. Inter- and intra-state conflict is sometimes aggravated by age-old ethnic loyalties, particularly with regard to border disputes, territorial encroachments, smuggling, access to water, water pricing, water pollution and illegal fishing. These conflicts are not military in nature—though they could conceivably escalate into violence—but are social and cultural.

For instance, the anti-Thai riots on 29 January 2003 in Phnom Penh, over a remark allegedly made by a Thai actress regarding Angkor Wat, reflects the historical legacy of competition between the two countries, even though the cross-border trade between the two is thriving. Neither side faced the core issue, much less accepted responsibility for resolving it, and instead brushed aside the matter through diplomatic apologies. But the apologies did not eradicate the historical mistrust. In the Mekong region, Thailand has long been perceived by its less developed neighbors as the overlord; and Thailand's advanced economy today and its wealth of resources, coupled with certain actions it has taken in the region, fuel this age-old perception. Just along the Cambodian-Thai border, Thai military exercises highlight Thai territorial sovereignty, in the process inciting anti-Thai sentiments. Similarly, along the Cambodia-Vietnam border, land encroachment by Vietnamese migrants generates local resentment against new settlers and resentment as well against local authorities for their inability to stop the encroachment.

Unfortunately, however, despite the growing urgency of upstream-downstream and inter-state issues, regional bodies do not possess a clear mechanism to resolve conflict and are not prepared or trained to handle various types of conflict (Chiengthong 2003). Given the historical baggage resulting from inter-state and civil wars, conflicts over borders and resources, territorial disputes and cultural animosities, all of which are undoubtedly obstacles to the peaceful development of the region, there is a pressing need for improved conflict resolution mechanisms.

Preventing and resolving conflict: not the same thing

It is true that in principle, ASEAN is committed to conflict management. The ASEAN Concord II, also known as the Bali Concord II, deals with preventive diplomacy based on the principles contained in the Treaty of Amity and Cooperation (Declaration of ASEAN Concord 1976). As the primary code of conduct governing relations between states and the diplomatic instrument for promoting peace, security and stability in the region, the agreement provides for distinct objectives and measures of conflict prevention. The objectives are to strengthen confidence and trust within the region and the larger international community; mitigate tension and prevent disputes from arising between member countries as well as between member countries and non-ASEAN countries; and prevent the escalation of existing disputes. The ASEAN member countries are expected to attain these goals by confidence-building measures, preventive diplomacy, the resolution of outstanding regional issues, and greater cooperation on non-traditional security issues (ASEAN Secretariat 2003).

But conflict prevention, while no doubt necessary, is not conflict resolution. When two or more if its members are in conflict, what is ASEAN to do? The Bali Concord II simply declares in the most general way that any dispute involving the ASEAN member-states should be resolved peacefully and in the spirit of fostering peace, security and stability in the region. While continuing to use national, bilateral and international mechanisms, the ASEAN countries may resort to existing regional dispute settlement procedures and in addition, work toward innovative modes of maintaining regional peace and better serve the collective and individual interests of members-state (ibid.).

In the absence of any new modality, however, the Mekong states have had to depend on the good faith and neighborly behavior of other states in the subregion to avoid conflict. But as we all know, being good neighbors does not always prevent conflict, and if conflict occurs, ASEAN—bound as it is by the principle of non-intervention in the internal affairs of its member-states—cannot be counted upon to step in and resolve the conflict or help mitigate the adverse effects of the dispute. As it is, the Mekong states are grappling with border disputes, conflict arising from overlapping territories and, in some cases, problems faced by indigenous communities. As members of ASEAN, they are expected to deal with these problems by preventive diplomacy as a norm of conduct rather than an obligation of membership in the community. The ASEAN declarations repeatedly speak of regional solidarity, cohesiveness and harmony (the "we" feeling) and the desire to build a democratic, tolerant, participatory and transparent community in Southeast Asia.

Norm-setting activities are expected to adhere to the fundamental principles of non-alignment, peace-oriented attitudes among member countries, use of non-violent means to resolve conflict, renunciation of nuclear weapons and other weapons of mass destruction and of threat and the use of force (ibid.). But norms cannot be enforced in the absence of legal obligations. The most that can be done with respect to these norms is to apply peer pressure, which parties in conflict can dismiss or consider depending on the strength and depth of a shared sense of community. Obligations, on the other hand, carry sanctions and provide for judicial recourse. Constructed and applied fairly, they exempt no one. At the moment, unfortunately, the Mekong does not have any formal subregional institution that focuses on conflict resolution, but as the Mekong's vulnerability to tension and conflict rises, so does the need for a binding institutional mechanism. Consequently, compensation for victims or the injured party, especially of indigenous groups whose rights remain woefully neglected (notwithstanding the ASEAN Cultural Community Plan of Action), is practically non-existent.

The Mekong turns inward

The MRC is perhaps the logical site for a conflict resolution mechanism because it directly addresses the Mekong states and the river that brings them together and yes, also sometimes drives them apart. As each of the former Indochinese states began to join ASEAN, Vietnam being the first in 1995, that same year four of the Mekong countries—Cambodia, Laos, Thailand and Vietnam—revived their old partnership, this time as the MRC. Like ASEAN, the MRC affirms the necessity of political cooperation in the utilization and development of the Mekong River basin and its resources. But because of its single-minded focus on the subregion, the MRC is a significant and special (sub)regional body. It serves as the forum for discussions of resource sharing and management of the Mekong River and provides technical expertise and advice for policy formulation and ecological management of shared resources.

The MRC cooperates in all fields of sustainable development relating to the utilization, management and conservation of water and related resources of the Mekong River basin, including though not limited to irrigation, hydropower generation, navigation, flood control, fisheries, timber floating, recreation and tourism (Table 5.1). Cooperative projects must possess two characteristics: mutual benefits to the riparian countries, and minimizing or avoiding harmful effects (Article 1, MRC Agreement).

From the perspective of regional cooperation, the MRC represents all the stakeholders, including international actors that have an interest in the development of the Mekong basin as expressed in the partnership agreement. In this cooperative scheme, the MRC deals with the technical aspects of the environment and other aspects of the river basin management, leaving the social and cultural aspects to national governments and ASEAN. The Commission's contribution to the latter aspects is indirect; by supporting the economic development of riparian states and communities, the MRC indirectly broadens the space for social and cultural growth.

Table 5.1. Programs of the Mekong River Commission

Programs	Goals	Environmental Components	Regional Issues
Core	Develops policies, rules and plans for sustainable, equitable development and management of basin resources	Basin development plan; water utilization program; environment program	Institutional capacity and delivery; equitable, transparent and democratic management of regional resources
Support	Builds administrative capacity		Organizational systems and human resources of MRC and riparian governments
Sector	Serves specific sectors or addresses particular regional issues	Fisheries, agriculture, irrigation and forestry programs; navigation program; tourism program; flood control and mitigation	Complementary initiatives at national and bilateral levels

Source: Mekong River Commission (www.mrcmekong.org)

Resolve conflict, not merely notify parties in conflict

However, much like ASEAN, the MRC does not have an institution-alized mechanism for conflict resolution. More fundamentally, the MRC does not have jurisdiction over conflict resolution because it has no authority to make political decisions for the region, its task being confined to the development of the Mekong River and basin. In case of an inter-state dispute arising from a breach of bilateral treaties, acts and other diplomatic agreements, each party's Ministry of Foreign Affairs is to deal with the conflict. If the dispute involves areas of jurisdiction or if a subject matter or operation of an entity created under an existing agreement conflicts with any provision of the MRC Agreement, the issue is to be submitted to the respective governments to address and resolve (MRC Agreement, Art. 36[a]).

To prevent disputes over the development and use of the Mekong's resources, the MRC links the member country's National Mekong Committee to the MRC's Joint Committee that reviews claims and disputes (Figure 5.1). This conflict prevention procedure provides a means of notifying the parties in conflict to resolve their dispute bilaterally in the spirit of transparency and good faith. The problem is, however, that the National Joint Committees reflect distinct individual, not collective (regional), interests. They exercise their authority by a voting process but neither conflict prevention nor resolution lies within their purview. The MRC is not a political organization and therefore does not craft development policy for the Mekong. It is the National Mekong Committee of each member state that makes political decisions on the development of the region. Left to settle their differences themselves, the parties tend to cling to their respective demands. Although Article 8 of the MRC Agreement provides equal sovereignty for members to request remedy for damages, there is still no legal recourse to remedy disputes on the utilization of the Mekong resource. As a result, damages are not often fairly compensated or compensated at all, and disputes remain unresolved.

Figure 5.1: MRC Organizational Chart

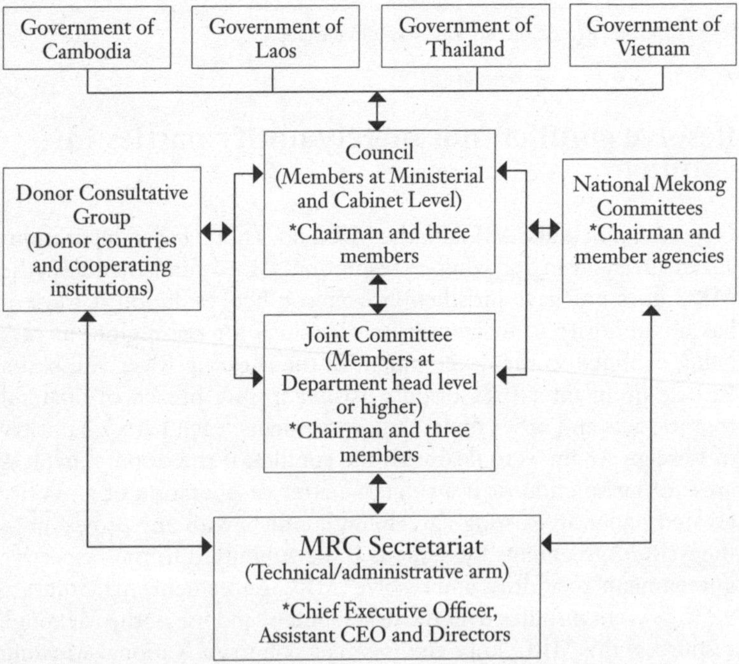

Source: Agreement on the Cooperation for the Sustainable Development of the Mekong River Basin, 5 April 1995, Chiang Rai, Thailand.

With respect to conflict resolution, therefore, the MRC has not been able to develop a legally binding instrument for judicial recourse. In the meantime, the institutional mechanism for notification will have to do—that, and the hopefully cooperative spirit of the national Mekong committee, the ASEAN spirit, and the ASEAN Declaration of 1967 disavowing aggression by parties in conflict. These principles do help bilateral initiatives, such as the ongoing effort by Cambodia and Thailand to work out the technical agreements over oil reserves in the Gulf of Thailand. But they could be assisted by more definite conflict resolution procedures.

The GMS is the other organization in the basin area but it is less formally organized and also operates within the ASEAN economic and political framework of non-intervention. The ASEAN Mekong Basin Development Cooperation (AMBDC 1996), whose purpose is to endorse development projects that would close the gap among the Mekong states and bridge regional integration, is also not endowed with a mechanism to resolve conflict. On the whole, therefore, conflict prevention as practiced in ASEAN and the MRC seems to privilege membership while remaining soft on the members' failure to live up to their responsibilities. While enjoying their privileges, members of these regional and subregional bodies have no obligation (or means) to help settle disputes between member countries. Because the ASEAN principle of non-intervention discourages the organization from stepping into conflict situations, good faith—which is unenforceable—virtually becomes the sole recourse. Therefore, dialogue and cooperation are the fundamental mechanisms for increasing the mutual understanding and hopefully mutual respect necessary to prevent conflict. But in the long run, how effective can non-binding mechanisms like dialogue and consultation be?

Rebuilding the Mekong

Let us now examine the role of regional organizations in reconstructing the Mekong region. Despite changes in the political leadership and the relatively slow institutionalization of policies and programs, the ASEAN and the MRC have had a positive impact in several areas, namely, security cooperation, economic and development cooperation, inter-state trade, and the development of the GMS. But in the Mekong, ASEAN's ultimate objective of regional integration remains a goal on paper. The historical legacy of hostility is difficult enough to hurdle over, and the diverse political regimes in the region are not easy to bring together even in the name of the common good. The "we" spirit is stressed often enough as part of ASEAN's endeavor to build trust and strengthen solidarity among all the member-states and peoples, but cultural tolerance is a continuing challenge. Above all, poverty reduction is the gravest and most demanding task of the region.

Thus apart from its policy on conflict management, ASEAN envisions a regional Economic Community (ASEAN Singapore Declaration of 1992) through the ASEAN Economic Framework. This framework includes elements of the ASEAN Investment Initiative and the ASEAN Mekong Basin Development Cooperation. Initiatives at the regional (ASEAN) and subregional (GMS and MRC) levels and economic reform by governments of the Mekong region have led to economic liberalization, allowing the Mekong countries to experience a double economic transition: from subsistence farming to more diversified economies, and from command economies to more open market-based economies. The double transition, in turn, has spurred foreign direct investment and donor assistance. As a result, commercial relations between the six GMS countries have rapidly expanded. Other economic mechanisms such as the Common Exempt Preference Tariff and the ASEAN Free Trade Agreement have facilitated freer flows of capital and goods within the region. Agreements particular to the Mekong region support these exchanges. For example, the Framework Agreement on the Facilitation of Cross-Border Movement of Goods and People was signed by Laos, Thailand and Vietnam in 1999, Cambodia in 2001, and China the following year. Another cooperative instrument was the Strategy for the Next Ten Years of the GMS Program, which sees a more integrated, prosperous and equitable region in the Mekong. At their Tenth Ministerial Conference in Yangon in 2001, the GMS member-states agreed on five "strategic thrusts": infrastructure, trade and investment, the role of the private sector, human resource development, and environmental protection. Tourism was subsequently added to the list, including visa facilitation. Economic corridors across all six countries aim to further facilitate the movement of goods and people from north to south and east to west.

The Asian Development Bank (ADB) is a key player in the reconstruction of the Mekong. Having initiated the formation of the GMS, the Bank is able to mobilize and finance development cooperation in the Mekong. The GMS's development priorities are sub-regional trade and investment (focusing on transportation and telecommunications infrastructure to facilitate trade and investment), energy generation, tourism promotion, and the resolution of transborder problems (e.g., spread of communicable diseases, human trafficking, downstream effects and drug trafficking). Transboundary issues alone are an overwhelming concern. Discussions between ASEAN, the AMBDC, MRC and ADB focus on improving living standards and mitigating cross-border problems by reducing poverty through economic growth and investment. Aside from the ADB, the Mekong regional organizations work closely with the World Bank, the United Nations Development Program and individual donor nations.

Inevitably, the implementation of the GMS programs will pose many challenges to governance and accountability. On the positive side, the GMS speaks loudly of pro-poor economic growth as the engine of the Mekong region's collective economic development. But the effect of development projects on the environment is tremendous and, in some cases, precarious. The dividends of economic cooperation are undeniably an important factor in creating a positive climate for investment and the rise of small- and medium-scale enterprises. But economic growth should not be a trade-off for the destruction of cultural riches and habitats of indigenous populations. The concern of regional bodies and their member-states for the development of the Mekong should be matched by conscious and deliberate action on the adverse effects of some of these projects for, in the final analysis, sustainable growth means people-oriented development.

Making regional bodies more effective

To improve the political, economic and cultural environment of the Mekong, a more solid relationship between state institutions and peoples in the region is necessary. One could argue that this is the business of states and not of regional development bodies. Yet states comprise regional institutions and inadequate, non-responsive governments put together can only produce a weak collective organization. The relationship between government and the people, furthermore, must be forged by the rule of law and democratic governance. The right to development, after all, demands an open and non-discriminating political system (Crawford 1998). People need to trust state institutions—an aspect of confidence building that tends to be neglected in the field of development cooperation. Yet that trust, though internal to each country, is crucial to peace and development of the region. Amid the pressure and impact of globalization, the breach of trust between state and society demands rapid institutional reform. For this reason, institutional growth and institutional capacity building are vital to regional develoment. Weaknesses of state institutions in the distribution of resources, for example, or the uneven or unfair representation of stakeholders eventually trigger internal and ethnic conflict, which in turn could affect the region as a whole. Therefore, the future of the Mekong region depends largely on the reforms, political and not just economic, that states individually undertake. And because regional bodies have little or no control over the policy changes of member nations, a fundamental component of an effective regional body lies outside its control.

At a broader level, perhaps because shared river resources leave the riparian countries little choice, cooperation in the development, use and allocation of resources is imperative. If political will is crucial at the national level, it is, too, at the regional level. ASEAN and the subregional organizations must be able to go beyond articulating principles to actually applying them so that in various ways, peoples of the region benefit from cooperative projects. More important, regional institutions must provide the people with a sense of ownership in development. For this reason, regional entities ought to exert greater effort to reduce development gaps not just among member-states but also between indigenous communities and populations at the center and alleviate other forms of social disparity. Development partnerships mean shared burdens and shared benefits, and not more of one and less of the other, whatever the development time frame. The question—development for whom?—must be asked again and again in every regional undertaking.

At present, regional institutions aim to make the Mekong region as attractive as possible to foreign investors, a laudable objective as long as the people of the region figure prominently in the picture and benefit from the planned investments. Regional organizations are also working toward a common economic system. Yet here again, the people and not just their governments must have a say and a role to play. The financial burden of development is so large and disproportionate to the financial capacity of the Mekong countries that the funding aspect tends to overwhelm other, equally pressing concerns.

Moreover, the institutional authority of regional bodies over the development of the region varies in scope and strength. The GMS, for example, is relatively weak because like the MRC, the GMS does not exercise political decisions but represents the economic interests of its member countries. But unlike the MRC and ASEAN, the GMS is not, to be precise, a regional institution. ASEAN is, although it is oriented more toward the larger Southeast Asian region than just the Mekong. The MRC also has a formal organizational structure and a specific mandate to provide technical assistance and implement development projects in the Mekong. The GMS, in contrast, is not an institution but rather a geographical entity initiated by the ADB. With no political or legal obligation, the GMS ministers work very closely with the Bank to develop the Mekong, and the relationship between the ADB and the GMS is a loose arrangement, high on policy advocacy, program planning and financial support, and low on the rest. Thus although some of the GMS objectives and programs overlap with those of ASEAN and the MRC, the GMS is not an institution in the way that ASEAN and the MRC are.

Against this background, it is difficult to forecast the effectiveness of the GMS programs in terms of their contribution to the livelihood and cultural development of the riparian people. The vision of the ADB-backed GMS is subregional prosperity, dynamic and equitable growth through the facilitation of market operations, delivery of goods and services across borders and the build-up of social capital for market management (GMS 2002). Specific measures to achieve this vision include the allocation of foreign direct investment, investment and tariff protocols, infrastructure development in transportation and telecommunications, transregional extradition treaties, credit schemes, transfer of skills and technology, and reduction of HIV/AIDS. In most of these programs the ADB plays a key role, not just as a source of funds (which includes soliciting investors) but also in implementation.

Despite their worthy intentions, the GMS programs face diverse challenges in a rather volatile region, challenges that are not always easy to anticipate and not easily overcome, owing to a combination of factors such as historical baggage, institutional weaknesses and the under-representation of basic sectors. Like the MRC and ASEAN, the capacity of the GMS to contribute to subregional growth is hampered by the absence of a conflict resolution mechanism.

In any case, all these regional and subregional bodies share a core concept of development cooperation in the Mekong, as evidenced by numerous statements that have concluded meetings and summits at various levels. The concept is backed by linkages that are necessary to implement cooperation projects. For instance, the trilateral linkage between ASEAN, the MRC and the ADB aims to close development gaps between the new (Cambodia, Laos, Myanmar and Vietnam) and the original members of ASEAN; the relationship has yielded concrete results for the Mekong. ASEAN makes collective decisions to promote the development of the Mekong region, while the MRC endorses decisions made by ASEAN that allow the ADB, World Bank and UNDP to mobilize their resources to finance development projects and provide the necessary technical assistance. To further crystallize its efforts on the Mekong, ASEAN created its own ASEAN Mekong Basin Development Cooperation, which focuses on infrastructure development programs in transportation, communication and energy, trade, cultural exchange, human resource development, tourism and environmental sustainability and, in the process, helping the transition of the Mekong states.

The development framework of these regional bodies suggests that interdependency and regionalism reduce barriers to regional cooperation. But in reality, the processes of economic interdependency and regionalism, actualized through inter-state trade, cross-border trade, shared infrastructure projects and the distribution of benefits such as improved access to markets and capital, goods and services, sometimes invite competitiveness and adversely affect the objective of regional cohesion. Governments in the region seem to work on the assumption that economic inter-dependency is apolitical in nature and that trade imbalance is a normal process of the free market economy. But on the other hand, the political and economic reality in the region indicates that these assumptions are at best naïve and that for planning purposes, it is better to assume that political competition is a fact of life affecting all facets of relations within the region.

Authorities in the region must thus be realistic about the limitations of interdependency and the market economy in terms of equitable growth and the capacity of these interdependent processes to resolve conflicting national interests. Even as neighboring states enter into regional alliances and cooperation agreements and do their best to realize the mutual benefits of economic interdependency, these states continue to compete with one another for power and resources in the exercise of their sovereign rights (Bunbongkarn 2000, 145–146). In the process, regional institutions and organizations committed to rebuilding the Mekong community in the spirit of "we" rather than simply "I", are weakened on the ground. The political realities of interdependency and regionalism do not necessarily ensure stability and equity.

Creating "caring societies"

In 1997 member-states of the ASEAN agreed to build a regional community of "caring societies", paying particular attention to improving the livelihood of its newest members, all of them from the Mekong: Cambodia, Laos, Myanmar and Vietnam (ASEAN Vision 2020). But institutional weaknesses in the subregion make the coordination and realization of this vision an extremely challenging task. On the ground, inefficient management and low levels of political commitment and political will undermine institutional projects of cooperation.

A second reality in the region is that developing members constantly face resource constraints that cause institutional disparities, gaps in capacity and human resources, in the long run also affecting the management and delivery of cooperation projects. Functional capacity thus remains a major challenge for the region.

In terms of policy, institutional reforms on the part of member nations are imperative but require strong political will. Regional cooperation serves two fundamental purposes: political stability and economic growth. These objectives in turn require policy reforms that will enable member countries to expand the market space in the region and allocate the benefits of growth equitably within a democratic and transparent environment. A reliable legal infrastructure is also necessary, one that is capable of enforcing laws, so that measures against corruption, smuggling, the drug trade and so on can be carried out. Equity and competitiveness in the region, after all, rest on fairness and accountability. External institutions, such as the ADB, World Bank and UNDP offer assistance for local reform in these areas.

The vision of "caring societies" will come closer to reality when the ASEAN member-states broaden their focus on conflict prevention to include the resolution of disputes with the help of the organization rather than just the parties in conflict. Managing contending interests of six different countries is no easy task, given different political regimes, cultures and economic systems. Regional organizations such as the MRC, especially its Joint Committee, must lead the way in addressing the problem of upstream-downstream development of the Mekong. The MRC could assert its mandate to ensure the sustainable development of the river basin in evaluating the impact of this development on various parts of the subregion.

Similarly, ASEAN could also be more pro-active in providing technical and financial assistance to the Mekong member countries not just by mobilizing funds but also by helping mitigate the ill-effects of certain development projects. While ASEAN and the ADB have been the link in bringing the GMS programs to the negotiating table, greater focus on the member countries that need help the most—the least developed economies—would demonstrate the true spirit of building a "community of caring societies". At present, the Mekong region continues to be highly dependent on outside capital, making it vulnerable to fluctuations in the global financial markets.

In sum, while regional organizations contribute to the development of the riparian communities along the Mekong, it is the responsibility of governments in the subregion to ensure good practices in public policy and administration. Democratic governance and accountability, especially to those who are not adequately represented such as women, children and indigenous communities, are essential to the making of caring societies. For their part, affected as they are by national politics and policies, regional organizations could use their combined influence to effect reform or more generally create an atmosphere conducive to reform.

References

ASEAN Secretariat. 2003. "Declaration of ASEAN Concord II" (Bali Concord II). 7 October.

———.2000. "Developing the Greater Mekong Sub-Region: The ASEAN Context." 10 February.

———. 1997. "ASEAN Vision 2020." 15 December.

———.1992. "Singapore Declaration of 1992." 28 January.

———. 1976. "Declaration of ASEAN Concord I." 24 February.

———.1976. "Treaty of Amity and Cooperation 1976." 24 February.

Baird, Ian, Monsiri Baird, et al. 2002. "A Community-Based Study of the Downstream Impacts of the Yali Falls Dam Along the Se San, Sre Pok, and Sekong Rivers in Stung Treng Province, Northeast Cambodia." Phnom Penh: Oxfam America Mekong Initiative.

Bunbongkarn, Suchit. 2000. "Security Challenges in the Greater Mekong Sub-Region." In *The Greater Mekong Subregion and ASEAN: From Backwaters to Headwaters*, edited by Kao Kim Hourn and Jeffrey A. Kaplan, pp. 143–153. Phnom Penh: Cambodian Institute for Cooperation and Peace.

Chiengthong, Jamaree. 2003. "The Politics of Ethnicity, Indigenous Culture and Knowledge in Thailand, and Vietnam and Lao PDR." In *Social Challenges for the Mekong Region*, edited by Mingsarn Kaosa-ard and John Dore, pp. 147–172. Chiang Mai: Chiang Mai University Social Research Institute.

Crawford, Beverly. 1998. "The Causes of Cultural Conflict: Assessing the Evidence." In *The Myth of "Ethnic Conflict": Politics, Economics, and Cultural Violence*, edited by Beverly Crawford and Ronnie D. Lipschultz, pp. 513–561. Berkeley: University of California Press.

Fukushima, Akiko. 2003. "The ASEAN Regional Forum." Reprinted in abridged form in *The Regional Organizations of the Asia-Pacific: Exploring Institutional Change*, edited by Michael Wesley, pp. 76–93. Hampshire: Palgrave Macmillan.

Greater Mekong Subregion (GMS). 2002. "Making it Happen: A Common Strategy on Cooperation for Growth, Equity and Prosperity in the Greater Mekong Subregion." Joint GMS Summit Declaration. Phnom Penh, Cambodia, 3 November.

Kao Kim Hourn and Doung Chanto Sisowath. 2001. "The Greater Mekong Subregion: An ASEAN Issue." In *Reinventing ASEAN*, edited by Simon Tay, Jesus P. Estanislao and Hadi Soesastro, pp. 163–182. Singapore: Institute of Southeast Asian Studies.

Kao Kim Hourn and Jeffrey A. Kaplan, eds. 2000. *The Greater Mekong River and ASEAN: From Backwaters to Headwaters*. Phnom Penh: Cambodian Institute for Cooperation and Peace.

Mekong River Commission. 1995. "Agreement on the Cooperation for the Sustainable Development of the Mekong River Basin." 5 April.

Ong Keng Yong. 2005. Address before the ASEAN People's Assembly, Manila, 11 May.

Pintobtang, Prapart. 2003. "The Role of NGOs and the People Sector's Movement in Building Good Governance and Democracy in Thailand." In *Challenges Facing the ASEAN Peoples*, edited by Hadi Soesastro, pp. 300–312. Jakarta: Center for Strategic and International Studies.

Royal Government of Cambodia. 2004. "Rectangular Strategy." Phnom Penh.

Sisowath, Doung Chanto. 2003. "The ASEAN Regional Forum—The Emergence of 'Soft Security': Improving the Functionality of the ASEAN Security Regime." *Dialogue + Cooperation* 3: 41–47.

Stensholt, Bob. 1997. *Developing the Mekong Subregion*. Clayton: Monash University Asia Institute.

Sudarsono, Juwono. 2003. "The Limits of Conflict Resolution in Southeast Asia." In *The 2ⁿᵈ ASEAN Reader*, edited by Sharon Siddique and Sree Kumar, pp. 297–302. Singapore: Institute of Southeast Asian Studies.

Thoraxy, Hing. 2003. *Cambodia's Investment Potential: Challenges and Prospects*. Phnom Penh: Cambodian Institute for Cooperation and Peace.

Toriumi, Iwao. 2000. The Final Report with Recommendations. Paper read at the conference, "Toward Vision 2020: ASEAN-Japan Consultation Conference on the Realization of the Hanoi Plan of Action." Nara, 26–28 March.

6

INTRA-REGIONAL AND CROSS-BORDER ECONOMIC COOPERATION

MYA THAN

The Mekong region, with a combined population of more than 300 million, is the poorest in Southeast Asia. Sandwiched between the booming part of Southeast Asia and rapidly emerging China, the region has immense potential. Yet, like the river that runs through it, the economic potential of the Mekong region[1] is so far just that—potential. Since the 1950s when the Mekong Committee was formed (consisting of Thailand, Cambodia, Laos and South Vietnam, as it was then known), the dream of harnessing the hydroelectric power of the mighty Mekong River has captured the imagination of politicians and planners alike. Almost fifty years later, it is estimated that only one percent of the region's potential hydroelectric energy is being exploited (Mya Than 1997). Today, the region's planners aim to transform the backwater region into an economically developed area by exploiting its resources.

Barely twenty years ago, the Mekong region was associated with bitter, seemingly unending armed conflicts, doctrinaire socialist ideologies, and an appalling lack of infrastructure. These negative factors resulted in an environment totally hostile to business and exacerbated the region's isolation from the rest of Southeast Asia. Even today, armed conflicts still exist in parts of the region, socialist governments still rule, and infrastructure remains poor at best. However, since the end of the Cold War and the shift of command/controlled economic systems to market-oriented ones in the late 1980s and early 1990s, the image of the Mekong region has undergone surprising changes. Moreover, since 1999, the four riparian Southeast Asian countries joined ASEAN and in October 2003, China signed the Treaty of Amity and Economic Cooperation. The vision of the Mekong region's development planners has thus become a distinct possibility.

In support of these moves, numerous multinational initiatives have been launched to boost, facilitate and, not least, cash in on the seemingly unlimited economic potential of the region. The region has even taken on a new name, the Greater Mekong Subregion (GMS), a term concocted by the Asian Development Bank (ADB), and has become one of Southeast Asia's 'growth triangles' (subregional growth zones).[2] The main objective of the GMS is to jointly develop natural resources and infrastructure by exploiting (presumably shared) geopolitical interest and geographical proximity among the Mekong basin countries.

To materialize the dreams of the region's development founders, economic cooperation among the member countries is absolutely essential. The aim of this chapter is to study the extent of economic cooperation in terms of cross-border movements of goods, finance and people, particularly, cross-border trade, investment and tourism among the six participating countries. The first section briefly traces the history of cooperation initiatives in the Mekong basin and points out salient economic and social indicators. The second analyses cross-border trade; the third, investment flows among member countries and foreign investments in infrastructure; and the fourth, movements of people in terms of tourism. The essay ends with issues and challenges for economic cooperation in the Mekong region.

International initiatives in brief

The tale of the Mekong is the history of six riparian countries bound by the Mekong River in alternate periods of conflict and peace. As the site of war and trade, the region is familiar with both hostility and cooperation. In fact, the first ever formal subregional economic cooperation among the states dates back to the later half of the 19th century and the first half of the 20th, when treaties regulating the navigational use of the lower Mekong River were concluded between Siam and France (the latter on behalf of its protectorates in Indochina). Since then, notes Prachoon Chomchai, "the non-navigational utilisation of the transboundary water resources of the Mekong basin has been characterised...by a virtual absence of hard and fast rules derived from international law" (1995, 1).

The postwar history of regional cooperation started in 1957, when the Mekong Committee was established under the auspices of the

United Nations (Economic and Social Commission for Asia and the Pacific, ESCAP), made up of Cambodia, Laos, Thailand and South Vietnam in the lower Mekong basin. With the Cold War at its peak, Burma and China were left out of the Committee. The objective was to promote, coordinate, supervise and control the Lower Mekong Basin (Statute, 1957, Art. 4) in other words, to commonly exploit the waterway for energy, irrigation, transportation and fisheries for the benefit of the riparian states. However, only a few projects were carried out as many political changes were occurring in the area. To reactivate cooperation, an Interim Mekong Committee was formed in January 1978 by three of the founder nations, Laos, Thailand and Vietnam. Owing to political and social upheavals at the time, Cambodia rejoined the group only in 1991.

The new phase of subregional cooperation occurred when the old Mekong Committee was reorganized by the original four members and renamed the Mekong River Commission (MRC) in April 1995. That same year, the last two of the riparian states, Myanmar and China, agreed to establish a dialogue mechanism with the MRC; the first was held in July 1996 in Bangkok. Most of the MRC's activities have focused on the inventory of resources, environmental monitoring, small-scale irrigation and the like. The MRC also formulated the Mekong Basin Development Plan for the "reasonable and equitable use" of Mekong water (for details, see Samran 1996). However, the Nam Ngum dam in Laos is the only significant hydroelectric project of the MRC to date.

A big boost came from the ADB in 1992, when it established the regional Technical Assistance Program to promote and facilitate economic cooperation among the six countries. The role of the ADB has largely been that of a catalyst; it encourages dialogue and assists in subregional cooperation through project identification and development. According to the ADB, its long-term objective is "to contribute to an ongoing process that will build confidence and trust among the participants and help provide an enduring framework for development assistance with a regional focus" (quoted in Mya Than 1997, 42). The ADB outlined seven areas of cooperation—transport, energy, environment, human resource development, tourism, trade and investment, and telecommunications—and identified over a hundred priority projects, with five road-upgrading projects at the top of the list. The Bank's current emphasis is to develop an attractive investment environment for the private sector.

Apart from the MRC and the ADB, there exist at least four international initiatives to develop the greater Mekong subregion, as follows:

- *Forum for the Comprehensive Development of Indochina*: This initiative deals mainly with infrastructure and tourism in Cambodia, Laos, Vietnam and Myanmar and is supported by Japan.
- *ASEAN-Mekong Basin Development Cooperation*: This framework was initiated by the ASEAN nations, primarily Malaysia and Singapore, in 1995 to promote the well-being of the people of the Mekong subregion. Several areas of cooperation were agreed upon: agriculture, minerals and forestry, industry, transport, telecommunications and energy, education and training, tourism, and trade and investment. Malaysia produced a project feasibility report on trans-Asia railway links between the ASEAN and the GMS countries and China. Thailand is also preparing an ASEAN Mekong Fund. Moreover, ASEAN is seeking support from other countries outside the region such as Japan, Korea, the European Union and Australia. The ASEAN-MBDC initiative links for the first time the non-Mekong and Mekong members of the ASEAN.
- *Golden Quadrangle (Quadripartite Economic Cooperation)*: The initiative came from Thailand in 1992 to strengthen economic cooperation and peaceful relations based on the concept of "turning battlefields into market places". This loose, informal arrangement links Thailand, Myanmar, Laos and Yunnan province of China and concentrates primarily on infrastructure development and tourism.
- *AEM-MITI Initiative*: In 1994 the ASEAN Economic Ministers and the Japanese Ministry of International Trade and Industry agreed to promote and maintain dynamic economic growth in Asia as a whole and strengthen economic linkages between the ASEAN and Indochina. Their initiative focuses on issues of transition by the former Indochinese countries and Myanmar to a market economy, with an emphasis on infrastructure, investment, trade and industrial policies.

Other initiatives have also been launched to support the region's development, such as the Mekong Fund, Mekong Development Bank, Thailand's Indochina Fund, and the Mekong Development Research Network initiated by the International Development Research Center. Many of these overlap and coordination among them is sorely needed (Stensholt 1996). Indeed, some analysts worry that such redundancies could be counter-productive. More significant, perhaps because it involves a major player, is the China-ASEAN Free Trade Area Agreement (ASEAN+1) signed in 2002 and the ASEAN Treaty of Amity and Cooperation concluded a year later.

The GMS economies: different yet similar

Of the six countries, China, Laos and Vietnam are officially Marxist Socialist states practicing one-party political systems. But each is transforming from a centrally planned economic system into a market-oriented one, albeit under different labels: 'Socialist Market Economy' (China), 'New Economic Mechanism' (Laos), 'Economic Renovation' (Vietnam). Despite differences in the pace and scope of reform, the essential elements are similar: the promotion of foreign investment, deregulation of domestic and foreign trade, price and enterprise reforms, and reform of the agrarian and financial sectors.

With the exception of Thailand, the Mekong region's economies are based on agriculture and are characterised by low per capita incomes. Thailand is in many senses the odd one out in this grouping for its per capita GNP of US$2,010 is two to three times higher than that of the other economies in the subregion. Yet, this statistic is misleading in that the Thai economy is so heavily centered on Bangkok, which is estimated to account for about 35 percent of Thailand's national product. The parts of Thailand located in the Mekong basin capture area (chiefly the north and northeast) are much poorer than the national average, suggesting that these areas more easily fit the characteristics of the other GMS members. Indeed the Mekong riparian economies, except for the Bangkok area of Thailand, are in roughly the same category as other "emerging growth areas" of Asia like eastern Indonesia, southern Philippines, parts of India and the interior of China. Competition for foreign investment in low-wage manufacturing over the next twenty years will likely be centered on these emerging areas.

Salient economic indicators of the six riparian countries are shown in Table 6.1. The economies of the region, with the exception of Thailand, are primarily agricultural economies with low per capita income. In 1999 total GNP accounted for about US$170 billion, with per capita income ranging from a low of US$280 (Laos) to US$2,110 (Thailand).

Table 6.1: Basic Indicators, 2001

	Yunnan	Myanmar	Laos	Thailand	Cambodia	Vietnam
Population (mil)	44	50	5	61	11	77
Area (1,000 sq km)	394.0	676.6	237.0	513.1	181.0	331.7
% cultivated land	7.3	15.8	3.9	41.0	17.4	21.6
% forest land	24.9	41.3	23.8	22.8	55.7	28.0
GNP per cap (US$) 1999	500	300	290	2,010	280	370
GDP growth (%)	8.0	6.2	5.8	3.8	5.0	5.7
Share of GDP (%)						
Agriculture	23.8[a]	43.3	51.3	8.0	32.0	22.7
Industry	45.6[a]	12.3	23.1	44.0	24.0	36.9
Services	30.6[a]	39.8	25.6	48.0	44.0	40.4
Exports (US$ mil)	910[b]	2,782	422	65,112	1,296	8,431
Imports (US$ mil)	434[b]	2,684	727	62,057	1,424	4,770
Inflation (%)	0.7[c]	34.5	7.8	1.7	5.2	0.8

Notes: [a] In 1998, [b] In 1994, [c] China

Sources: ADB, *Asian Development Outlook* 2002, Manila; ADB, *Key Indicators 2001*; *Asiaweek*, 16 February 1996; *Yunnan Statistical Yearbook*, 1991–1998; IMF, *Direction of Trade Statistics 2002*, Washington, D.C.

Despite these figures, economic growth in the GMS in recent years has been impressive, with economic outputs increasing at an average annual growth rate of 5.3 percent, making the region one of the world's fastest growing in 2001. Total exports and imports of the entire Mekong region in 2001 accounted for approximately US$80 billion and more than US$82 billion, respectively, including Yunnan.

As all but one of the six participating riparian countries of the region are transforming from a rigid centralized economy into a market-oriented system, foreign trade and investments are welcome in the GMS. Now wide open, borders are absorbing a burgeoning trade to an extent that in some places, unofficial trade is estimated to equal or exceed official trade.

Moreover, the region's relatively educated and disciplined pool of labor gives it strong comparative advantage in labor-intensive industries. Also, the resource-rich economies are already plugged into the world's fastest growing economies of East Asia like China and the other ASEAN nations, whose economies are complementary. The dominant characteristic of the subregion and its biggest economic weakness is the lack of infrastructure.

Based on 1995 performance, the ADB expects the GDP of the region to expand six-fold in the next 20 years to about US$1,250 billion (in 1995 dollars). The ADB further estimates that by 2020, the GMS will have a population of about 350 million, half of whom will be living in cities; a labor force of nearly 200 million; and a per capita GDP around the same level as Malaysia's in 1997 (EAAU 1997, 342).

Intra-Mekong basin trade

Three reasons are often cited as the rationale for economic cooperation among developing countries: to increase market access and promote the gains from trade occurring as a result of rationalization and specialization; to enhance political cohesion; and to further other trade and economic policy goals (OECD 1993, 25). With respect to the GMS, cooperation has been pushed by such factors as the collapse of the Soviet Union and Council for Mutual Economic Assistance, the fear of protectionism, the US embargo, and competition for foreign direct investment. The pull factors, on the other hand, are geographical proximities, existence of old trade routes, historical links, cultural, language and ethnic affinities, thawing of political tensions as a result of the end of the Cold War, economic reforms carried out in formerly centralized planning economies, regional and subregional groupings, and the then imminent membership of the Southeast Asian member countries of the GMS in ASEAN (Mya Than 1997, 43).

A crucial aspect of economic cooperation is intra-regional trade which to some riparian countries is more significant than their trade with others outside the region. As shown in Table 6.2, for example, in 1999 the (formal) trade of Laos, Cambodia and Myanmar with other Mekong countries constituted nearly 59 percent, 31 percent and 29 percent, respectively, of their total external trade. In contrast, the Mekong trade is far less important to China (5 percent of total external trade), Thailand (6 percent), and Vietnam (12 percent). Note also that if the informal cross-border trade were included in the table below, the volume of intra-regional trade would rise considerably.

Table 6.2: Intra-Mekong Formal Trade, 1999 (US$ million)

Country	Camb.	China	Laos	Myan.	Thai	Viet.	Total External Trade		Mekong as % of Total
							Mekong	World	
Cambodia	n.a.	95	--	--	214	478	787	2,564	30.7
China	160	n.a.	31	508	4,216	1,318	6,233	124,843	5.0
Laos	--	33	--	--	475	30	538	911	59.1
Myanmar	--	539	--	n.a.	538	--	1,077	3,748	28.7
Thailand	392	4,617	441	538	n.a.	903	6,891	115,004	6.0
Vietnam	509	1,382	101	--	940	n.a.	2,932	23,620	12.4

Source: IMF, Direction of Trade Statistics Yearbook 2000, Washington.

Furthermore, again with the exception of Thailand, the economic structures of most GMS member economies are competitive rather than complementary. As Figure 6.1 indicates, the major exports are agricultural products and major imports, manufactured goods, machinery and equipment.

Fig. 6.1. Major Exports and Imports of GMS Countries

Major Exports

Yunnan	tea, cigarettes, wood products, textiles, chemicals
Myanmar	rice, teak & hardwoods, rubber, beans & pulses, fish
Laos	timber & forestry products, electricity, coffee, metals
Thailand	rice, shrimps, rubber, textiles, maize, rubber, tin, manufactured goods
Cambodia	timber, soya bean, rubber, maize, tobacco, gems
Vietnam	rice, coal, rubber, tea, footwear, crude petroleum

Major Imports

Yunnan	machinery, equipment, chemical products
Myanmar	manufactures, raw materials, machinery, equipment
Laos	machinery & raw materials, fuels, rice & foodstuff, machinery, equipment, sugar
Thailand	mineral fuels, machinery, chemicals, iron & steel
Cambodia	machinery, transport equipment, base metals, manufactures, foodstuff
Vietnam	chemicals, fertilizers, cement, machinery, equipment, raw materials, petroleum products

Trade across borders, legal and not

The most interesting feature of the economic renaissance of the Mekong riparian countries is not, as in the typical East Asian newly industrializing country, the growth of exports to industrialized country markets based on low-wage manufacturing. Rather, it is in the explosive growth of cross-border trade within the Mekong region. With the end of hostilities in the region, borders previously closed for decades were thrown open towards the end of the 1980s. Since then, all riparian countries have formalized their border trade. In 1996, for example, a rail link between China and Vietnam was reopened, after being closed for 18 years following a short but bitter border conflict.

However, the opening of borders in itself has not resulted in a free flow of goods. Customs regulations, rules governing the movement of vehicles, arbitrary 'transit taxes' and other red tape have forced much of the intra-regional trade to go underground. Indeed, some estimates put 'unofficial' or informal trade at as much as officially recorded trade, if not more. In any case, the volume is large. Discussions with government officials indicate, for example, that the informal border trade currently amounts to between one-third and one-half of Thailand's informal trade with Laos and Myanmar. Other estimates place the informal trade between Laos and Thailand at between one-third of and equal to the level of formal border trade, and that between Thailand and Myanmar at about two times the volume of formal border trade (ADB 2001c, vol. 6, 6).

Goods smuggled into neighboring countries are almost the same as those in the formal trade, such as consumer goods, medicines, vehicles and spare parts, gemstones, cattle, tobacco, liquor, and electrical appliances, in addition to banned goods such as teakwood, drugs, small arms and ammunitions, alcohol, and so on. Smuggled goods are transported by hired laborers—many of whom are aged between 20 and 45, according to Myanmar sources—on behalf of traders on one or the other side of the border, or by small-scale traders, tourists, the general population and, of course, professional operators (ibid.).

Myanmar's cross-border trade

Table 6.3 presents data on the formal border trade of Myanmar with Thailand and China (Yunnan). Because Myanmar has no border checkpoint with Laos—the border being only a few kilometers along the Mekong River in the hinterland of both countries—no trade has ever been recorded between the two, although trade undoubtedly takes place.

Between 1992–1993 and 2000–2001, Myanmar's overall exports to its Mekong partners increased at an average annual growth rate of 9.3 percent. However, its overall imports decreased at an average annual growth rate of -3.1 percent. The country's total cross-border trade grew slowly at an average annual rate of 1.8 percent although in terms of overall trade balance, Myanmar's position has been positive.

Over the same period, Myanmar's exports to China rose at an average annual rate of 12 percent, while its imports from China increased at the rate of nearly 3 percent. The total cross-border trade between the two neighbors grew at an average annual rate of 6.1 percent. Among Myanmar's cross-border trading partners in the Mekong, China is the largest exporter to and importer from Myanmar; China's share in Myanmar's total cross-border trade increased from 54.5 to 75.6 percent during the period. Yunnan's (China's) imports from Myanmar include fish and fisheries, beans and pulses, fruits, paddy, maize, and rattan, whereas Myanmar's imports from Yunnan are raw materials (cotton yarn), manufactures (fertilizer, dry cell batteries, office paper, cigarettes, textiles), machinery and equipment (tractors, diesel engines, transformers).

In contrast to the trade flows between Myanmar and China, trade between Myanmar and Thailand declined between 1992–1993 and 2001–2002: exports from Myanmar to Thailand, at the rate of 1.3 percent; and imports, at 2.4 percent. Informal cross-border trade, however, appeared to thrive. After 2002 the formal border trade between the two improved significantly because political relations

Table 6.3: Myanmar's Formal Border Trade Flows in the Mekong Region, 1992/93–2000/01 (US$ million)

Country	Item	1992–1993	1995–1996	1996–1997	1997–1998	1998–1999	1999–2000	2000–2001	Average Annual Growth Rate (%)
Total	Exports	104.7	43.2	58.4	155.0	146.3	196.4	212.5	9.3
	Imports	249.9	292.8	298.7	102.1	154.0	148.0	196.3	-3.1
	Total	354.6	336.0	357.1	257.1	300.3	3444	408.8	1.8
	Balance	-145.2	-249.6	-240.3	52.9	-7.7	48.4	16.2	n.a.
Yunnan	Exports	54.8	22.0	30.1	86.4	104.1	108.9	136.1	12.0
	Imports	138.5	229.3	158.4	59.4	126.9	130.5	173.5	2.9
	Total	193.3	251.3	188.5	145.8	231.0	139.4	309.6	6.1
	Balance	-83.7	-207.3	-128.4	27.1	-22.8	-21.5	-37.4	n.a.
	Exports	40.4	16.0	20.4	52.1	24.1	50.1	36.5	1.3
	Imports	102.6	47.4	124.1	31.2	24.9	14.3	17.4	-24.8
	Total	143.0	63.4	144.5	83.3	49.0	64.4	53.9	-13.0
	Balance	-62.2	-31.4	-103.7	20.9	-0.8	35.8	19.1	n.a.
As % of Total									
Yunnan	Exports	52.3	51.0	51.5	55.8	71.1	55.5	64.0	
	Imports	55.4	55.4	53.0	58.2	82.4	88.2	88.4	
	Total	54.5	54.5	52.8	56.7	76.9	40.5	75.7	
Thailand	Exports	38.6	38.6	34.9	33.6	16.5	25.5	17.2	
	Imports	41.1	41.1	41.5	30.6	16.2	9.7	8.8	
	Total	40.3	40.3	40.5	32.4	16.3	18.7	13.2	

Note: Mathematically, a country's exports to the importing country's imports should be equal. However, owing to different national recording systems and the FOB (free on board) and CIF (cost, insurance, freight or charged in full) shipping systems, the two figures are usually not the same.

Source: ADB, *Country Economic Report: Myanmar*, Vol. 2: Statistical Appendices, December 2001: 34.

between them warmed up. In terms of total cross-border trade, Myanmar grew at an average annual rate of only 1.3 percent mainly due to frequent trade policy changes in Myanmar and political tensions between Thailand and Myanmar. For the same reasons, Thailand's share in Myanmar's total cross-border trade decreased from 40.1 percent in 1992–1993 to 17.3 percent in 2000–2001. It is important once again to note that the data on cross-border trade does not include informal trade (smuggling), which is substantial. Myanmar imports animal and vegetable oils, footwear, organic chemicals, vehicles, knitted and crocheted apparel, plastics, electrical machinery and equipment from Thailand, while Thailand imports live animals, fish and crustaceans, edible vegetables, raw hides and leather, ores, slag and ash, oil seed, oleaginous fruits, and machinery from Myanmar.

Cross-border trade from the Thai side of the border

During the period 1991–1999, as shown in Table 6.4, Thailand's total cross-border trade grew at an average annual rate of 25.6 percent, whereas its total exports to and total imports from fellow riparian countries increased at 37.7 percent and 6.3 percent, respectively. Throughout the period except in 1999, Thailand enjoyed a positive trade balance.

After Cambodia formed a coalition government following the general election in 1992, cross-border trade between Thailand and Cambodia grew substantially, from a total of just US$12.7 million in 1991 to US$493.6 million in 1999—an increase of 58 percent. Cambodia's share in Thailand's total cross-border trade also increased from four percent in 1991 to 24.9 percent in 1999. During the period Cambodia was the second largest border trade partner of Thailand after Laos.

As for the Thai-Lao trade, the relationship is akin to the colonial bond: one supplies raw materials to the other, which in turn imports back manufactured consumer goods. Like Thailand's other neighbors, Laos' border trade with Thailand increased significantly since the country shifted to a market-oriented economy in the late 1980s. The total cross-border trade between the two increased from US$142.7 million in 1991 to US$1,094.6 million in 1999—an annual increase of 29 percent. Laos quickly emerged as Thailand's largest border trade

Table 6.4: Thailand's Formal Border Trade Flows in the Mekong Region, 1991–1999 (US$ million)

Country	Item	1991	1994	1995	1996	1997	1998	1999	Average Annual Growth Rate (%)
Total	Exports	129.5	752.4	822.6	903.1	1,192.9	792.3	1,671.6	37.7
	Imports	190.3	257.7	279.1	158.9	227.7	96.2	310.2	6.3
	Total	319.9	1,010.1	1,101.7	1,062.0	1,420.6	887.5	1,981.8	25.6
	Balance	-60.8	494.7	534.5	744.2	965.2	696.1	1,361.4	n.a.
Cambodia	Exports	1.9	260.2	334.2	362.7	306.7	300.1	463.0	98.9
	Imports	10.8	126.3	160.1	56.8	102.2	24.4	30.6	5.7
	Total	12.7	386.5	494.3	419.5	408.9	324.5	493.6	58.0
	Balance	-8.9	133.1	174.1	305.9	204.5	275.7	432.4	n.a.
Laos	Exports	79.0	280.1	317.8	346.1	491.1	333.8	876.4	35.1
	Imports	63.7	58.7	77.6	81.0	96.3	42.5	218.2	16.6
	Total	142.7	338.7	395.4	427.2	586.4	376.2	1,094.6	29.0
	Balance	15.3	221.4	240.2	265.1	394.8	296.3	658.2	n.a.
Myanmar	Exports	48.6	212.1	170.5	194.3	395.1	158.4	332.2	27.2
	Imports	115.8	72.7	41.4	21.1	30.2	28.3	61.4	-8.3
	Total	164.5	284.8	212.0	215.4	426.3	186.7	393.6	11.5
	Balance	-67.2	139.4	129.1	173.2	364.9	130.1	270.8	n.a.
As % of Total									
Cambodia	Exports	0.2	34.6	40.6	40.2	25.7	37.9	27.7	n.a.
	Imports	5.7	49.0	57.3	35.7	44.9	25.7	9.9	n.a.
	Total	4.0	38.3	44.9	39.5	28.8	36.6	24.9	n.a.
Laos	Exports	61.0	37.2	38.6	38.3	41.2	42.1	62.4	n.a.
	Imports	33.5	22.8	27.8	51.0	41.8	44.6	70.4	n.a.
	Total	44.7	33.5	35.9	40.2	41.3	42.4	55.2	n.a.
Myanmar	Exports	37.5	28.2	20.7	21.5	33.1	20.0	19.9	n.a.
	Imports	60.8	28.2	14.8	13.3	13.3	29.7	19.8	n.a.
	Total	51.4	28.2	19.2	20.3	29.9	21.0	19.9	n.a.

Source: Thailand Department of Customs, *Thailand's Border Trade*, 2000.

partner, with its share of the total border trade of Thailand rising from 44.7 percent in 1991 to 55.2 percent in 1999. Thai exports to Laos at the Mukdahan-Savannakhet checkpoint consist of vehicles, electrical machinery and equipment, mineral fuels, fertilizers, salt, cement, and pharmaceuticals, among others. For its part Laos exports such articles as oilseed, oleaginous fruits, cotton, wood and wooden articles, live animals, carpets and floor covering to Thailand.

Like Thailand's border trade with Cambodia, that with Myanmar depends heavily on political relations between the two and trade policy changes in Myanmar. Generally, total cross-border trade between Thailand and Myanmar increased at an average annual growth rate of 11.5 percent between 1991 and 1999. During the same period, exports from Thailand increased at the rate of 27.2 percent annually, while imports from Myanmar contracted at the rate of 8.3 per cent per annum. The total cross-border trade between the two increased from US$164.5 million in 1991 to US$393.6 million in 1999, an increase of 11.5 percent over the period. At the same time, however, Myanmar's share in Thailand's total cross-border trade declined from 51.4 percent to 19.9 percent. Border tensions between the two countries in 2001 and 2002 adversely affected Thailand's exports to Myanmar.

Laos-Vietnam and Yunnan's cross-border trade

Trade across the border of Laos and Vietnam increased significantly between 1991 and 1999, as shown below. At their border checkpoint, Lao Bao, formal border trade grew at an annual rate of 27.6 per cent during this period primarily because both countries moved toward a market-type economy at almost the same time. At the border, Vietnam exports cement, construction steel, livestock, sawn timber and marble to or through Laos; Laos exports gypsum to Vietnam.

Table 6.5. Laos-Vietnam Total Formal Cross-Border Trade (at Lao Bao), 1991–1999 (US$ million)

Year	1991	1992	1993	1994	1995	1996	1997	1998	1999
Value	86.6	54.9	62.8	158.7	108.1	122.3	334.2	148.9	607.5

Source: ADB, *Pre-investment Studies: Trade and Investment, Final Report*, Vol. 1-6, February, 2001.

Yunnan's formal border trade with the Mekong, on the other hand, tends to be underestimated. Though outdated, the data in Table 6.6 suggests the importance of certain articles of trade and Yunnan's trading partners.

Table 6.6: Yunnan's Formal Cross-border Trade with Mekong Countries,* 1991 (US$ '000)

Exports	Laos	Myanmar	Thailand	Total
Cereals and oils	10	--	--	10
Local produce for industry	--	--	80	80
Light industry products	40	7,240	5,990	13,270
Machinery	550	11,730	720	13,000
Others	180	--	--	
Sub-total	780	18,970	6,790	26,360
Imports				
Radio equipment	--	--	200	200
Pesticide	--	--	900	900
Others	--	19,800	--	19,800
Sub-total	--	19,800	1,100	20,900
Grand Total	780	38,770	7,890	47,260

Note: * Yunnan-Vietnam border trade figures are not available.

Source: ADB, *Subregional Economic Cooperation: Initial Possibilities for Cambodia, Lao PDR, Myanmar, Thailand, Vietnam and Yunnan Province of PRC*, Manila, 1993.

As shown above, Yunnan's border trade with Laos in 1991 amounted to less than one million dollars. Informal trade actually outweighed formal border trade and imports from Yunnan were not even recorded. In the mid-1990s, imports of vehicles from Laos (as a transit point) were very popular and made huge profits. Similarly, Yunnan's exports to and imports from Myanmar are highly underestimated. In 1988–1989, for example, the total Myanmar-Yunnan border trade was recorded at US$273.6 (ADB 2001a, 34), whereas Table 6.6 shows only US$38.77 million in 1991. In the informal as well as formal trade, Myanmar imports mostly consumer goods and exports various agricultural and forest products (see Table 6.3 for updated statistics on Myanmar-Yunnan trade).

Unlike Yunnan's trade with Laos and Myanmar, that with Thailand is conducted via the Mekong River. The Yunnan-Thailand border trade is also large, though inclined to be under-reported. In 1991, for example, the total volume of border trade was reported at a mere US$8 million. Exports from Yunnan consist of raw materials, vegetables and consumer goods. Yunnan also imported chemicals and pesticides from Thailand in 1991. According to the Thai Farmers Bank Research Center, over the period of January–June 2002 alone, Thailand exported 1,110 million baht (about US$26 million) worth of goods and imported 270 million baht (about US$6.5 million) worth of commodities.

Statistics on the Yunnan-Vietnam border trade are not provided because published data in English on the 1980s is either not available or inaccessible. But trade did take place, considering the common land border (1,350 km) between six Vietnamese provinces and two Chinese autonomous regions (Yunnan and Guangxi[6]), and border trade agreements between Vietnam and China. Among the latter, the two outstanding ones were the Temporary Agreement on Border Trade (1991) and the Agreement on Trading in Border Areas (1998). Official sources put the trade between Vietnam and China in 1992 at around US$320 million, with some 70 percent of it estimated to be a result of smuggling (Mya Than 1996).

Yet another kind of cross-border trade takes place between Yunnan and the Mekong countries. Known as the 'transit trade', the final destination of goods is not the immediate border but another country beyond it. For example, vegetables and fruits from Yunnan cross the Myanmar border checkpoint and then enter Thailand through the Myanmar-Thai border checkpoint and vice versa. Yunnanese traders pay a transit tax to Myanmar customs in addition to the Thai customs tax. Statistics on the transit trade are intermittently available because most of it is registered as formal border trade since most traders attempt to evade the transit tax. In the early 1990s, highly visible items such as cars and motorcycles were smuggled from Thailand to Yunnan through Myanmar and Laos. The smugglers had to pay the transit tax (mostly 5 percent customs duties) to the transit countries. The trade was accompanied by rampant corruption.

A study of the cross-border trade brings up many interesting faces and types of people. In the case of Myanmar, experts and personal observation point to at least six types: former big-time black market players and dealers (*daings*); people allowed to trade as a reward by the authorities; private businessmen with export and import permits; people with good connections who trade freely without legal permits; small traders who had been involved in the illegal border trade; and carriers who transport goods between Myanmar and neighbouring countries. It is also worth noting that many, if not the majority, are young women, especially in the last two types, perhaps because of their traditionally accepted role as traders and entrepreneurs. Also, young boys are used as carriers.

Investments flows

Foreign direct investment (FDI) in the region has expanded since the economic transformation of the Mekong's formerly planned economies. The Asian countries, not the West, are the largest investors in the region except in Thailand. For this reason, when Asia was hit by the financial crisis in 1997, FDI inflow into the Mekong countries slowed down. Since most of the largest investors in the Mekong countries are East Asian countries including the original ASEAN member countries, almost all of the riparian countries were affected. Nonetheless, as a whole, the Mekong region's FDI grew rapidly at an average annual rate of 20.7 percent between 1991 and 1999.

Table 6.7: Foreign Direct Investment in the Mekong Countries, 1991–1999
(US$ million)

Country	1991	1992	1993	1994	1995	1996	1997	1998	1999
Cambodia	---	33	54	69	151	294	204	121	126
China	4,366	11,156	27,515	33,787	35,849	40,180	4,4237	4,3751	3,8753
Laos	7	8	30	59	95	160	86	45	79
Myanmar	238	172	105	126	277	310	382	315	216
Thailand	2,014	2,113	1,804	1,366	2,068	2,336	3,895	7,315	6,213
Vietnam	229	385	1,002	1936	2,349	2,455	2,745	1,972	1,609
Total	20,772	26,012	46,492	58,182	65,723	76,884	83,034	91,619	93,758

Source: ADB, *Key Indicators* 2001: 71.

Except for investments from Thailand, most investments in the region are directed at tourism and the extraction of natural resources. During a meeting of leaders from Europe and ASEAN in Bangkok in March 1995, participants from both sides expressed interest in supporting infrastructure projects in the Mekong, including the railway line linking Europe and Asia proposed by Malaysia. However, the financial crisis in the region and the inclusion of Myanmar in ASEAN set back these plans (Mya Than 1997).

Intra-regional FDI is another important aspect of economic cooperation. Thailand is the largest investor in the Mekong followed by China. Thus far Myanmar, Laos, Cambodia and Vietnam have not invested in any of the riparian countries mainly because of their weak economies. Thailand is the largest investor in Laos (US$2,296.6 million as of end 1995) and the third largest in Myanmar (US$1290.89 million as of end February, 2003) after Singapore and the United Kingdom. Thailand is also the one of the largest investors in Vietnam (US$700 million as of November 1996).

Table 6.8: Intra-Mekong Foreign Direct Investment, Various Years (US$ million)

Investor	Myanmar[a]	Thailand[b]	Yunnan[c]	Laos[d]	Vietnam[e]	Cambodia[f]
China	58.50	525.2	n.a.	38.1	71.0	72.9
Thailand	1,290.89	--	33.5	2,296.6	700.0	0.9
Myanmar	n.a.	0.03	--	--	--	0.03
Total	1,355.49	525.2	33.5	2,334.7	771.0	73.803

Notes: As of 28 February 2003
[b] 1986–1994, [c] 1994, [d] End 1995, [e] As of 13 November 1996, [f] End December, 1995

Sources: Myanmar Central Statistical Organization, *Selected Monthly Economic Indicators*, February 2004, Yangon; Cambodian Investment Board, August 1994; Permanent Office of the Foreign Investment Management Committee, Lao PDR; State Committee on Cooperation and Investment, Vietnam, 1994; Ministry of National Planning and Development, Myanmar, 1995; and Yunnan Nien Jian, Yunnan, China, cited in Mya Than 1997.

China's FDI in Myanmar is underestimated, accounting for only US$58.5 million as of February 2003. Its beer factory, cigarette factory and casinos operating in Mongla, a border town on the Myanmar-Yunnan border belie this figure. China has also invested in Laos and Cambodia. Myanmar, on the other hand, has slight investment in Laos. On the whole, intra-regional investment in the region exists but is small by international standards. The ADB encourages joint investments especially in infrastructure, such as the East-West Economic Corridor road project connecting Mawlamyine in Myanmar to Da Nang in Vietnam, passing through Thailand and Laos, with investments from these countries.

Although FDI laws of the GMS countries are relatively liberal and attractive, and there is an abundance of natural and human resources in the region, investment inflows are nevertheless slow due to the lack of infrastructure, inefficient bureaucracies, and the impact of the 1997 regional financial crisis on the top investors—who also happen to come from the more developed ASEAN economies.

The Mekong as a single tourist destination

The fact that the Mekong hosts some of the world's greatest cultural treasures and is still perceived as a 'last frontier' makes the region a major historic and natural tourist attraction. The Mekong countries are aware that tourism plays an important role in generating much needed foreign currency and contributing to economic growth and employment. Although the six member countries of the GMS region do have varying degrees of tourism programs and facilities, the potential associated with a distinct regional grouping surpasses that of any individual country. Tourism is also one of the few industries that can encompass the entire Mekong region and convert it into a single destination for tourists. New vacation packages, airfare deals, and easier access to and within the Mekong area are some of the strategies that can encourage tourism. It is no surprise that tourism today is emerging as an important industry in the GMS.

Since the early 1990s, tourist arrivals in most Mekong countries have increased significantly. Notwithstanding the short period since the opening of the borders and the lack of infrastructure and support services, the performance of the tourist industry has been impressive. This is partly because there is institutional support from several sources at the regional and national levels. At the regional level are the Working Group of the Greater Mekong Subregion Tourism Sector, supported by the ADB, the Agency for Coordination of Mekong Tourism Activities, and the Pacific-Asia Travel Association. Their activities include marketing, training, management of natural and cultural resources, and facilitation of travel. At the national level are organizations devoted to tourism in individual Mekong countries, such as the National Tourism Authority of Lao PDR, the Ministry of Hotel and Tourism of Myanmar, the Tourism Authority of Thailand, the Vietnam National Administration of Tourism and similar tourism organizations in Cambodia and China.

Tourist arrivals and projected estimates of arrivals by year and by country are presented in Table 6.9 from 1992–2003. Of the total projected arrivals in 2003, Thailand would account for 63 percent. Tourist arrivals in the region are expected to grow at an average annual rate of 10.4 percent. A study projected an average growth of about 7 percent per annum in tourist arrivals, or about 23 million in the year 2007 (Thailand Institute of Scientific and Technological Research, quoted in ABD 2001, Vol. 5). This high growth projection arises from the economic transformation of Cambodia, Laos, Myanmar, and Vietnam, the expansion of air routes and tourism promotion activities.

Table 6.9: Tourist Arrivals and Arrival Projections[a] in the Mekong, 1992–2003

Year	Thailand	Yunnan	Myanmar[b]	Laos	Vietnam	Cambodia	Total
1992	5,136	132	153	87	440	75	6,023
1993	5,761	405	155	103	600	118	7,142
1994	6,167	522	185	146	1,018	177	8,215
1995	6,952	597	203	347	1,351	220	9,688
1996	7,192	752	314	403	1,607	261	10,529
1997	7,832	839	313	480	1,929	312	11,704
1998	8,362	946	349	567	2,238	359	12,821
1999	8,893	1,052	387	654	2,546	406	13,938
2000	9,423	1,159	423	742	2,854	453	15,056
2001	10,483	1,266	460	829	3,163	501	16,173
2002	11,014	1,373	497	917	3,472	548	17,290
2003	11,543	1,480	543	1,004	3,780	595	18,407

[a] Estimates made in 1997.

Sources: Thailand Institute of Scientific and Technological Research, cited in ADB 2001, Vol. 5; Myanmar, Central Statistical Organization, *Selected Monthly Economic Indicators*, Yangon.

Laos has experienced a significant increase in tourist arrivals since 1992 (from 87,000 in 1992 to 480,000 in 1997—an increase of about 40 percent), when the government started to implement the policy of promoting tourism. According to its National Tourism Authority, 346,000 foreign tourists visited Laos in 1995 and the number increased to more than half a million in 1998. The tourism sector contributed US$80 million in 1998 compared with US$40 million in 1997 (ibid., 11).

Myanmar, in contrast, has recorded the lowest tourist arrivals in the Mekong for political and security reasons. The European Union, for one, and some human rights groups imposed sanctions on Myanmar because of its human rights record. Between 1994–1995 and 2001–2002, an average of 267,180 tourists arrived in Myanmar by air, sea and land. On average, tourists stayed seven days and spent some US$80 a day. In all, the tourism sector earned more than US$67 million in 1996–1997 (Myanmar Ministry of Tourism, 1997) partly because of the government's promotion, "Visit Myanmar Year", in 1996.

As with other transitional economies of mainland Southeast Asia, Vietnam's *Doi Moi* opened up its economy in the late 1980s. Since then, the tourist sector has grown significantly in terms of foreign visitors and earnings from tourism. The Vietnam National Administration of Tourism reported 93,000 foreign visitors in 1988 and 1.8 million in 1999 (ADB 2001, 5), putting the average annual growth rate at about 30 percent. In 2000, the number of tourist arrivals grew to 2.15 million, mainly owing to 'software' improvements such as the grant of visa-free status to tourists from selected countries, cuts in visa fees, simplification of visa categories, improved access with new air linkages between Vietnam and major cities in Asia, active participation of the country in regional tourism cooperation schemes, and improvement in skills of tourism personnel. Improvements were also undertaken in the 'hardware' section, such as better accommodation and tourism facilities.

Of all the Mekong countries, Thailand stands out as the leading tourist attraction, occupying one of the top 20 tourist destinations in the world and with tourism contributing heavily to the country's GDP. In 2000 Thailand received about 9.5 million foreign guests, an increase of 11 percent over the previous year and nearly five times the equivalent figure for Laos, Myanmar and Vietnam combined (ADB 2001, Vol. 5, 13). This growth is attributable to Thailand's mature and robust tourist industry, which is backed by domestic economic growth. Travel restrictions are few; tourist attractions, easily accessible; tourist facilities (accommodation, better network of transportation), good and reasonably priced; and workers in the industry, highly skilled. Geography no doubt helps, given Thailand's position as the gateway to the region, and so does relative political stability. The majority of tourists in 1998 came from East Asia (60 percent of the total)—Japan tops the list, followed by Europe (23 percent), and North America (6 percent).

Table 6.10: Arrivals by Country of Tourist as Percent of Total Arrivals,
Various Years

Tourist	Cambodia[a]	Thailand[b]	Myanmar[c]	Laos[b]	Vietnam[d]	Yunnan[a]
Australia	3	1	5	--	--	13
China	8	2	4	27	n.a.	11
France	3	9	9	5	--	17
Germany	4	7	4	--	--	--
Hong Kong	3	--	--	--	45	--
Japan	13	11	7	6	5	5.3
Korea	5	2	--	--	--	--
Malaysia	12	5	--	--	--	--
Singapore	6	5	--	--	13	12.8
Taiwan	7	19	n.a.	9	--	--
Thailand	n.a.	6	19	--	15	14.8
UK	6	4	9	3	--	--
USA	5	6	11	12	5	3.5
Vietnam	--	--	11	n.a.		
Others	25	23	25	37		

[a] 1993, [b] 1998, [c] 2000–2001, [d] 1999

Source: ADB, *Economic Cooperation in the Greater Mekong Subregion*, 1996: 141–146;
and Mya Than 1997.

Like Thailand, Yunnan province of China has performed
remarkably well in the tourism sector, with tourist arrivals growing
from 131,462 in 1992 to 1,266,262 in 2001, an increase of 29 percent
per annum. This is a surprising achievement for Yunnan, a landlocked
and backwater province in southwest China, and can be explained
by the introduction of market-oriented reforms, transportation
networks, training of tourist guides and development of tourist
facilities. Most of the tourists in 1993 came from Hong Kong, Macau,
and Taiwan; overseas Chinese constituted 45 percent of all foreign
tourists. The remaining tourists came from Thailand (14.8 percent),
Singapore (12.8 percent), Japan (5.3 percent), and lastly, 3.5 percent
from the United States (Mya Than 1997, 52).

Cambodia's tourist arrivals between 1992 and 2003 were also
impressive, increasing from 75,000 in 1992 to 595,142 in 2003—an
average annual rate of increase of 48.8 percent. Transportation
networks in the country improve year after year; accommodation is

rapidly expanding, accompanied by human resource development in the tourism sector since the late 1990s. Reduced travel restrictions and visa regulations have also spurred growth. In 1993, the majority of tourists were from France (16.7 percent), followed by Australia (13.1 percent), China (11.1 percent), and Japan (7.7 percent). Tourism in Cambodia is expected to play an ever-increasing role in the country's economy.

Intra-Mekong tourism is also gaining momentum as Thais and Chinese, in particular, travel more and more to their Mekong neighbours (Table 6.10). Plans for tourism promotion in Cambodia, Laos, Myanmar and Thailand are based on Buddhist religious, cultural and heritage sites, whereas Yunnan's ethnic cultures and natural beauty are its main attractions.

On the other hand, tourism in the Mekong region (except in Thailand) suffers from several constraints, such as the lack of information about tourist sites, inadequate accommodation and basic facilities, absence of a legal framework for tourism development, and weak private sector participation. Apart from basic facilities, numerous aspects of tourist infrastructure—transport, quality standards, safety, security, and travel and customs regulations—remain obstacles to the rapid development of the industry. Unless addressed, these issues will slow down tourist arrivals and reduce potential earnings from tourism.

Impact of cross-border economic cooperation

The end of the Cold War opened the opportunity for economic cooperation in the Mekong region. The old bloc of East (Vietnam, Cambodia, Laos and China), West (Thailand) and Non-Aligned (Myanmar) have been replaced by ASEAN, the GMS and ASEAN+3 of which China is part. Moreover, China signed the ASEAN Treaty of Amity and Cooperation, binding it to cooperate with ASEAN in political, security, economic, and social matters. These arrangements have, of course, encountered problems arising from historical baggage, border disputes and refugees. But as demonstrated earlier, cross-border trade, investment and tourism have on the whole improved substantially.

The impact of intra-regional and cross-border cooperation is felt most strongly in the border towns, cities and villages. New buildings mark the landscape and property prices are rising. For example, in

Tachilek on the Myanmar side of the Myanmar-Thai border, one square foot of land in the early 1990s cost about 200 baht (Dana 1994, 72), 15 times that a decade ago. In Thailand's Chiang Rai city, real estate prices increased up to 20 times between 1990 and 1993. In Maesai, Thailand, just across the Myanmar town of Tachilek, it is no longer possible to buy land within half a kilometer of the frontier (ibid.). Many in Myanmar complain that those buying land and buildings in prime urban sites in the upper part of the country are Chinese from the border areas. Economic growth without equity among the races constitutes a social time bomb, especially in Mandalay, the former capital of Myanmar.

The uneven distribution of gains from cross-border trade applies to individual member countries of the GMS as well. For Laos and Myanmar, flows of goods at border points, against the claim of mutual benefits, tend to favour China and Thailand by siphoning out precious raw materials in exchange for a flood of consumer goods. In the course of these exchanges, border areas in Laos and Myanmar are developing closer links to Kunming in China and Chiang Rai and Maesot in Thailand than to the more distant capitals of Vientiane or Yangon (Mya Than 1996).

Opening the Mekong borders has led to other deleterious effects: illegal migration, illegal labourers, refugees, cross-border prostitution, human trafficking, spread of HIV/AIDS and sexually transmitted diseases, and environmental degradation. Of these, illegal migration is open to conceptual challenge. Viewed from a nation-state perspective, it is patently illegal, but from a regional standpoint, it is not quite so. Most migrants are from Cambodia, Laos, Myanmar, and Yunnan; and Thailand is, not surprisingly, their main recipient. There are approximately 1.5 million documented migrant workers in Thailand and 165,497 undocumented workers from Myanmar alone (Asian Migration Centre 2002, 39). The latter are sometimes caught at border checkpoints.

In 2003, Thai immigration authorities arrested 280,937 illegal migrants, mostly from Myanmar (*Bangkok Post*, 5 January 2004). Of the total number, 189,486 were illegal migrant workers, 115,633 of whom were Myanmar nationals; 54,738 came from Cambodia; and 19,115, from Laos. Of the remaining 91,451 illegal migrants, 52,781 were Myanmar nationals, 23,700 were Cambodians and 6,098, Laotians. A portion of migrant activity involves the sex trade. In addition to migrants, estimates of refugees in Thailand run to as high as 100,000 (ibid., 142).

Cambodia, too, receives illegal immigrants, though on a much smaller scale. The estimates run to some 70,000, including overstayers and smuggled people. Out of the total immigrants (both legal and illegal) inside Cambodia as of 2002, about a million were from Vietnam and 55,000 were Chinese citizens (ibid., 52).

Yunnan hosts a relatively low number of refugees (29,230 in 1998), coming from Myanmar, Vietnam and Laos. Laos, in particular, appears to be a large human exporter. In March 2002, more than 42,000 Laotians were documented as working outside the country (mostly in Thailand) and about 100,000 were undocumented migrants. At the same time, Laos also plays host to illegal immigrants, mainly from China and Vietnam, although their numbers are minimal. There are no official figures on illegal migrants, illegal workers and refugees in Vietnam (ibid., 114).

Another negative result of cross-border movements is the spread of HIV/AIDS and sexually transmitted diseases. In the Mekong region, these diseases pose a serious health problem with potentially disastrous economic and social implications. So far, China has the largest number of victims of HIV/AIDS numbering 600,000; Thailand, 755,000; Myanmar, 530,000; Cambodia, 220,000; Laos, 1,400; and Vietnam, 100,000 (ibid., 4). Among the six riparian countries, the rate of increase of HIV/AIDS is highest in Cambodia at 2.8 percent (*ADB Review*, November–December, 2002).

Drug trafficking has also increased with infrastructure improvements in the region where opium production is based. Myanmar alone produces an average of 350–450 tons a year and traffickers find Thailand an ideal springboard for drug trafficking. Although opium production has been reduced in some areas, the production of the whole 'golden triangle' area seems intact. Trafficking of heroin, an opium derivative, to South Asian countries such as India and Bangladesh has also increased significantly. Even the Mekong River has not escaped the drug trade route (Lintner 1991, 1–4).

In addition to drug trafficking, women and children are illegally transported and traded in the region. The Asian Migration Centre (2001, 171) reports that Thailand has become the major hub for human trafficking from neighbouring countries. More than 3,000 Vietnamese women are said to be trafficked annually across the national borders to China; 1,428 women were recorded to have been trafficked to Cambodia in 1995–1996.

The impact of cross-border cooperation on the environment is another serious issue. Already complaints have arisen regarding the effect of dams and hydropower stations along the Mekong River on both local and downstream inhabitants of the Mekong basin. Despite these concerns, Yunnan continues to build eight more dams and blast rocks along the river in order to sell electricity to Thailand from 2013. Yunnan also has a US$30 million project to blast away the Mekong River rapids near the Yunnan-Laos-Myanmar border. These blasting of rapids and dams have a negative effects on fisheries, vegetable gardening along the river banks, paddy fields and the ecology of the river, affecting the livelihood of 60 million people in the downstream countries. Some experts argue, however, that the magnitude of the effect of rapid-blasting remains inconclusive since only 20 percent of the water comes from China. Note also that Thailand, Laos and Vietnam are increasingly drawing water from the Mekong River to support the expanding farmlands converted from tracks of forests.

Finally, there is the issue of the "centre-periphery" relationship that challenges the notion and practice of nationhood. While one could expect such a challenge to arise from regionalism, whether in the form of a cooperation agreement or a binding union, on the ground the challenge has greater implications. Cross-border movements and exchanges link border towns and peoples of neighbouring countries more closely and exacerbate the distance between these towns and their respective capitals. In the process, new centres are emerging that could compete with, and at various levels of, the nation-state.

Issues and challenges

Regional cooperation does not sweep differences under the rug. Sometimes, cooperation heightens these differences especially if they remain unattended. The Mekong region already suffers from historical baggage. Though no longer a violent ideological battlefield, political differences hound the region on some sort of spectrum, with Myanmar at one end, having to answer to charges of human rights violations, and Thailand at the other, enjoying relative political stability (at least compared with its neighbours). In between are communist states struggling to forge some kind of democracy. Also, there are still territorial disputes among members, for example, between Thailand and Myanmar, Cambodia and Thailand, Cambodia and Vietnam, not to mention the maritime disputes between Vietnam and China. At times, there have even been armed clashes, though limited to border areas, as in 1997, 2001 and 2002 on the Myanmar-Thai border.

As suggested earlier, the status of the nation vis-à-vis the region is a challenge that every member country of the Mekong must address. One can accept as natural a country's resistance to giving up part of its national sovereignty. But when an entire river is shared by six countries, not to mention the borderland areas, the management, use and distribution of shared resources become potentially controversial issues that not only heighten national interest but also block cross-border infrastructure and financial cooperation (Mya Than and Abonyi 2001, 160). This explains why the most important regional development projects have taken place within national boundaries rather than across the region. Moreover, the complexity of the Mekong region's multi-country, transborder nature, and its varied political, legal and economic environments make project preparation and implementation difficult (ibid.).

There are also organizational issues that spring from different political management styles. The transitional economies, for example, are still run by control-oriented governments and their bureaucracies have not changed. Designed to prevent abuse, these bureaucracies are not, however, efficient. As a result, delays in the approval and implementation of projects are not uncommon. State-owned enterprises, in addition, still stifle competition and nurture economic inefficiency.

The economic issues are just as challenging. Accounting systems in the Mekong region vary, and foreign investors must adjust to them. Legal systems in the transitional economies are ambiguous and not always transparent; clear-cut property rights are needed as well as laws relating to companies, bankruptcy, and monopolistic practices. More serious are the differences in the level of development of the GMS countries, making economic integration a distant possibility. Consider ASEAN, for example. It took the Association 25 years to create the ASEAN Free Trade Association and 11 years after its founding, AFTA has yet to be implemented in a substantive way. The GMS economic cooperation could take longer because of the particular requirements of the transitional economies. In addition, the infrastructure in most Mekong countries is woefully inadequate. Roads are poor and power, telecommunications and water supply, still in the early stages of development. These conditions raise the costs of projects since investors would have to provide back-up power, water and other utilities. Apart from the need for 'hard' infrastructure, tariff and non-tariff issues must also be addressed, including pricing policies, foreign exchange controls, procurement policies, and the role of state enterprises trading monopolies ('software issues'). Furthermore, there is the risk of severe debt since multilateral development loans for regional infrastructure projects involve large amounts. Debt management, therefore, is an urgent consideration.

Against this backdrop of challenges and difficulties, one must however consider that four of the GMS countries are now full-fledged members of ASEAN and China has formally bound itself to the ASEAN Treaty of Amity and Cooperation. China (in 2002) and Myanmar (in 2003) became parties to the GMS Cross-Border Land Transportation Facilitating Agreement. In addition, Thailand, Myanmar, Laos and Cambodia formed an Economic Cooperation Strategy to enhance intra-group trade and eventually pull Myanmar, Laos and Cambodia out of poverty while addressing economic and political problems in border areas. Some could argue, of course, that these are merely agreements that need to bear fruit. But in fact, some already are albeit to a small degree. The Thailand-China free trade agreement, for example, cut tariffs on fruits and vegetables in October 2004 as an early harvest of the free trade agreement. These recent developments are incremental steps that help create a more conducive environment for intra-Mekong regional economic cooperation. Considering its not too distant past of conflict and warfare, huge steps have no doubt been taken to improve life in the Mekong region.

Notes

1   The terms "Mekong Region" and "Greater Mekong Subregion" (GMS) are used interchangeably.
2   The rationale for a growth triangle is to exploit the economic complementarities of geographically contiguous areas to achieve accelerated economic development through the inflow of foreign investment, development of infrastructure, joint development of common natural resources, and/or promotion of industries for the export market (Chia 1993).

References

Asian Development Bank (ADB). 1993. *Subregional Economic Cooperation: Initial Possibilities for Cambodia, Lao PDR, Myanmar, Thailand, Vietnam and Yunnan Province of the People's Republic of China*. Manila: ADB.

————. 1996. Unpublished papers from the Sixth Conference on Subregional Economic Cooperation in the Greater Mekong Subregion, Kunming, 28–30 August.

————. 1996. *Economic Cooperation in the Greater Mekong Subregion: Facing the Challenges*. Manila: ADB.

————. 2001a. *Key Indicators 2001: Growth and Change in Asia and the Pacific*. Manila: ADB.

————. 2001b. *Preinvestment for the Greater Mekong Subregion: East-West Economic Corridor*. Vols. 1–6. Manila: ADB.

————. 2001c. *Country Economic Report: Myanmar*. Manila: ADB.

————. 2002a. *Asian Development Outlook*. Manila: ADB.

————. 2002b. *ADB Review* 35, 6 (November–December).

Asian Migration Research Center. 2002. *Migration: Needs, Issues and Responses in the Greater Mekong Subregion*. Bangkok: AMRC.

Bradley, D. 1994. "Languages: The Tool of Trade in the New Circles of Growth." Paper presented at the conference, Asia's New Growth Circles, Chiang Mai, 3–6 March.

Central Statistical Organization (CSO), Myanmar. 2004. *Selected Monthly Economic Indicators* (February). Yangon: CSO.

Chia Siow Yue and Lee Tsao Yuan. 1993. "Subregional Economic Zones: A New Motive Force in Asia-Pacific Development." In *Pacific Dynamism and the International Economic System*, edited by C. Fred Bergsten and Marcus Noland, pp. 225–269. Washington, D.C.: Institute for International Economics.

Ministry of Finance, Thailand. 2000. "Thailand's Border Trade". Bangkok: Customs Department, Ministry of Finance.

East Asia Analytical Unit (EEAU). 1997. *The New ASEANs: Vietnam, Burma, Cambodia and Laos*. Canberra: Department of Foreign Affairs and Trade.

————. 1995. *Growth Triangles of Southeast Asia*. Canberra: Department of Foreign Affairs and Trade.

International Monetary Fund (IMF). 2000. *Direction of Trade Statistics Yearbook 2000*. Washington, D.C.: IMF.

Lintner, Bertil. 1991. *Cross Border Drug Trade in the Golden Triangle*. Durham: Boundaries Research Press for the International Boundaries Research Unit, Department of Geography, University of Durham.

Mya Than. 1996. "The Golden Quadrangle of Mainland Southeast Asia: A Myanmar Perspective." Singapore: Institute of Southeast Asian Studies Working Paper No. 5.

———. 1997. "Economic Co-operation in the Greater Mekong Subregion." *Asian-Pacific Economic Literature* 11, 2 (November): 40–57.

Mya Than and George Abonyi. 2001. "The Greater Mekong Subregion: Co-operation in Infrastructure and Finance." in *ASEAN Enlargement: Impacts and Implications*, edited by Mya Than and Carolyn L. Gates, pp. 128–163. Singapore: Institute of Southeast Asian Studies.

Mya Than and Y.P. Woo. 1997. "A River Runs through It: Peace Brings the Promise of Growth to the Mekong." *Asia Insights* 1, 3 (November).

Organization for Economic Cooperation and Development (OECD). 1993. *Regional Integration and Developing Countries*. Paris: OECD.

Chomchai, Prachoon. 1995. "Transboundary Protection of the Environment: A Mekong Perspective." Paper presented at the conference on International Boundaries and Framework for Regional Cooperation, 14–15 June, Singapore.

Samram, C. 1996. "The Mekong Basin Development Plan." In *Development Dilemmas in the Mekong Subregion*, edited by Bob Stensholt. Clayton: Monash University Asia Institute.

Stensholt, Bob 1996. "The Many Faces of Mekong Cooperation." In *Development Dilemmas in the Mekong Subregion*, edited by Bob Stensholt. Workshop Proceedings. Clayton: Monash University Asia Institute.

Yunnan Statistical Yearbook 1991–1998. 1992–1999. Kunming: People's Publishing House of Yunnan.

7

THE ADB'S DISCOURSE ON POVERTY AND WATER

CHAIYAN RAJCHAGOOL

...since the world is going on, since research is proliferating, and on the other hand since God's share must be preserved, some failure on the part of Einstein is necessary....Einstein fulfils all the conditions of myth, which could not care less about contradictions so long as it establishes a euphoric security: at once magician and machine, eternal researcher and unfulfilled discoverer, unleashing the best and the worst, brain and conscience, Einstein embodies the most contradictory dreams, and mythically reconciles the infinite power of man over nature with the "fatality" of the sacrosanct, which man cannot yet do without.

Roland Barthes, *Mythologies*

The agenda

Being both the architect of the concept and the arbiter of development of the Greater Mekong Subregion (GMS), the Asian Development Bank (ADB) has, and will continue to have, an impact on the region which goes beyond that of an international financial lending institution that is pouring large sums of money into the region. Its influence is not confined to the sphere of socio-economic change but also extends into the realm of ideas. It is, therefore, important to try to understand the Bank's objectives, its mode of thinking, and of working, in particular on the issues of poverty reduction and water management.

Given the plight of the poor and the extent of poverty in the GMS, the interest in poverty reduction is self-explanatory. Water management, on the other hand, is a component of the overall ADB water policy as well as part of its integrated approach to poverty reduction, in particular in terms of rural and agricultural development (ADB 2004, passim). The ADB's working ethos and approach to development can thus be examined through its perspective on poverty reduction and its corollary, water management. Additionally, water as both symbol and substance is of utmost importance to the GMS because all the member countries are "tied" to the Mekong River, and the river system and its water resources are at the core of all livelihoods in the region.

This essay examines the ADB's policy statements, using discourse analysis to focus on the structure of the Bank's arguments, its modes of reasoning and ideological assumptions. The essay points out the inherent and troubling contradictions between the assumptions of the Bank's prescriptions and its pro-poor or "people-centred development" policies, which threaten to render the ADB's anti-poverty programs ineffective, amongst other things.

Discourse in a nutshell

The concept of "discourse" as a methodological device is helpful for it allows us to see a certain logic in the agenda and mission of important actors in the GMS. With the interconnection between thought and practice, the discursive approach reveals views (ideas/beliefs/attitudes)-cum-actions, which could be applied to individual as well as organizational actors.

"Discourse", however, is not a straightforward concept. The proliferation of meanings and hair-splitting debates on the concept of discourse make its application a daunting task. Borrowing heavily from the guru of the concept, Foucault discourse here is defined as a body of statements in which ideas and values are ingrained and form relationships with other statements (see Danaher et al. 2000; Smart 2002; Kendall and Wickham 1999; Brown 2000; Hall 2001). Together, these statements articulate the conditions for evaluating truth and regulating practices within a certain field or discipline. For example: "Water is a socially vital economic good," says the ADB. (The assertion is not necessarily shared by the peasant or the ecologist, who may each have their own statements.) It is juxtaposed with other statements such as, "Capacities need to be sustainably built to manage water use more efficiently." As more and more statements are joined together, they constitute a certain way of "making sense" of and "seeing" things. This is a process ("construction of subjectivity") by which an entity (in this instance the ADB) presents a certain, distinctive way of formulating ideas.

Put in another way, discourse is about the production of knowledge. As discourse constructs the topic, it defines and produces the objects of our knowledge, directing the way the topic can be discussed and understood. Discourse also influences how ideas are put into practice and used to regulate the conduct of others. Each field, though not independently of one another, has its discourse (e.g., development discourse, US foreign affairs discourse, academic discourse). Since all social practices entail meanings, which shape and influence what we do, all practices have a discursive aspect. In short, discourse here is taken to mean "a system of statements within the world and by which the world can be known" (Ashcroft and Ahluwalia 2001, 14) and upon which action/interaction occur.

The GMS itself provides a good example. The region as a geographical, ecological (and to some degree, cultural) space has always been there. But when it was "amalgamated" into a social, political and economic arena by the ADB, it became a new configuration endowed with new meaning. The implication is that the disappearance of antagonisms across political, economic and other systems in the region will reaffirm the region's natural geographical dimension. In other words, the physical entity can become "natural" only when the "unnatural"—the socio-eco-political repositioning—has come into play.

There is, too, the view that development can take place only when the enmity among the different socio-political systems in the region has subsided. For example, in line with the ADB's outlook:

> The region is enjoying a relatively unprecedented era of widespread peace between the countries in which geographical, ecological, social, cultural, political and economic links are being reconsidered and evaluated....The Mekong Region's abundant natural resources, such as water, forest, fisheries, biodiversity, minerals and energy,... provide enormous wealth creation possibilities. Those who hold this view see the potential economic benefits from the use of some of these resources as still untapped. (Kaosa-ard and Dore 2003, 1)

What the statement in fact means is that it is high time to bring these countries formerly outside the capitalist sphere into the orbit so that their natural resources can be exploited, more investments launched, business ventures entered into, and so on. Moreover, once the walls are no longer there, the resources, especially transboundary water resources and water from rivers or reservoirs, can also be "shared" (siphoned off from one to another). As a result, higher profits can be made. This is the process that underlies the invention of the "Subregion".

The Mekong is thus used as metonym for the GMS: as both reality and trope, the Mekong indicates and symbolizes the region. The demarcation of the region is a construct, starting with its initial imagination as a spatial concept, and then engaged with practice, evolving into "a spatial reality". This is known as "discursive practice".

"Discourse analysis" has metamorphosed in two directions. On the one hand, it has become highly theoretical and used in conjunction with other complex concepts (ideology, culture, consciousness). On the other hand, it has been loosely applied to everything from highly sophisticated ideas such as madness, civilization, power, and democracy, to simpler notions like advertising catchphrases.

In the wider context of the development of ideas, no organization, let alone individual, is entirely its own creation of ideas. The ADB has inherited ideas and concepts from various sources, and works and decides in the course of intellectual exchange and negotiation within the larger intellectual and ideological climate. This context of ideas can be equated with what Foucault called the "episteme", which is, in Hall's words, "the way of thinking or the state of knowledge at any one time" (Hall 2001, 73).

With or without self-awareness, the ADB lays down development rules and procedures, ways of thinking and reasoning, all relating to what can be said and what is or is not valid. For instance, it links poverty reduction and water management and subsequently produces a certain kind of knowledge that helps the organization formulate policies and actions such as its water pricing policy. In terms of our analysis here, the ADB's discourse on poverty and water management, backed by its formidable funding capacity (over the region that it has "constructed"), enables it to put its own policies and ideas into practice, giving that discourse ever more of a hold over the region, and so on. In short, with the invention of the GMS, the ADB has assumed a more influential role over this new entity, providing credit and assistance to GMS-related programs to the tune of more than US$2 billion since 1992, with about half of this devoted to poverty reduction.

Poverty: the business of definition and identification

For the poor and those with direct experience of poverty, poverty is self-evident. However, for those (usually outside the poverty realm) whose tasks are to reduce poverty, the concept seems to need a precise definition. The importance given to these efforts to define poverty has turned a seemingly easy-to-understand matter into a large, complex enterprise. Like all phenomena, poverty can be looked at from different angles that are multi-dimensional and historically and culturally bound. Since a definition is an abstraction of realities, being diverse and wide-ranging in essence, any definition of poverty rarely finds common agreement. The lack of agreement fundamentally lies in differences of perception: poverty can be assigned into the polarity of a "subjective view" at one end and an "objective reality" at the other. The underlying assumptions determine different positions within this spectrum, and hence different approaches to poverty.

In the last three decades the field of "poverty studies" has flourished. In addition to a wealth of data from case studies around the globe, some new theoretical grounds have been established, addressing the questions of how poverty can be accurately identified and explained, respectively. The first is principally divided between the above-mentioned polar assumptions, while the second has its own assumption of how socio-economic phenomena are conceptually and causally related, namely, by structural determinants or by actor attributes.

Let us consider first the question of identification. Among the social science disciplines, economics pioneered and still dominates poverty studies, developing indices to define poverty in terms of income and consumption, each with a poverty line as the benchmark to indicate the state of poverty. The income index adopts the monetary measure of the standard of living, with "a-dollar-a-day" poverty line. The consumption index, in contrast, sets the poverty line in terms of calorie consumption (2,100 calories of energy and 58 grams of protein per person per day) plus some allowance for non-food intake such as clothing and shelter (SEDP-II 2001, 1). Due to the exclusion of non-economic facets of poverty, critics of these perspectives have labeled the indicators "income poverty" and "consumption poverty".

Of the two, the income index is better known and more popular among practitioners in the field of poverty reduction, even as both indices ultimately point to the same requirement, namely, a certain level of food intake required to sustain life. Other more novel and telling poverty indices, such as the Gini coefficient,[1] are not as popular as the easily grasped notion of a minimum earning. Despite the shortcomings of the income index, it is often applied for practical comparative reasons.

Furthermore, the income perspective sees itself as a science. Grounded on massive data and measurements, it tries to steer clear of what it regards as subjective views or biases. Hence its defense is that it represents "the objective worldview" which is compatible with the principle of science (verifiable reality). Critics of this perspective point out its narrowness in terms of applicability to developing countries, and in terms of theorizing, its reductionist tendency, given its emphasis on statistics. The index overlooks non-measurable qualitative factors such as mortality from illness, homelessness, unsafe environments, social discrimination and exclusion, lack of participation in decision-making and in civil, social and cultural life, all of which are other internationally recognized parameters of poverty (e.g., Copenhagen Declaration of the World Summit of Social Development 1995).

It is rather curious how the basis of the income perspective—"a-dollar-a-day" —was made. There are two major problems with the methodology and resulting conclusions here. First, it falls into the notion of "one size fits all". Second, its underlying assumptions are contentious. Physical consumption is naturally related to a number of attributes, such as age, gender, type of food, life activities, life expectancy, etc. All these vary according to culture and history. On the question of longevity and quality of life, for example, who can say how long a human life should last and in which way one should spend one's life.

In addition, the very unit of analysis may be called into question. Whether person or household, the unit is taken to be individualist, without regard for the social configurations of an individual's life. Thus, contrary to its claims of objectivity, the income index approach does not present an objective picture of social reality or indeed of poverty. It ignores the social and cultural facets of humanness. In the final analysis, then, different views of poverty can be seen to be grounded in theories of what constitutes a human being, a fact that rarely finds space in studies of poverty.

Economists' explanations of poverty generally fall into two camps: structural and behavioral. The structural explanation emphasizes power relations, the distribution of resources, and the socio-political and economic mechanisms by which opportunities and deprivation work differently on different categories of people. This position examines the macro-economic impact of institutionalized systems in seeking the essential remedy to poverty.

The behavioral explanation sees the characteristics of people (individual attributes, styles of life, motivation, etc.), and culture as the important link with, if not the cause of, poverty. If the structural perspective sees the radical reorganization of the distribution and production system to redress poverty—a strategy that would require state intervention, the behavioral perspective, on the other hand, is generally critical of the role of the state in economic intervention. Too much intervention would, according to behaviorists, discourage people's own efforts, distort market forces, and institutionalize dependency on government.

Between these two poles a number of positions can be seen. If all the causes are attributable to the structure, the role of agency is altogether disregarded. But to attribute all the blame to individuals or groups of people is to negate the power of gigantic institutions and ongoing exploitative conditions. The dichotomous way of thinking does not correspond well to the complexity of realities. The phenomena of poverty are multidimensional and multi-layered, which is why the search for a definitive definition has proved futile. So is the search for a definitive explanation. Since each position can always be criticized from another viewpoint, a variation of combined positions would be more acceptable.

Returning to the questions of identification and explanation raises an underlying concern: in Mingsarn Kaosa-ard's words, it is "...not how poverty is measured, but how poverty is created" (Kaosa-ard 2003, 94). The ADB has impressively capitalized on scholarship in the field, going beyond the monetary measure of poverty into the more considered notion of consumption, and even looking at how the poor themselves, rather than professionals and academics, view poverty. The ADB poverty studies on Laos and Cambodia—*Poverty Diagnostics Study: Lao People's Democratic Republic* (ADB 2000); and *Participatory Poverty Assessment in Cambodia* (ADB 2001)—are good illustrations.

In both studies, the ADB applied "Participatory Poverty Assessments" (PPA) in order to obtain indigenous views of poverty. PPA adherents believe that knowledge and understanding of poverty ought to come from the poor themselves so that key poverty issues in specific places are correctly identified. They do not believe in a general definition of poverty, but in the specific and culturally bound nature of the meaning of poverty.

The Cambodia study focuses on what the poor are concerned with, namely: lack of food security, life crises (e.g., bad health and illness, flood and drought), lack of assets, little or no access to land, water and basic services, poor physical infrastructure, and decreasing access to hitherto shared natural resources. They are also affected by social exclusion and the erosion of family and community relationships. These findings are solidly grounded in the lives of the poor. In the case of Laos, in addition to deficiencies in health and lack of income, the important characteristics of poverty include such notions as helplessness, vulnerability, geographical remoteness, feelings of inferiority, and social isolation.

In both case studies, accounts of poverty differ from those worked out by professionals. On the one hand, the self-perception of the poor—the "actor's orientation"—is believed to be more illustrative than the definitions by professionals. Given that the phenomena of poverty are multidimensional and complex, they cannot be easily simplified or reduced to a singular facet. The representation of poverty through the eyes and senses of the folk could also lead to strategies far more effective than those promulgated by states or corporate bodies.

On the other hand, the PPA suffers from methodological flaws. Data collection is unsystematic and the data itself too specific to a site/community and highly qualitative. The tendency toward subjectivity is thus apparent. To solve problems of poverty, reality must be testable and falsifiable in the Popperian sense of the term.

As with the earlier polar positions, neither position is complete or fully able to define, explain or account for poverty. The point of this exercise is to provide the broader context in which positions taken by the ADB are negotiated and concluded.

Poverty Reduction

Poverty reduction is the ADB's overarching goal, its vision of the Asia Pacific region being one rid of poverty. "All of ADB's other goals and strategic objectives should contribute to poverty reduction" (ADB 1999, 1). The terms "poverty alleviation", "reduction" and "eradication" are of recent appearance for in the past, ideas of working for the betterment of the poor were expressed in terms of development, improving the conditions of the deprived, raising the standard of living for low income groups, targeting the have-nots, and so on. Aside from the ADB, other international organizations like the UNDP, UN-ESCAP and the World Bank have embraced the new term, and while some institutions lean more toward advocacy and others, actual practice, the ADB is both vocal and active in the arena of poverty reduction.

The ADB's Lao and Cambodian case studies, which apply the PPA, illustrate the organization's thinking and practice. The Laotian case study links the characteristics of poverty as perceived by the poor with the causes of poverty, but the case study of Cambodia is silent on the causes of poverty.

Let us start with the study of Laos. Here the causes of poverty are attributed to "restrictions to earning". The list of restrictions is comprehensive, with water, land, insects, drought, flood, credit, knowledge, and transport ranking highly. As viewed by the poor, poverty is caused by conditions within the realm of their direct experience. The wider issues at the macro (sometimes "global") level, described as structural factors of poverty, often lie beyond their plane of perception and understanding. Generally these causes, such as competition in the world market and international trade agreements that affect the prices of poor people's produce, are not readily apparent in the community field of vision. For this reason, local/community explanations of poverty could limit the solutions to poverty.

Understandably, the ADB formulates its concept of poverty and poverty reduction differently from perceptions on the ground. Well informed in the field of poverty research, the organization defines poverty broadly and quite simply as the state of deprivation. People are being denied what they are entitled to, which is defined in terms of ownership of, opportunity for and accessibility to education, health care, nutrition, water and so on, ending with income, jobs, and wages (ADB 2004, 5).

Consciously or not, it is interesting that the monetary aspect is at the end of the list of entitlements. Moreover, the chapter opens with the mistakes of the past and then proceeds to the right path, as it were.

In the past, ADB relied heavily on income level as the basic measure of poverty. However, there is now universal agreement that dimensions of poverty far transcend this traditional definition. In ADB's view, poverty is a deprivation of essential assets and opportunities to which every human is entitled. Everyone should have access to basic education and primary health services....(ADB 2004, 2)

A textual analysis of the full passage reveals three parts to it: the statement of having been in the wrong, the statement of the (universal) truth, and the statement of the correct(ed) view. Precise and concise in its composition, the passage moves from negation to confirmation. This form is akin to a confession in which one states the sin of the past, the (absent) priest preaches the divine truth, and the sinner amends his/her way. One's wrong is thereby righted and the sin, absolved, and the forgiven now sets out to perform the virtuous deed.

While the text above suggests a paradigm shift and hints at a new course of action, the next passage reverts back to the old quantitative indices for practical (comparative) reasons:

In practice, the most broadly used standard for measuring poverty will continue to be the adequate consumption of food and other essentials. This yardstick (the poverty line) varies from country to country, depending on income and cultural values. While national measurements are essential for measuring the impact of efforts to reduce poverty, ADB's priority is on absolute poverty, and international comparisons will also be necessary. (ADB 2004, 2)

Hence the yardstick is not only still regarded as "universal"; the economic and monetary aspects, which appear last in the list of entitlements in the earlier passage, appear to be the overarching criteria.

The conception of poverty reduction also offers a curious domain to explore the heart and mind of the bank. In the same text, ADB states:

For all stakeholders, the strategies chosen to reduce poverty must be comprehensive enough to address all of its many causes. For this reason, ADB sees the *twin pillars* of pro-poor, sustainable economic growth and social development as the key elements in any framework for reducing poverty. Successful achievement of either element requires sound macroeconomic management and good governance, the third pillar. Together the three pillars result in socially inclusive development. (ADB 2004, 2, emphasis added)

Although management and good governance are presented as a third pillar, they are essentially presented as a requirement for the success of the two other, presumably more important, pillars. Curiously though, another text by the ADB sums up the foregoing statement as "*three pillars* of interrelated themes: pro-poor sustainable growth, social development, and good governance" (ADB 2003, 4; emphasis in the original), with governance taking on equal significance as the first two. Perhaps the difference is merely a matter of semantics but if construed as a difference in emphasis, there could be an effect on the strategy.

A comparison with the Second Socioeconomic Development Plan 2001–2005 (SEDP-II) of Cambodia is instructive. The SEDP-II poverty reduction strategy is built on three main pillars: economic growth that covers sectors where the poor obtain their livelihood; social and cultural development; and the sustainable use of natural resources. Support for these pillars is expected to come from a package of reforms in governance (p. 15). In other words, the prime edifice on which the SEDP-II goals rest is the mechanism of the state. In contrast, the ADB elevates management and governance to the same level as the other pillars of sustainable growth and social development even as it refers to governance as a requirement for economic and social development.

Perhaps because of Cambodia's painful experiences, the SEDP-II sees the achievement of poverty reduction predominantly in the realm of the political. It is in this arena where poverty is to be fought and the measures for poverty reduction, crafted. Indeed it has been often argued that in the last analysis, poverty is a political problem manifested in socio-economic phenomena. While the ADB does mention good governance as one of three pillars, the SEDP-II relies on governance reforms as the key to attaining its three main objectives. The discourse of SEDP-II on poverty reduction, in terms of direction and the degree of emphasis, is therefore political. ADB discourse, on the other hand, places management and good governance on another terrain not quite as fundamental as that of SEDP-II. Placed along with other pillars, it suggests a matter of (technical) adjustment rather than that of significant change ("reform"). Compared with SEDP-II, ADB's discourse on poverty reduction is tilted toward the realm of economics.

Furthermore, SEDP-II identifies poverty indicators drawn from the views of the poor and their corresponding key areas of work. The correspondence enables a convergence of policies and action plans.

However, such correspondence is absent in the ADB documents, for while views of the poor about poverty are solicited, the strategies for poverty reduction do not reflect a correspondence between poverty indices and what is to be done to alleviate poverty.

Even as the ADB cites poverty reduction as its "overarching goal", it does not seem to have an "overarching" discourse on poverty and poverty reduction. There are a number of ADB discourses such as those on economic efficiency/strategy, resource development, the legal framework of development, and national socio-economic policy, including those of the Washington Consensus. While these discourses are evidently very broad and encompassing, the question remains as to how all these relate to the primary objective of poverty reduction.

For example, documents show that the ADB outlook varies from the conventional belief in trickle-down effects to more progressive views in favor of social development. What is consistent is the ADB focus on economic growth, derived from a simple and logical proposition: the antonym of "to reduce" is "to grow". Hence to reduce poverty is to make wealth grow. In terms of logical validity this reasoning is beyond dispute. Combating poverty is seen through an economic perspective and consequently, by economic means.

Given this perspective, the matter of wealth distribution—which could stimulate poverty reduction (certainly in terms of relative poverty)—is not amply discussed. Other issues that have bearing on poverty reduction, particularly in the GMS, are the deterioration of natural resources (partly due to population pressure and partly to policies and institutions that govern the use of natural resources); conflicts between customary rights and national laws, between national policies and certain international projects; allocation of public resources to large construction projects rather than social investments; unequal distribution of the benefits from globalization; tension between development-oriented and the protection-oriented agencies; the participation of people in decisions and projects that directly affect them; and adverse effects of large-scale projects on certain communities (Kao-sard and Dore, ibid., 103–4).

What is also of interest here is ADB's outlook on Asia as a whole as displayed in the *Asian Development Outlook 2001* (ADB 2001a). As in a painting, its perspective places all the countries in Asia (except Japan) at the rim of the frame, with the economies of the United States, Japan, and Europe at the center. A prominent stroke is the 11 September 2001 terrorist attacks on the United States, which is placed right at the beginning of the introduction, overshadowing the strokes and color of the economies of Asia. The picture of Asian economies is thus cast within an American-centric composition and each country is merely portrayed as a variation on the theme.

The same publication situates the United States not just as a context within which each Asian country operates, but as the organizing principle of Asian economies. This, however, is not (and should not be) the only possible way of constructing Asian economies. In contrast to the American-centric cast, for example, one could examine the impact of the Asian crisis in 1997 on Cambodia, which was much greater than other international economic forces. In the case of Thailand, the rupture of the bubble economy, which changed the label of Thailand overnight from an emerging roaring tiger to a moaning cat, had greater impact on the economy as a whole and that of the neighboring countries of Cambodia and Laos, than any international event (Chan Sophal et al., 1999). Noted Thai economists commonly argued that the main causes of the Thai financial disaster were internal institutional failures rather than the forces of globalization with the United States at the core. The United States is not the only context within which each Asian country functions. There are other overlapping contexts at different levels, and some are more powerful than others.

Water: fluid substance, solid problem

Turning now to water management as one of the solutions to poverty, water, like poverty, can be viewed from different angles and assigned different meanings, from being an economic commodity, to a production factor, to a gift of nature. These descriptions are not as innocent as they seem. If water is a production factor, for instance, it has a cost just like other production factors (fertilizers, pesticides). If treated as nature's gift, it should be freely utilized. Hence the definition can be as fluid as water itself.

Like the previous section, this one attempts to demonstrate the way in which the ADB constructs knowledge regarding water management. A general profile of the ADB's position here is necessary. Water management is necessary for the following reasons. Water supply in the Mekong is under threat not simply because of rising demand caused by population growth but also because of the injury to the environment. The quality of water is also deteriorating. Water resource management requires comprehensive national and regional water policies on conservation, resource allocation, environmental protection, equity, regulation, education, pricing, and efficient and sustainable use. Water resource management can also be considered a strategy of poverty reduction and access to water by means of sound water management to benefit the poor is high on the ADB agenda (ADB 2001, passim).

Based on this reasoning, the ADB's water policy, as explained by McIntosh, aims to: (i) promote national focus on water sector reform, (ii) support the integrated management of water resources, (iii) improve and expand the delivery of water services, (iv) conserve water and increase system efficiencies, (v) promote regional cooperation and increase the mutually beneficial use of shared water resources within and among countries, (vi) facilitate the exchange of water sector information and experiences, and (vii) improve governance (McIntosh 2003, 18).

The ADB discourse is premised on water scarcity; hence the necessity of efficient water management. The management, in turn, is to be worked out from both the demand and the supply sides. As with poverty reduction, the fundamental premise is the definition of water. The ADB sees water as a good or commodity which carries a price. The economic perspective, however, is not the only angle from which to view water management. As has been argued, water management issues are rooted in interactions between water resources and environmental, cultural, institutional and social determinants in a complex way (Moench et al. 1999). A well-known study of the introduction of irrigation in southern India has shown the changes water can bring to villages (Epstein et al. 1998). People with stronger means gain far greater benefits than those with slender means. Land adjacent to the water supply changes hands usually at the expense of the poorer owner. Water management without the foresight of equitable development may not result in poverty reduction but the reverse.

The ADB publication on water, *Water for All: The Water Policy of the Asian Development Bank* (2001), is the bank's key statement on water management. It lays out, in ADB's own words, "a comprehensive water policy that recognizes the Asia and Pacific region's need to formulate and implement integrated, cross-sectoral approaches to *water management and development*" (emphasis in the original). Unless otherwise indicated, the quotes in this section are from this publication. The features of the ADB discourse on water are examined in the following section.

Noble in preamble, marketing in means

The preamble opens with an assertion of the link between access to water and the condition of poverty. "The poor are particularly vulnerable when water is either unclean or in short supply. The Asian and Pacific region is home to nearly 900 million of the world's poorest people; accessing adequate clean water is one of their principal concerns" (ADB 2001, 1). In support of this noble objective, the document cites the types and amount of assistance the ADB has extended to the water sector (more than US$15 billion or about 19 percent of the banks" total lending). To translate these aims into action, the ADB applies marketing means; for example: "...ADB needs to promote efficiencies in water use by supporting demand management, including water pricing" (ibid., 12).

Water pricing is not the sole measure but one among others, such as an effective legislative framework for water user rights, and the empowerment of communities. But for the poor, it is the pricing measure that is contentious and here, small-scale farmers and farm tenants do not share the view of the ADB. Price and value are, to them, different things. The former is adhered to by the bank, the latter by the folk.

The ADB foresees that demand will continue to outpace supply. Consequently, demand cannot be curbed if "water is treated as a social, not an economic good." This view is premised on a cost/benefit analysis of a market economy. If water could be used for higher yield, why waste it on relatively less productive purposes?

A price charged on water use can be regarded either as a fixed tax or a service charge but both pose practical and conceptual problems. More important, they rest on unsound assumptions. However, as Molle points out in his manuscript of a well substantiated empirical research project (2001), this does not mean that regulation and intervention are unnecessary or that the principle of free access should prevail. It is the line of reasoning that is called into question here. With respect to Thailand, for example, Molle argues the following:

- farmers do not *guzzle* water but have been very responsive to water scarcity;
- water shortages are caused by *management failures*, not by the lack of water per se;

- farmers do not use water free of charge because on top of excessive taxes imposed on the agricultural sector, they have to invest in pumping devices to access water;
- the function of a water market is not preferable to the system of (state) centralized allocation;
- the operating costs are not as high as they are made out to be (it amounts to 0.61 percent of the national income) and could be considered an indirect subsidy to an already heavily taxed agricultural sector (emphasis added).

Molle concludes that affixing a water fee to volumetric use will have no effect on water use efficiency. Moreover, the supply of water cannot be guaranteed either in terms of quantity or timing.

Following the ADB perception of water as a marketable good, water users will then be related to and within a water market that is hardly ever equitable. Taken in light of the preamble's noble aims, the means do not match the objective.

Water management in a water-tight regime

As the mainstream neo-liberalist argument goes, since the construction and maintenance of water infrastructure cost money, beneficiaries should be responsible for the expenditures at least in part or, better still, in whole. The use of water at no cost entices an uneconomical treatment of water. Intervention and regulation are therefore imperative. A water fee, an essential component of the water pricing policy advocated also by ADB, should do the trick. As an ADB senior official put it, "...farmers have to share responsibility with governments [for] the cost of water provision." Then Thai Finance Minister Tarin Nimmanahaeminda, who chaired the ADB's board of governors, echoed this position in 2000, claiming that the people and the environment would benefit in the long run (Tadem 2003, 391). Yet other sectors like industry and tourism, in accordance with government policies, tend to receive better treatment. Recently, for instance, the Thai government spent huge amounts for tourist promotion but did not ask tour operators, hoteliers, and other related businesses to share the cost. Consider also the kinds of subsidies and investment incentives offered by some governments in the GMS that waive costs for industry in the name of national development.

It is also striking that the ADB starts off its discourse on the problems of water supply from a macro perspective at regional and even global scale, but when it comes to the matter of policy implementation, it considers only the micro level. On the other hand, micro measures could be informed by macro perspectives. Water pricing, for example, can be considered in the larger (universal) framework of water rights, but applied in conjunction with local water-users' input.

The ADB discourse on water management looks at the water situation and its relation to (some of) the water use variables, giving greater value to certain controllable variables over others. Hence the conclusion that water management by means of water pricing is an answer to the looming water crisis.

For their part, farmers are more often concerned with the fluctuation of farm prices that the ADB, in its present discourse on water and water management, may regard as given at least for the time being. The absence and presence of variables under consideration are pivotal to one's discourse and conclusion. Such variables as farm prices, farm subsidies (or the lack of them), farm-related taxes and the overall tax structure, and macro policy on the use of natural resources are overwhelmingly important for small-scale farmers. The ADB does recognize the relationship between water use and land use—"...today, food production can be efficiently increased by improving the utilization of water and other resources, rather than by expanding the land frontier" (2001, 2) —but precisely because of the connection between land and water uses and needs, the charge on water use will not be viable unless other burdens of the poor are addressed. The crisis of crop prices could be even more devastating than the water crisis. In the poor farmers' logic, land encroachment incurs less cost than investment in water use and soil improvement. In light of the ADB's professed objectives, the impact of competing needs on poverty ought to be of foremost consideration. But as things stand on the issue of water price, the farmers and the ADB are at odds with each other.

Conflict-free operation

While flood and drought are seen as "natural" occurrences, water use is a matter of how nature is related to human beings. Usually there is less water than required. If water is then to be used efficiently, it has to be managed carefully. The concerns of ADB's water management policy are "allocation, distribution, equity, conservation, pricing, regulation, education, participation, and sustainable use" (ibid., 9).

These aspects principally suggest the notion of some best possible way in dealing with a limited resource. There is a sense, too, that specific interests would be better served in the context of general interests and that the interests of different social sectors are in any case reconcilable. Throughout the text, there is no discussion of conflict in terms of interests or of rights, let alone of culture and other aspects. The text abounds with such terms as "partnership", "participation", "cooperation", "regulation", "the mutually beneficial use of shared water resources within and between countries", and so on. With the conspicuous absence of any anticipation of conflict, an essential component of policy operation, measures relating to conflict resolution are non-existent.

In addition, if the water problem is approached from the perspective of human/nature relations, water management becomes basically a technical matter. But if viewed from the standpoint of social relations, water management enters the socio-political terrain where different interests of diverse and stratified groups contest one another and conflict becomes ubiquitous. The socio-political dimension is complex for different kinds of conflicts take place in different circumstances, as human experience continually shows. While undoubtedly pleasant, a "conflict-free" orientation that prefers to see the win-win solution may not necessarily solve the problem.

Take the case of the farmers" recent protest against the ADB water price policy, which caught the bank unawares. The protesters' question was basic: In which way does the water pricing policy conform to the strategy of poverty reduction? Water pricing as a measure in the overall water management scheme may not yet be compatible with the present situation of inadequate water supply infrastructure, as demonstrated in Molle's thoughtful research. Good intentions turn sour when policies are formulated without substantial studies. The conviction of the ADB is evident in its comparative perspective.

Comparative argumentation

Statistical information such as that below is often used to draw a comparison and, if necessary, send off an alarm in response to an acute problem.

The pressure on water resources is compounded by Asia's limited freshwater endowments, which are among the world's lowest. South

Asia, home to over a sixth of the world's population, has the lowest level of water resources per capita. Its per capita availability of water has dropped by almost 70 percent since 1950. During the past 50 years, per capita availability has declined by 60 percent in North Asia and 55 percent in Southeast Asia. (ADB 2004, par. 5)

Globally, water withdrawals have increased by over six times during the last century, or at more than double the population growth rate.... Within the Asian and Pacific Region, water withdrawals are the highest in Central Asia (85 percent), followed by South Asia (48 percent), and Mongolia and northern PRC (25 percent). (ibid., par. 6)

The increasing use (or in banking terminology, withdrawal) of water will considerably upset the balance sheet ("ecological balance" in the text, the metaphor "balance" again conveying a familiar understanding in the banking business). Asia is already in the red. As a result, corrective actions are needed and prescribed by the bank.

Narrative Patterns

The ADB narrative starts off with an apocalyptic picture of the larger Asian region.

... Salinization and aquifer depletion are the typical consequences of overuse of water. Once fertile lands in India, Pakistan, and Central Asia have been laid waste due to salinization. It has driven small and marginal farmers into penury. Widespread water pollution has resulted in increased water scarcity; poorer public health; lower agricultural yields; and a declining quality of aquatic life in lakes, rivers, and coastal waters. Because the poor are often landless and farm marginally productive areas, forests get depleted, biodiversity is lost, catchment areas deteriorate, flooding is frequent, and groundwater recharge is diminished. Farm livelihoods, including those of the poor, become precarious and the poverty cycle is entrenched. Watersheds and ecosystems have been severely degraded in most countries of the region. (ibid.)

If this picture is not alarming enough, a stronger stroke is added.

... Floods and droughts are a common natural hazard in Asia and have strong links with water and its management. Watershed degradation (comprising mainly deforestation and soil erosion) and unplanned urbanization (where urban settlements disrupt natural drainage systems) are the two principal factors for flooding. Ill-conceived river improvements and flood control measures also exacerbate natural flooding. (ibid., par. 11)

The ADB's line of argument proceeds from a dichotomy between abundance and scarcity, wasteful withdrawals and efficient use, anarchy and sound management. Additionally, it magnifies the problem from "people" to "humanity": "...just as its abundance and efficient management enhance quality of life, its scarcity and wasteful use impact acutely on humanity" (ADB 2001, 1). The "calamities" (ADB's own word) are not merely of natural phenomena but also of bad management or no management at all. Without proper human intervention, countless numbers of human lives would be at great risk, as described earlier.

Riding a white horse, the ADB is endowed with a mission: "ADB has intervened actively in the water sector and financed projects for irrigation, drainage, flood control, water supply and sanitation, hydropower, fisheries, forestry and watershed management, navigation, or multiple uses" (ibid., 11). The ADB, too, knows better than most. "ADB will consistently advise governments of the need to adopt cost recovery principles in their water policies and strategies" (ibid., 27). Because the Bank's "perspective on water issues derives from a review of lessons learned from previous interventions in the sector, the distillation of good practices in the region and elsewhere, and current contexts" (ibid., 11). Naturally, the ADB will show governments the way out of the water crisis. One principal point of understanding is that water must be regarded as an economic good that comes with a price. As a matter of course the basic economist's reasoning is the rule of the game. To appreciate its "sense and sensibility", a lengthy quote is perhaps necessary.

> Conservation of water and its sustainable use are increasingly critical factors in managing a scarce resource. Governments and civil society need to see water as an economic good. Financial incentives for optimizing water use will be strengthened through a mix of water charges, market-based instruments, and penalties. Public awareness programs will reinforce the incentives. The incentives include water use rights, licenses and charges, tradable permits, effluent charges, water treatment fees, access fees, environmental liabilities, fishing rights, and tax incentives. Managing water demand is a function of

efficient pricing, effective regulation, and appropriate education and awareness. ADB will promote tariff reforms through its water-related projects and programs to modify structures and rates so that they reward conservation and penalize waste....Consumers will be expected to meet the full operating and maintenance costs of water facilities and service provision in urban and rural water supply and sanitation schemes subject to subsidy considerations. (ADB 2001, 26–27)

The "advice", however, is seen by social movements as an exertion by the bank of "its political leverage with client governments to impose far-reaching policy changes including sectoral reform, structural adjustment, privatization, and the removal of state subsidies and social services..." (Tadem 2003, 383). The bank's position is unassailable: "Evidence from scores of water projects shows that the poor are increasingly willing to pay for water services that are predictable and effective. Governments have been consistently mistaken in their assertions that charging farmers for irrigation services is not possible because of their inability to pay" (ADB 2001, 27). Perhaps for this reason it does appear to have been disconcerted by the farmers' protest. Notably, the bank offers no proof of the "scores of water projects" that show the poor's willingness to pay the water charge.

In any case, from the apocalyptic state of affairs, the ADB comes up with a (the?) solution.

In the past, few projects were derived from a comprehensive water resource strategy. Even fewer took account of other water uses in the project area. The emphasis was mainly on the productive use of water resources, with little attention paid to managing the resources themselves. To meet the increasing challenges of water scarcity, pollution, and degradation of watersheds and ecosystems, water and related resources need to be managed in an integrated manner. Integrated water resources management (IWRM) is a process to improve the planning, conservation, development, and management of water, forest, land, and aquatic resources in a river basin context, to maximize economic benefits and social welfare in an equitable manner without compromising the sustainability of vital environmental systems. (ibid., 19)

Furthermore, and the policy seeks to enhance the quality and productivity of water resources, by promoting national water sector reforms through a river basin approach to IWRM. This approach is also extended to a subregional and regional basis, in the case of transboundary river basins, recognizing that careful management of water resources is essential to achieve and sustain equitable, pro-poor economic growth. (ADB 2001, 36)

Using words coined in the school of international development agencies, the narrative pattern of the ADB discourse is very revealing. It begins with a message of doom, followed by an assertion of superior knowledge based on lessons the ADB acquired from the past. By means of the bank's prescriptions, the problems can be solved; disorder will be transformed into order.

In this sense the narrative structure is akin to a religious mode of narration. The two strong actors, sinner and savior, and the connection between them comprise the underlying line of the action story. Impending calamities are delivered with a threatening message (e.g., water scarcity, water-borne diseases are real and worsening); and failure to redeem oneself will make human downfall inevitable. The way to redemption is there, laid out by the bank, for enlightened governments and peoples to embrace. Embrace them or be damned!

A juxtaposition of religious text and ADB language suggests a well-crafted bank "theology".

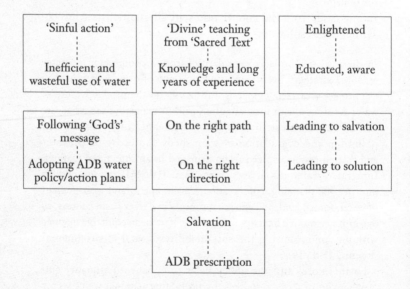

To reiterate, ADB's discourse on poverty follows contradictory modes of reasoning, i.e., market-oriented economics coupled with a kind of "ethical economics" (pro-poor orientation). The question, however, is whether the latter is to be subsumed under the former. Is pro-poor economics not really substantive but merely decorative? If decorative, one can see old wine in a new bottle, i.e., development discourse in the post-Cold War era. Similarly, the ADB's discourse on water, on the whole, has a dual nature. On one hand, it is unarguably well intended, but on the other, its frame of thinking and working are embedded in the system and method of business. With its head inclined toward profit and its heart toward the poor, the ADB faces its biggest challenge yet in carrying out its development mission.

Notes

1   A ready-made description can be taken from a quotation in *The International Glossary on Poverty*: "If we choose two people at random from the income distribution, and express the difference between their incomes as a proportion of the average income, then this difference turns out to be (on average) twice the Gini Coefficient: a coefficient of 0.3 means that the expected difference between two people chosen at random is 60 per cent (2 x 0.3) of the average income. If the Gini coefficient is 0.5 then the expected difference would be the average income itself" (Gordon Spicker 1999, 71).

References

Asian Development Bank (ADB). 1999. *Fighting Poverty in Asia and the Pacific: The Poverty Reduction Strategy*. Manila: ADB.

———. 2000. "New Challenges for Social Development," Proceedings of the Regional Social Development Advisors' Meeting, 23–24 November 2000, Social Development Division, Office of Environment and Social Development, Manila.

———.2000a. *Water for All: The Water Policy of the Asian Development Bank*. Manila.

———.2000b. *Poverty Diagnostics Study: Lao People's Democratic Republic*. Manila.

———.2000c. *New Challenges for Social Development*, Proceedings of the Regional Social Development Advisors' Meeting, 23–24 November.

———.2001a. *Asian Development Outlook 2001 Update*. Manila.

———.2001b. *Participatory Poverty Assessment in Cambodia*. Manila.

———.2003. *ADB-Government-NGO Cooperation*. Manila.

———.2004. *Fighting Poverty in Asia and the Pacific: The Poverty Reduction Strategy of the Asian Development Bank*. Manila.

Ashcroft, Bill and Pal Ahluwalia. 2001. *Edward Said*. London: Routledge.

Barthes, Roland. 1970. *Mythologies*. Paris: Seuil.

Brown, Alison Leigh. 2000. *On Foucault*. Belmont: Wadworth/Thompson Learning.

Chan Sophal et al. 1999. "Impact of the Asian Financial Crisis on the SEATEs: The Cambodian Perspective." Working Paper 12, Cambodia Development Resource Institute in collaboration with the Cambodian Institute for Cooperation and Peace, Phnom Penh.

Danaher, Geoff et al. 2000. *Understanding Foucault*. London: Sage Publications.

Gordon, David and Paul Spicker, eds. 1999. *The International Glossary on Poverty*, London: Zed Books.

Epstein, T. Scarlett et al. 1998. *Village Voices: Forty Years of Rural Transformation in South India*. New Delhi: Sage Publications.

Hall, Stuart. 2001. "Foucault: Power, Knowledge and Discourse." In *Discourse Theory and Practice*, edited by Margaret Wetherell et al., pp. 72–81. London: Sage Publications.

Kaosa-ard, Mingsarn and John Dore, eds. 2003. *Social Challenges for the Mekong Region*. Chiang Mai: Chiang Mai University Social Research Institute.

Kendall, Gavin and Gary Wickham. 1999. Using Foucault's Methods. London: Sage Publications.

Mafeje, Archie. 2001. "Conceptual and Philosophical Predispositions." In *Poverty Reduction: What Role for the State in Today's Globalized Economy?*, edited by F. Wilson et al., pp. 15–32. Cape Town: Cooperative Research Program on Poverty (CROP), International Studies in Poverty Research and New Africa Education Publishing.

McIntosh, Arthur C. 2003. *Asian Water Supply Reaching the Urban Poor*. Manila and London: ADB and International Water Association.

Ministry of Planning. *Second Socioeconomic Development Plan 2001–2005 (SEDP-II)*. 2001. Phnom Penh: Royal Government of Cambodia.

Moench, Marcus et al. 1999. *Rethinking the Mosaic-Investigations into Local Water Management*. Jaipur: Institute of Development Studies.

Molle, François. 2001. *Water Pricing in Thailand: Theory and Practice*. Bangkok: Kasetsart University Doras Centre.

Sangkhamanee, Jakkrit. 2003. Charting the Mekong: A Configuration of the GMS "Geo-body" for Development. Paper presented at the Regional Center for Social Science and Sustainable Development International Conference, "Politics of the Commons: Articulating Development and Strengthening Local Practice." Chiang Mai University, Thailand, 11–14 July.

Smart, Barry. 2001. *Michael Foucault*. London: Routledge.

Tadem, Teresa. 2003. "Thai Social Movements and the Anti-ADB Campaigns." *Journal of Contemporary Asia* 33 (3): 377–398.

Wilson, Francis et al. 2001. *Poverty Reduction: What Role for the State in Today's Globalized Economy?* London: Zed Books.

World Bank/The International Bank for Reconstruction and Development. 2001. World Development Report 2000/2001: Attacking Poverty. Oxford: Oxford University Press.

ABOUT THE AUTHORS

Maria Serena I. Diokno is a Professor of History and former Vice President for Academic Affairs of the University of the Philippines. She obtained her doctorate in History at the School of Oriental and African Studies, University of London. Recent publications include articles on the history of imperialism in Southeast Asia, perspectives of Southeast Asian studies in the region, history and identity studies, and memory, power and the construction of history. She is a co-founder and leading member of SEASREP (Southeast Asian Studies Regional Exchange Program). She also sits on the International Steering Committee of SEPHIS, a South-South exchange program for research on the history of development.

He Shengda is a Professor at Yunnan University, Vice President of the Yunnan Academy of Social Sciences and Vice President of the Association for Southeast Asian Studies in China, and Special Research Fellow at the Center of Economic and Technological Studies, Government of Yunnan Province. His publications deal with relations and economic cooperation between ASEAN and China (Yunnan). He received his bachelor's degree in history from Yunnan University.

Armando Malay, Jr is Associate Professor at the Asian Center, University of the Philippines Diliman and was formerly Dean of the Center. He specializes in Southeast Asian history and politics, with a focus on Vietnamese history and contemporary foreign relations in the region. Published in both French and English, he obtained his master's degree in Asian Studies at the University of the Philippines and his doctorate in history at the Université de Paris VII.

Mya Than is Visiting Fellow at the Institute of Security and International Studies in Chulalongkorn University, Thailand and Associate Senior Fellow at the Institute of Southeast Asian Studies in Singapore. He was a Senior Researcher at the Institute of Economics in Yangon. An economist, Mya Than has worked on regional and sub-regional cooperation and economic and social development in Southeast Asia, with an emphasis on Myanmar and the Mekong region. He earned both his MSc (Management in Agriculture) and PhD degrees from the University of Agriculture in Prague.

Nguyen Phuong Binh is Deputy Director at the Institute for International Relations, Ministry of Foreign Affairs, Hanoi. Her research and publications focus on security and diplomacy issues in Asia and the Pacific region, with particular interest in economic security, ASEAN, and multilateralism. She obtained both her master's and doctoral degrees from the Moscow Diplomatic Academy.

Nguyen Van Chinh is Senior Lecturer in Social Anthropology and Deputy Director of the Center for Asian and Pacific Studies at the Vietnam National University (Hanoi). He has been consultant to various international organizations such as the World Bank, the Asian Development Bank, Save the Children, United Nations Development Program, and the World Health Organization. His works cover rural education in Vietnam, rural politics, family and fertility practices, child labor, and issues relating to ethnicity in Vietnam and the Mekong region. He received his doctorate from the University of Amsterdam.

Vatthana Pholsena is Assistant Professor at the Southeast Asian Studies Programme, National University of Singapore. In January 2007, she will join the Institut d'Asie Orientale (Lyon) as a CNRS research fellow. Her research interests are the impact of the American/Vietnam war on the ethnic minority population living along the Lao-Vietnamese borders in Southern Laos and central Vietnam; connections between history, historiography and memory in Laos; and post-Cold War relations among Laos, Thailand and Vietnam. She earned her master's degree in political science from the Institut d'études politiques de Grenoble, France and her doctorate in Southeast Asian studies at the University of Hull.

Chaiyan Rajchagool is Assistant Professor at the Department of History, Faculty of Humanities, Chiang Mai University. His publications span a range of topics, from the Thai monarchy to contemporary issues such as HIV/AIDS, land transport and sustainable development, armed conflict and conflict resolution, ethnicity, and ongoing debates in postmodern thought. He received his master's degree in peace studies from Bradford University and his doctorate from the University of Manchester.

Doung Chanto Sisowath is Assistant Dean and Professor at the Faculty of Social Sciences and International Relations, Pannasastra University of Cambodia. In 2000 he joined the Cambodian Institute for Cooperation and Peace in Phnom Penh as Deputy Executive Director and Research Fellow. He earned his master's degree in political science at Florida International University.